IMAGES
of America

BARRE

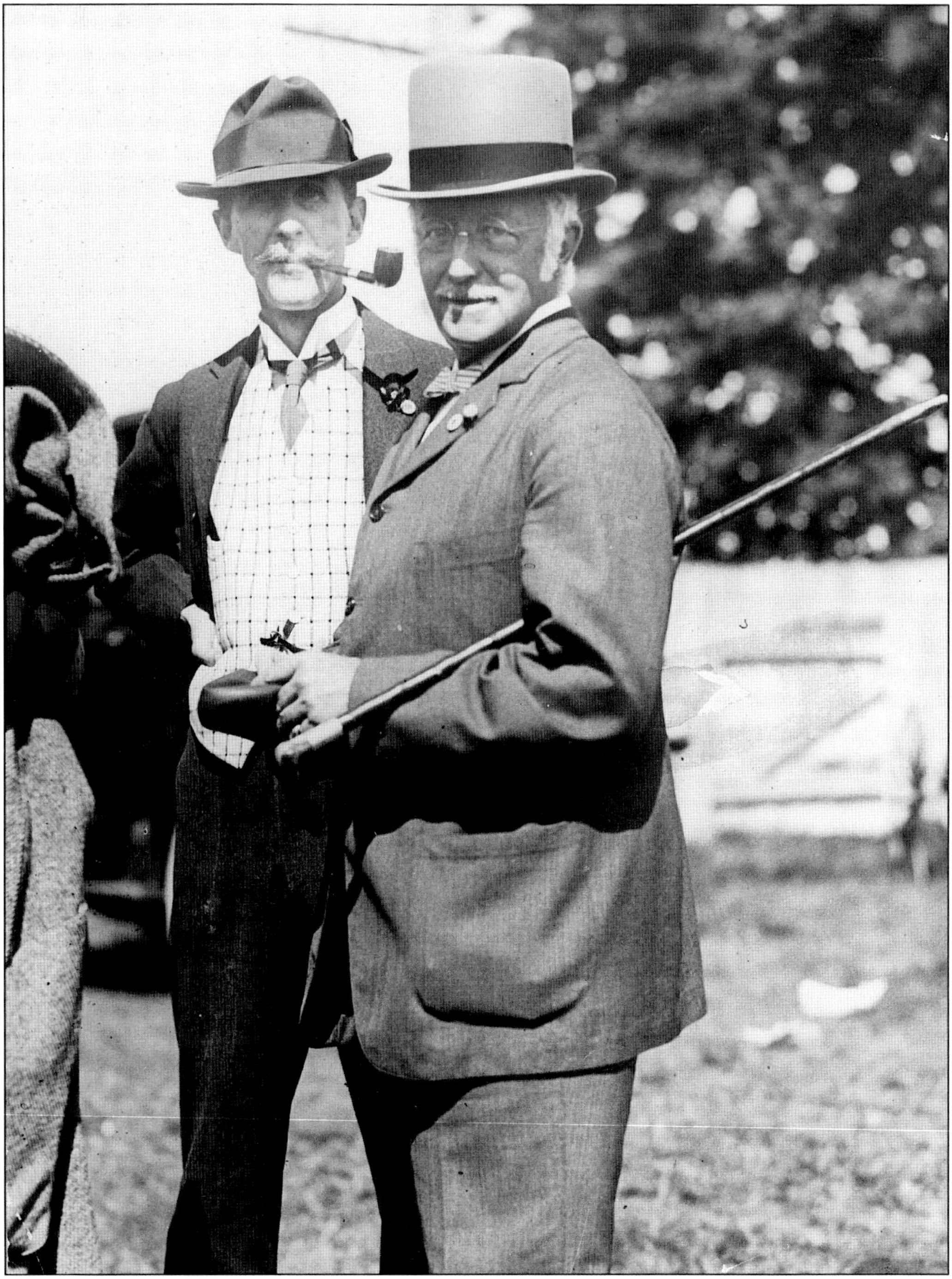

We would like to dedicate this book to all members of the Barre community who have dedicated themselves to making our town so special through the years. Shown here are two unidentified dapper gentlemen at the Barre Fair around 1920. We value and appreciate everyone . . . past, present, and future.

IMAGES
of America

BARRE

Barre Historical Society

ARCADIA
PUBLISHING

ISBN 978-0-7385-0001-0

Published by Arcadia Publishing
Charleston, South Carolina

Printed in the United States of America

Library of Congress Catalog Card Number: 99-62496

For all general information contact Arcadia Publishing at:
Telephone 843-853-2070
Fax 843-853-0044
E-mail sales@arcadiapublishing.com
For customer service and orders:
Toll-Free 1-888-313-2665

Visit us on the Internet at www.arcadiapublishing.com

Contents

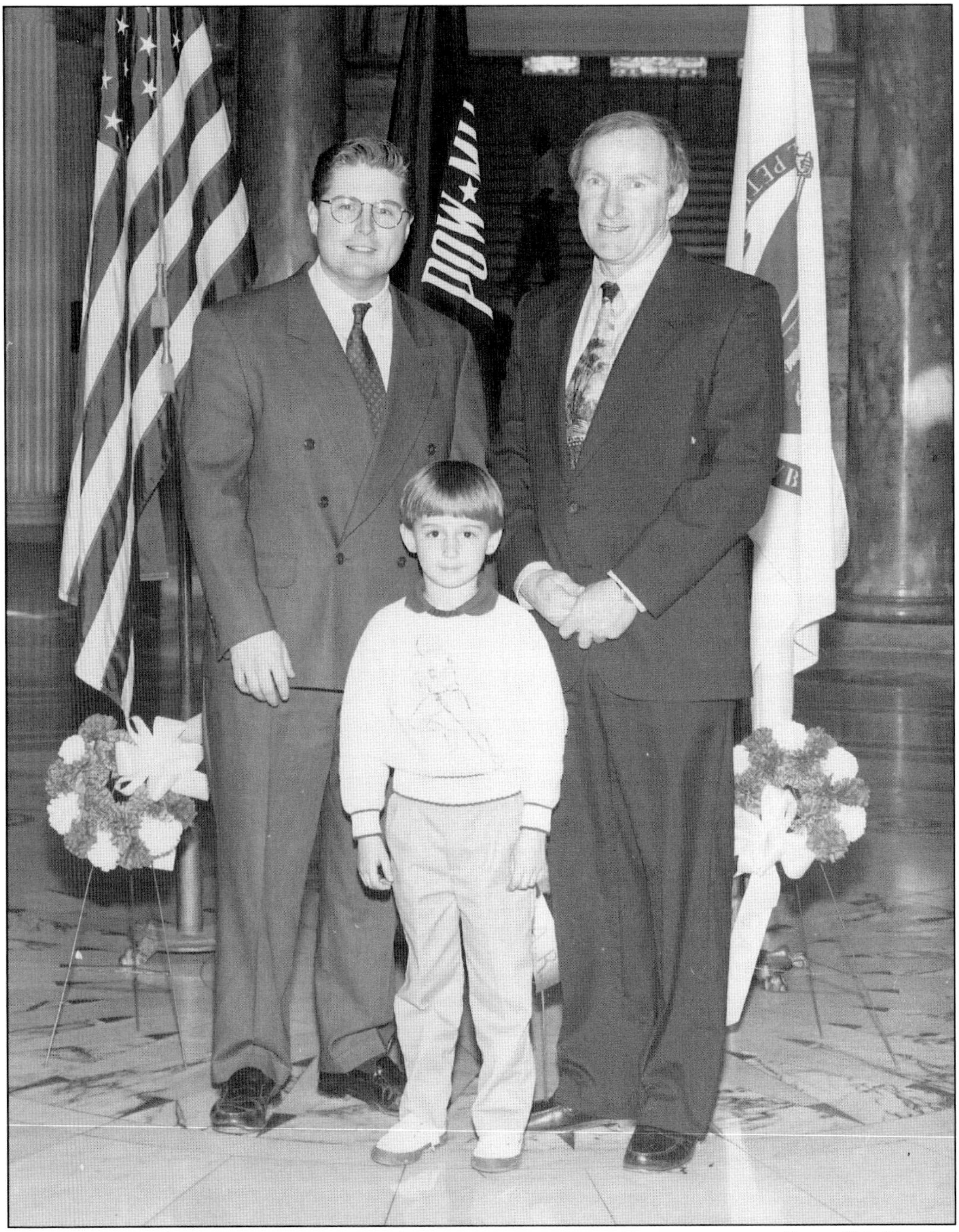

This photograph of State Senator Stephen M. Brewer, State Representative David H. Tuttle, and his nephew, Michael R.H. Tuttle, was taken at the Massachusetts State House, c. January 1997.

INTRODUCTION

The Town of Barre is set among the hills and valleys of Central Massachusetts like a gem. From several vantage points, Mt. Wachusett's rounded slopes may be glimpsed, and in the distance, in the opposite direction, is the lengthy shoreline of the Quabbin Reservoir. Lying between these natural landmarks, Barre is geographically a diamond. Demographically, it has a population approaching 5,000 residents. The area of more than 40 square miles has many entities as owners. These include the Metropolitan District Commission, which cares for Boston's water supplies, and conservation organizations attempting to keep parts of the state green. Together, they protect more than one-third of the community from residential development.

Before Barre became a town, it was simply called the Northwest District of Rutland. Then, as settlers became numerous enough to maintain some degree of self-government, it became Rutland District. Twenty-five years saw the evolution completed, because an act passed on June 14, 1774, by the Massachusetts General Court, as our state legislature is called, incorporated what had been Rutland District as the Town of Hutchinson, honoring a former royal governor. The name was unpopular with the townspeople. Like other colonists, they were struggling for their own identity and freedom. They felt Thomas Hutchinson had been one of the impediments in that endeavor. Soon after the first guns of the Revolution were fired, the town petitioned to have the name replaced. In June of 1776, it was accomplished and the name chosen was Barre, honoring Colonel Isaac Barre, a member of the British Parliament who espoused the cause of the colonists.

In its infancy, Barre, like the new nation, was predominantly rural in nature and farming was the principal economic activity. But with freedom came the right to experiment, to invent, to manufacture the goods previously forbidden by royal proclamation. The Industrial Revolution reached Barre and many villages bloomed within the town, sustained by shops, mills, and stores. For a time, several successful industries—including textiles, gunpowder, and wood products—operated continuously, but in the 20th century these were narrowed down to two major companies: the Charles G. Allen Co. in Barre and the Barre Wool Combing Co. Ltd. in South Barre.

Now, tourism has become a major business. Fall foliage, hunting, fishing, the Woods Memorial Library and its museum, and the Barre Historical Society with archives valuable to genealogical researchers and historians are among the attractions. Tourism is enhanced by suitable accommodations. For slightly more than 100 years, the Hotel Barre graced the western perimeter of the Common and truly was the "Jewel of Central Massachusetts," but a tragic fire in 1990 ended its reign. We have moved forward and bed-and-breakfasts at the Harding Allen Estate, the Wholesome Hearth, the Jenkins Inn, Hartman's in the western part of town, and the Stevens Farm in the eastern section have filled the void and become attractions in themselves with fine lodging and delectable food.

To nourish the spirit, Barre has several religious denominations and churches. There is also the Insight Meditation Society, the Barre Center for Buddhist Studies on Pleasant Street, and a magnificent cross at John Harty's.

We are fortunate that, in 1834, a weekly newspaper called the *Barre Gazette* was established and the history of the town has been documented continuously in its pages through all the intervening years. Since the invention of the camera, the resulting pictures, which have been collected, are generously accessible. This book, using photographs from Barre's past and present, is a gift to all who peruse these pages. The changes that have taken place since many of the pictures were taken prove that Barre is a wonderful, resilient town and is still one of the best places in the world to live. The town motto "Tranquil and Alert" still holds true.

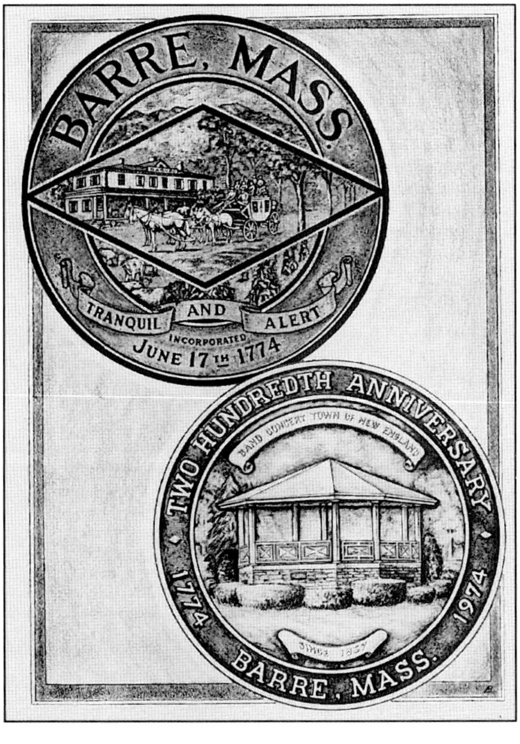

One

Around the Common

Whether you say the "village," "uptown," or the "center," you are probably referring to Barre Common, which has been the focal point of our history since the first settlers constructed a rustic meetinghouse there in 1753. By 1807, the Common consisted of eight houses, four shops, three stores, a tavern, a lawyer's office, and the second meetinghouse. During the next 60 years, the area grew rapidly as the townspeople approved the acquisition of the nine parcels of land that comprise the grassy area today. At least two dozen structures became commercial in nature as three hotels, four churches, and scores of small businesses flourished and a new meetinghouse, our present town hall, was erected.

As we approach the 21st century, the role of the Common has changed, but the town government, greatly enlarged, is still nearby and many events and celebrations are still held here annually. The beauty and availability of our Common is one of the joys of living in Barre.

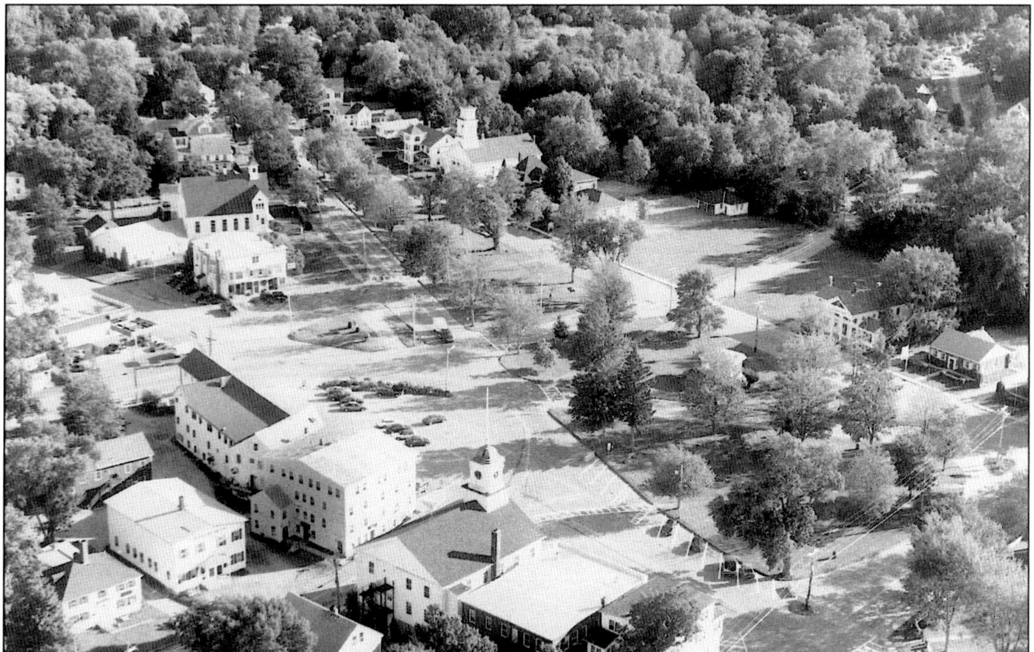

This view of the Common as it looks in 1999 was taken from above and behind the Barre Town Hall.

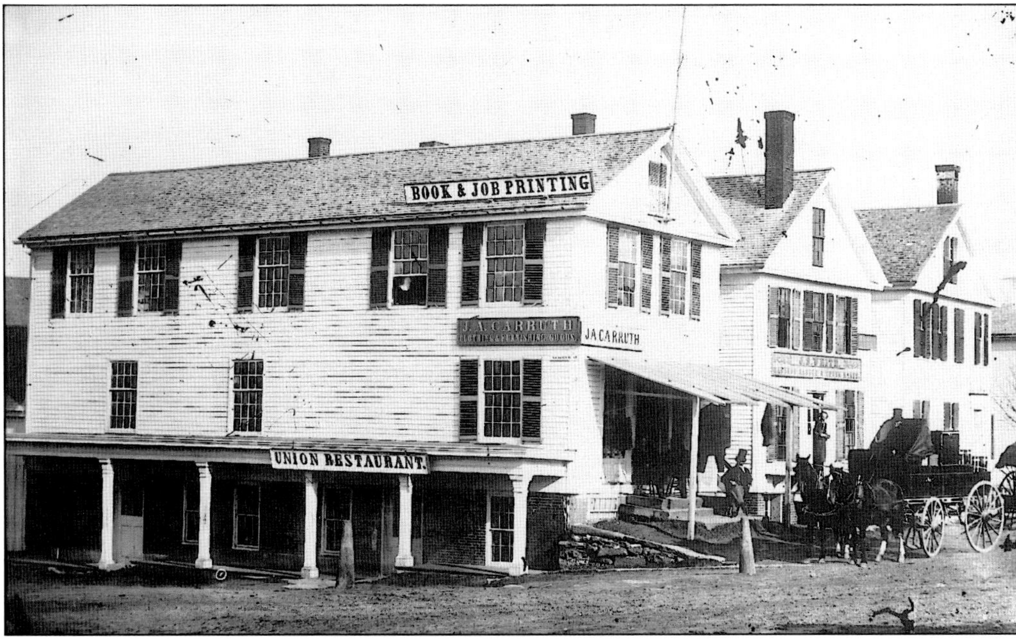

For many years, this complex of buildings stood side-by-side on the east side of James Street at the corner of Summer Street. Dozens of shops were located here over the decades. There were restaurants, clothing stores, printers, harness makers, and a laundry; however, it was a popular grocery that produced the name "South End Market."

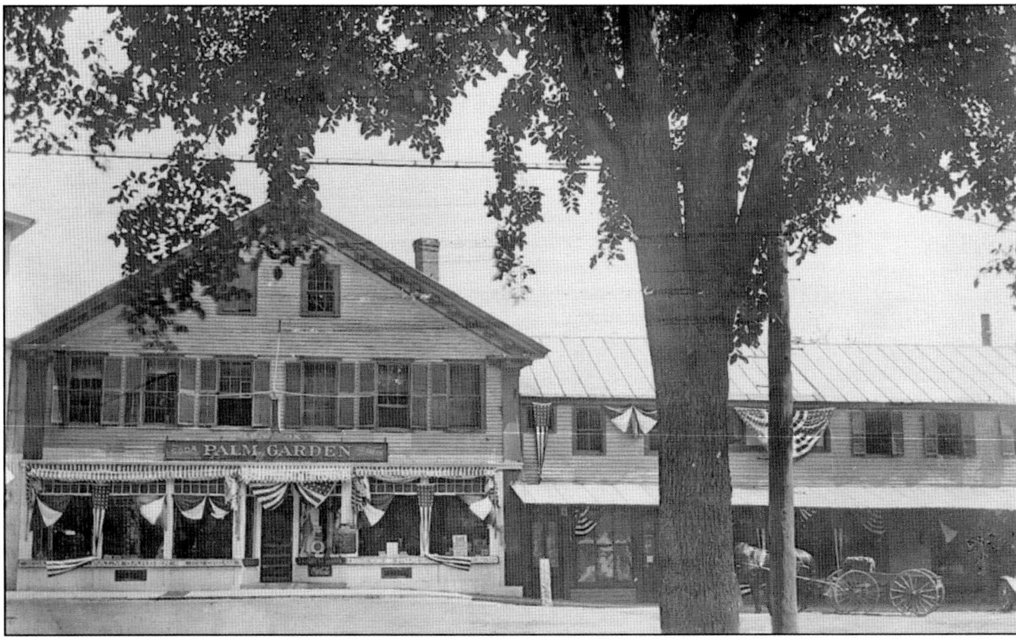

On the east side of the Common on Exchange Street, there were once four buildings. Moved into one line in 1855, they were later joined together. The central section, originally the emporium of Jenkins and Lee, has undergone many changes. Now called "The Colonel Isaac Barre," it appears here as "The Palm Garden," decorated for a national holiday in thelate 1800s.

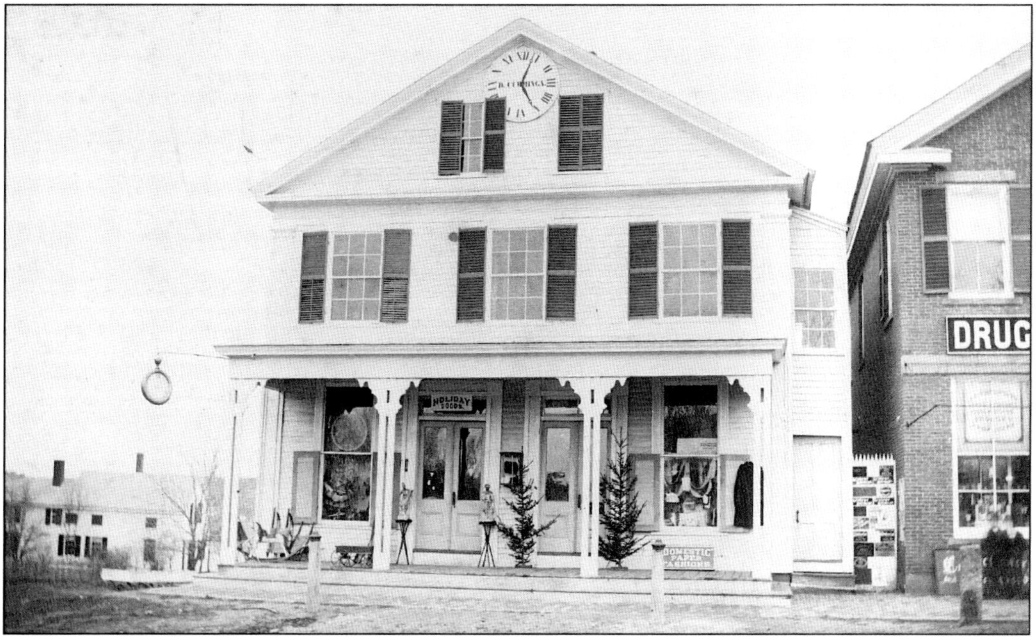

The building that still stands on the southeast corner of Exchange and School Streets was originally the Union Store. For many years, it often displayed a watch or clock indicating a jeweler within. A succession of dentists had their quarters on the second floor during much of the 20th century.

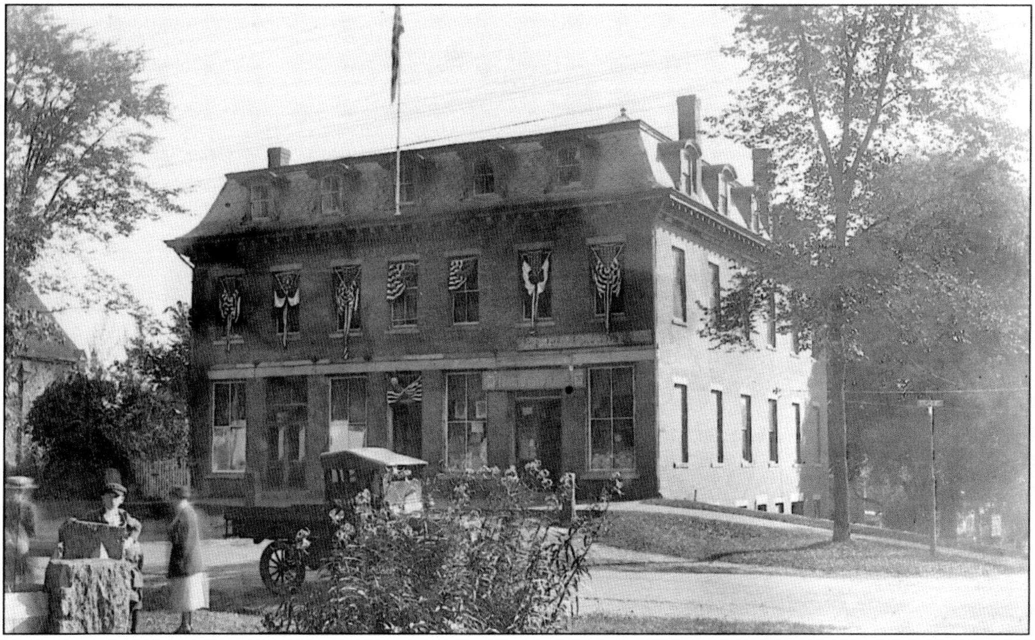

Soon after the Colonnade Building burned in 1862, the Smith Block of brick construction was erected in its place. A saloon, shops, professional offices, a bank, and the *Barre Gazette* were all located on the first two floors; an ever-present photographer's studio utilized the top floor, which contained a convenient skylight. Extended and without the third floor, the building now contains a business that caters to automotive needs.

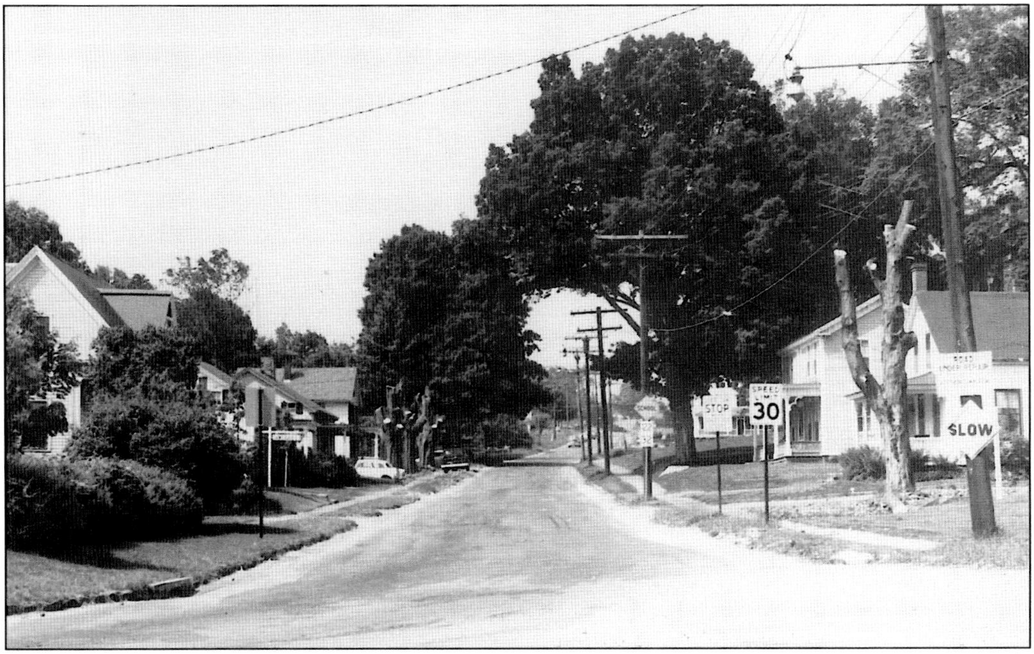

With growth and progress has come the necessity of widening roads and removing roadside trees. This view of West Street shows the beginning of the process in the early 1960s that removed verdant shade trees.

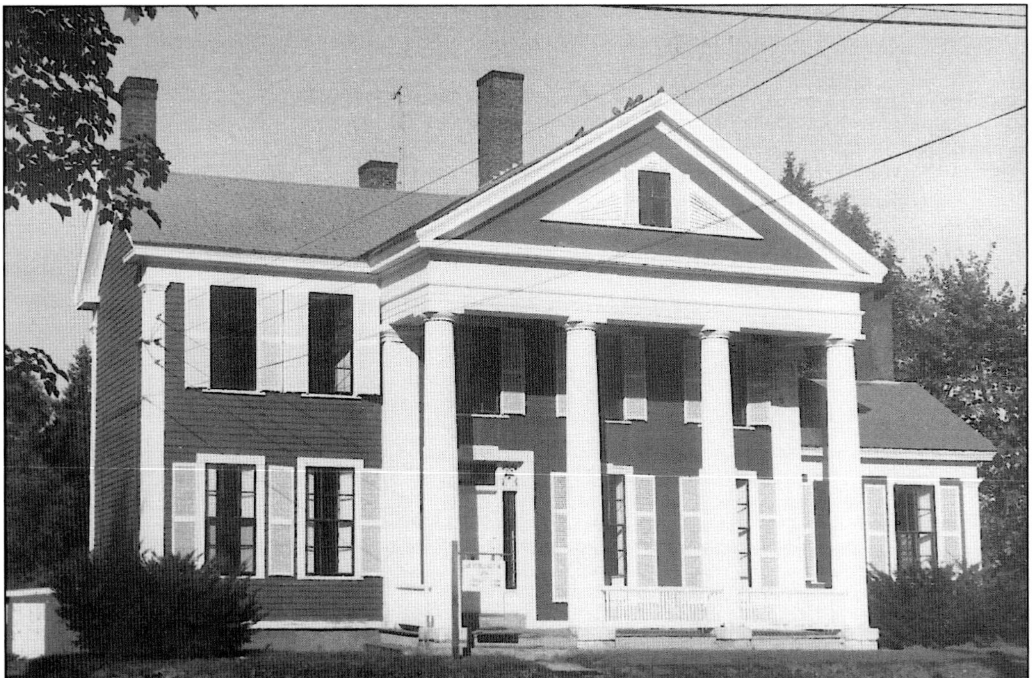

This building on the west side of the Common was built and occupied by Spencer Field, partner of Harding P. Woods in the general store next door. It became the home of the Barre Historical Society in 1962.

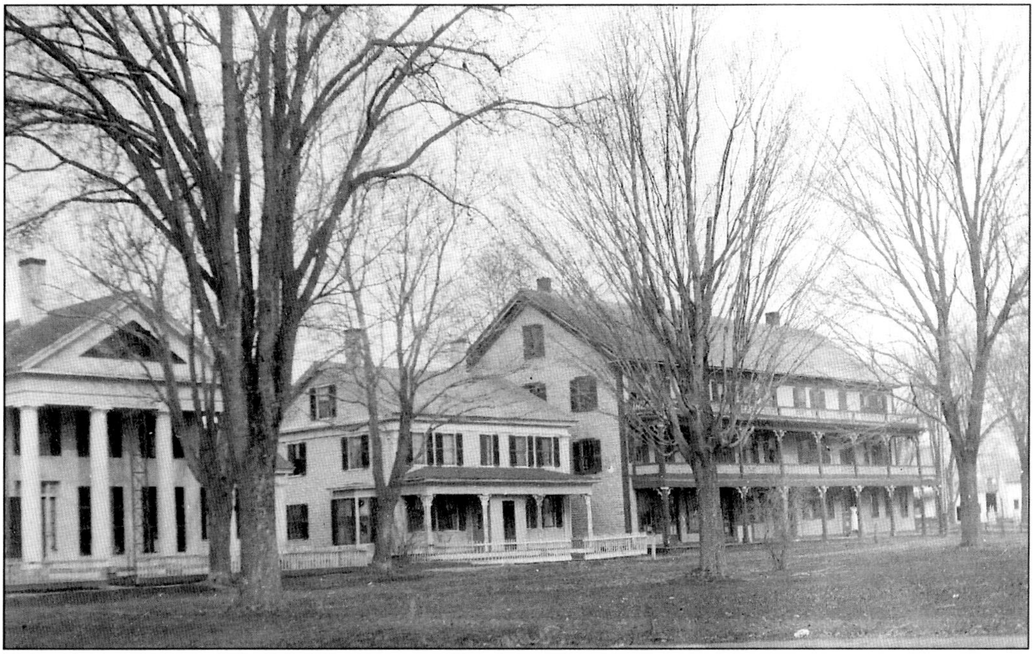

A hotel from early in the 19th century, the Massasoit House stood at the site of the present post office and was a terminus for several stagecoach lines. It was flanked on the south by the imposing home of Edwin Woods.

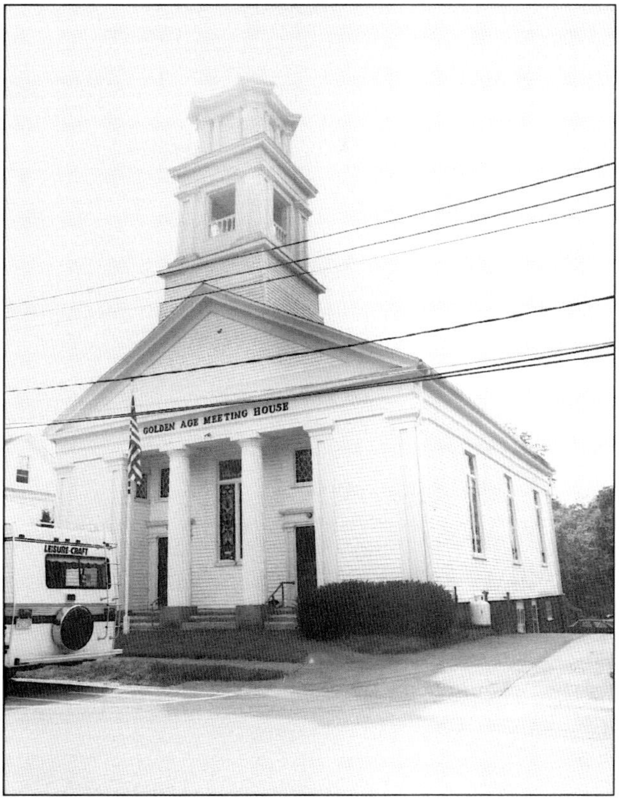

The Universalist church was built in 1840, but within a decade became the property of the Methodists. It was an active church for more than 100 years. When that church disbanded, its members transferred the building to the Golden Agers. In 1992, Barre Players Inc. assumed ownership. The building is now a theater.

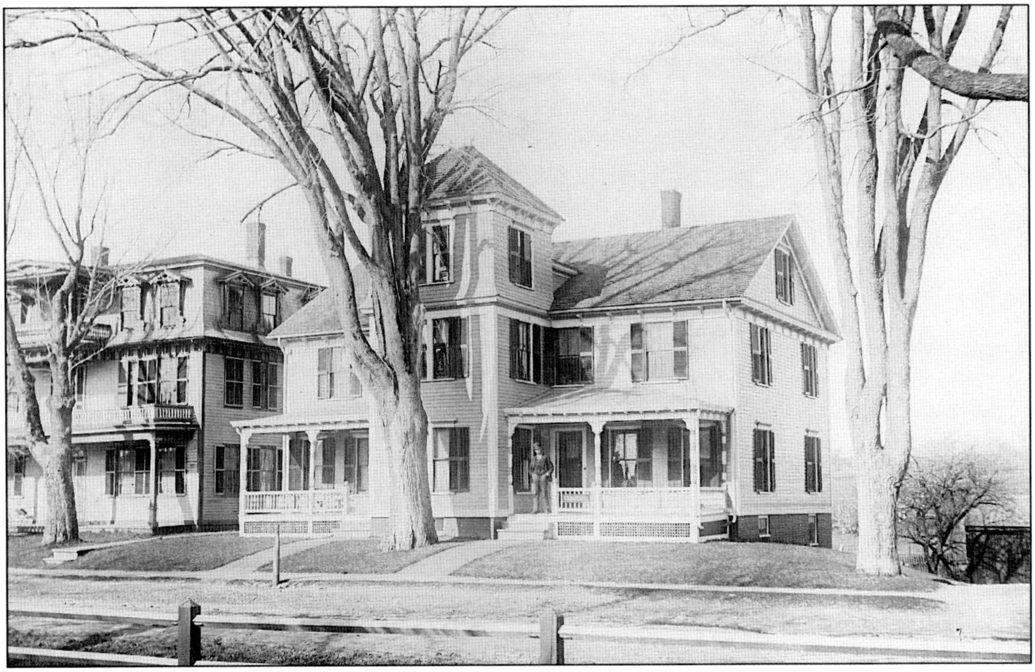

The Kilner House was the location of our earliest tailor; it was moved down Common Street to make room for the Hotel Barre. The Kilner House still stands as an apartment house and jewelry store, while the dwelling to the left, the home of William Tay, Barre's "ice man" at the turn of the century, was razed years ago.

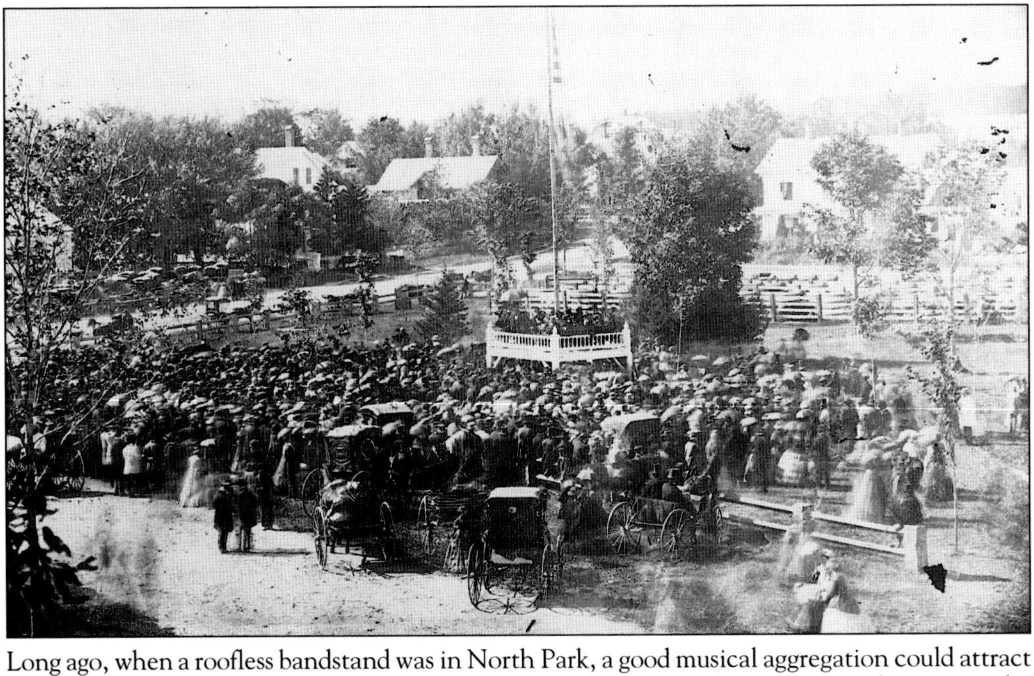

Long ago, when a roofless bandstand was in North Park, a good musical aggregation could attract crowds of men in coats and straw hats and ladies wearing shawls and gowns that swept the ground. One hundred and fifty years later, band concerts are still held on our annual schedule.

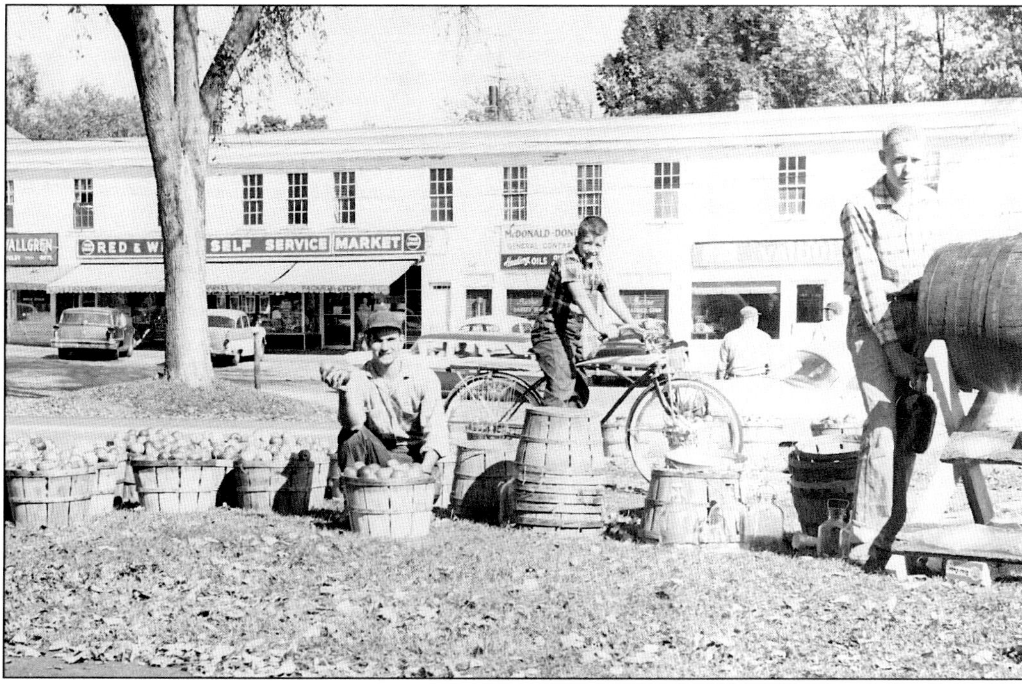

The Common has often been a free venue for groups to raise money. Here, Barre High School students dispense cider in 1959. An apple and cider festival has been a frequent fall fund-raiser for students.

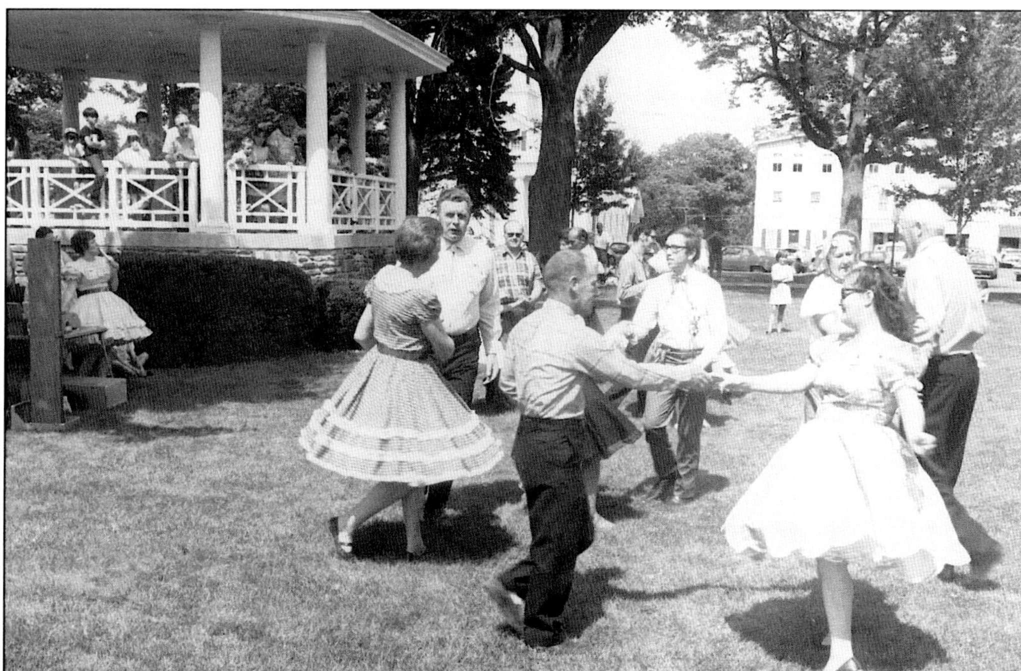

The carefully manicured grass makes a most suitable "stomping ground" for this enthusiastic group call "The Earth Turners."

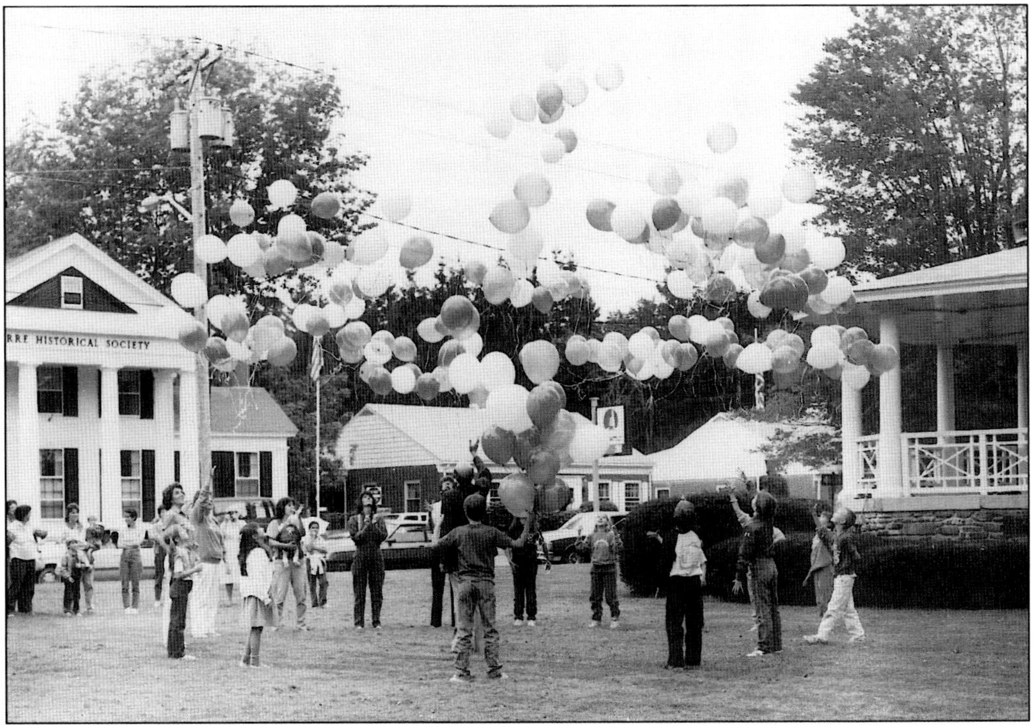

During an occasion for remembrance and celebration, the Common is the place to free a multitude of balloons, in this case for the 200th anniversary of our nation's constitution.

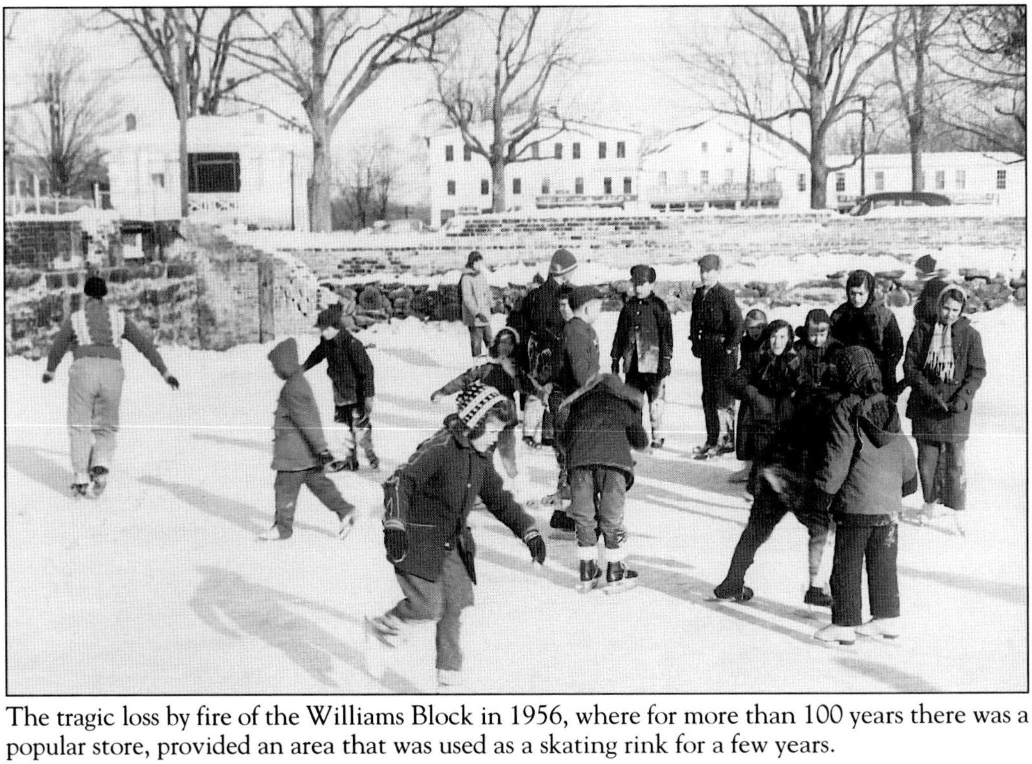

The tragic loss by fire of the Williams Block in 1956, where for more than 100 years there was a popular store, provided an area that was used as a skating rink for a few years.

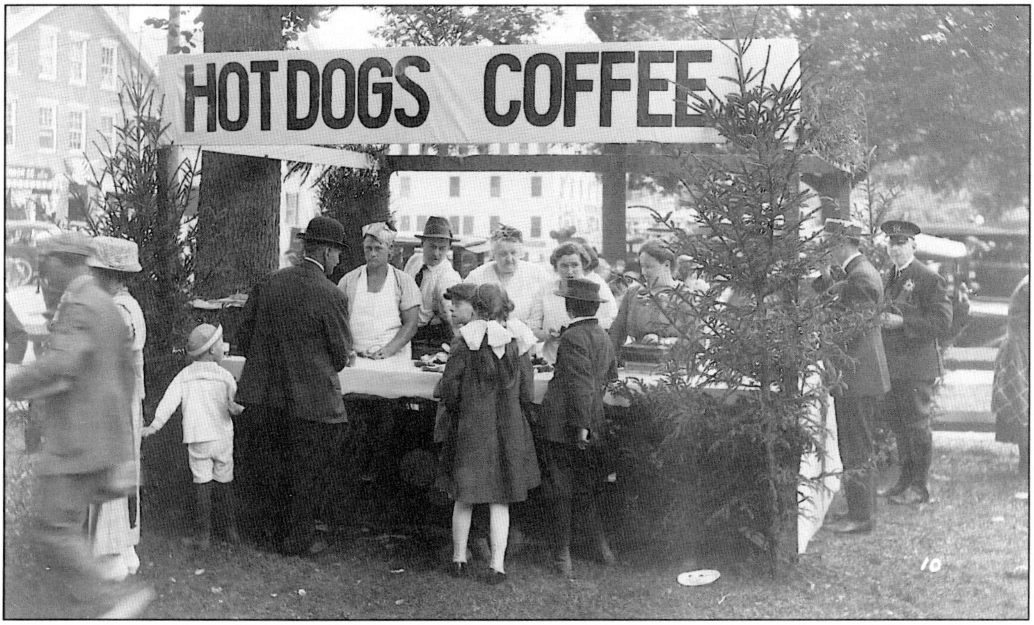

Church fairs, sales, flea markets, and carnivals have all abounded on the Common. The food booth is always a popular part of an affair, as seen in this picture of an unidentified civic group of long ago.

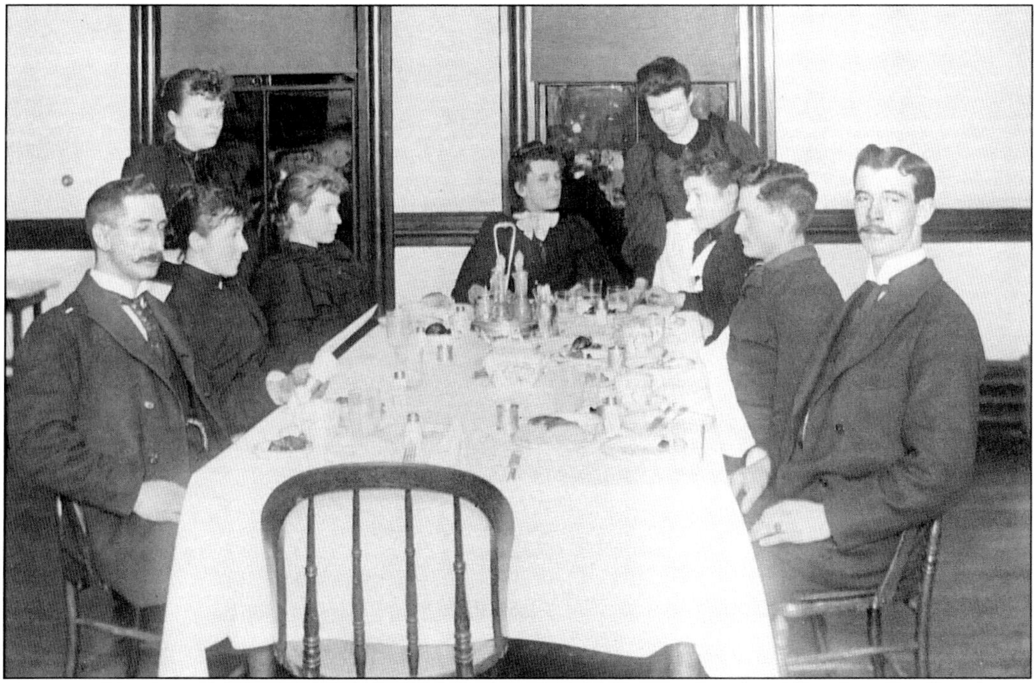

Eating establishments have always been on the Common, but none was better or more sadly missed than our jewel of Victorian dignity, the Hotel Barre. Shown in this group from 1893, from left to right, are Mr. Will Spooner, Mrs. Spooner, Miss Crosby, the high school assistant, Mrs. Ella Cole Whitman (head of the table), Phronia Kimball Bruce, Arthur Sawyer, and Mr. Shearn.

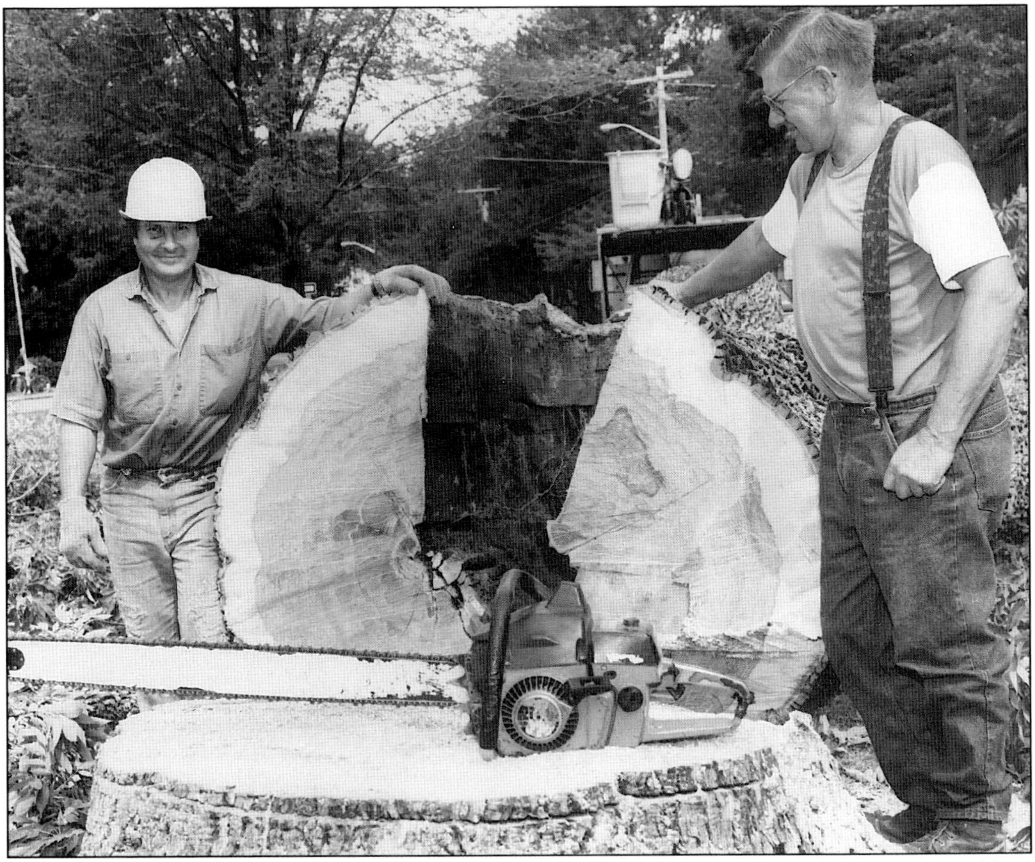

The trees on the Common were giants, but some became dangerous in their antiquity and had to be removed.

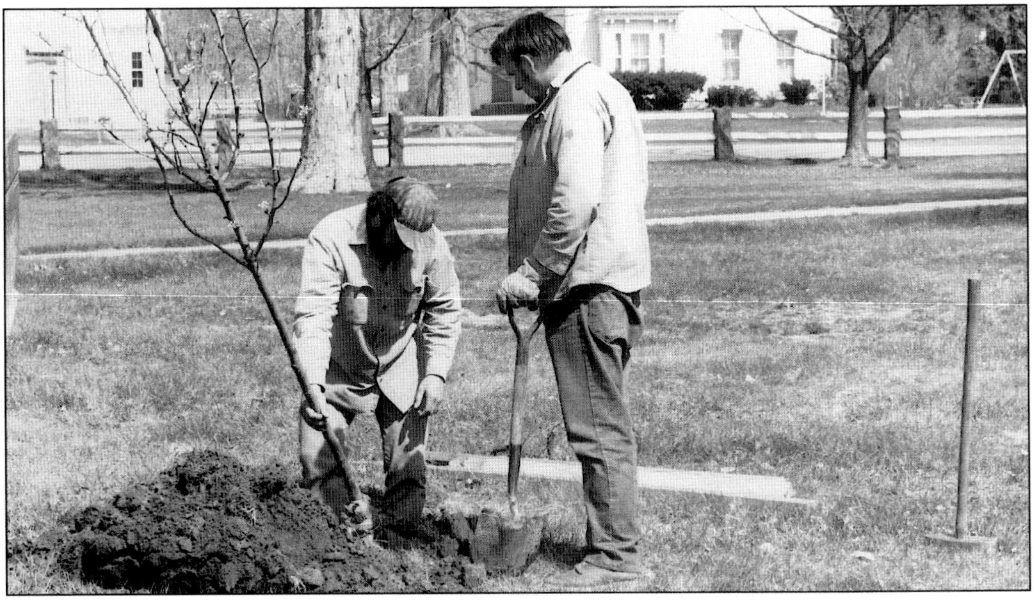

Trees are replaced regularly by some that may also become giants in their time.

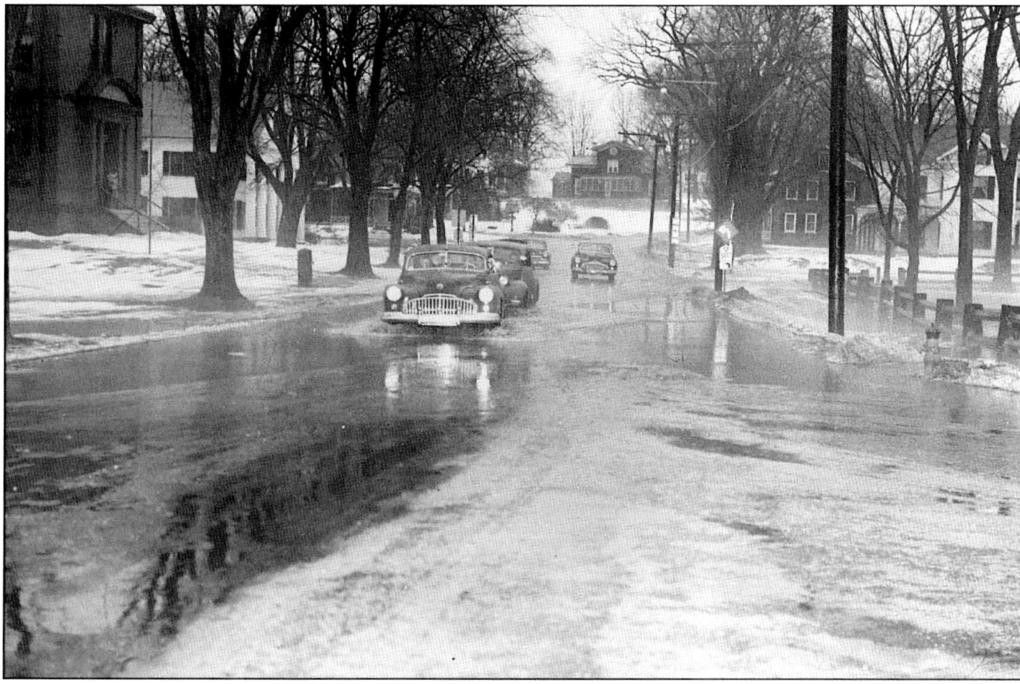

The Common has seen floods, such as this one caused by a mid-winter thaw in January 1953.

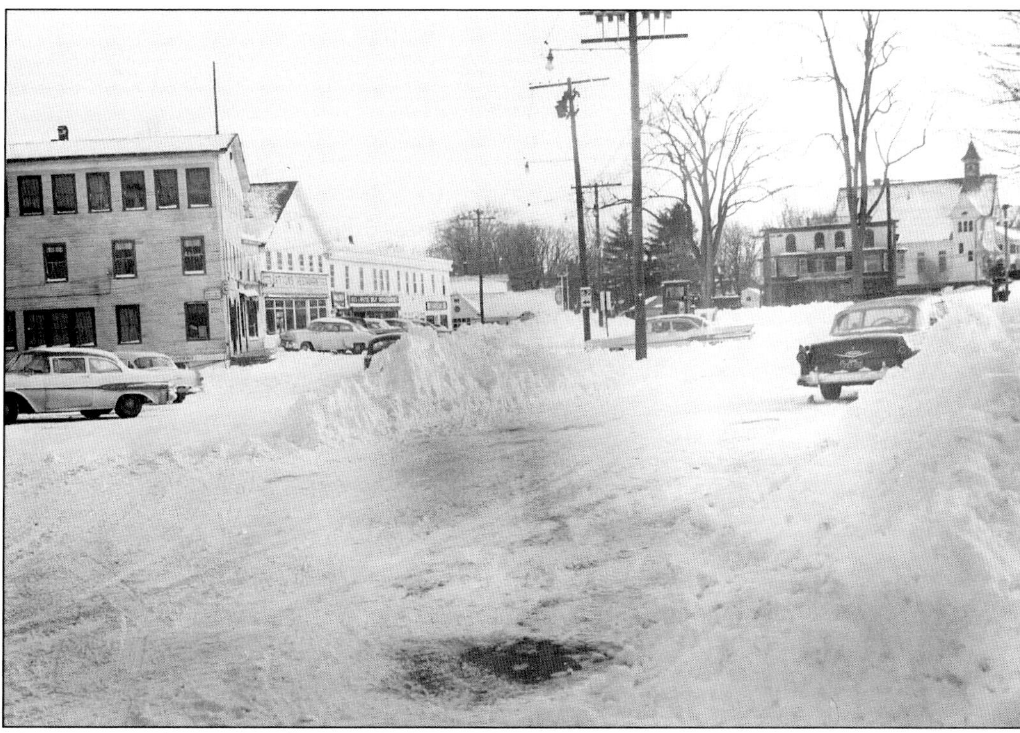

The Common has endured blizzards that made scenes invisible from one end to the other, as in this 1958 photograph.

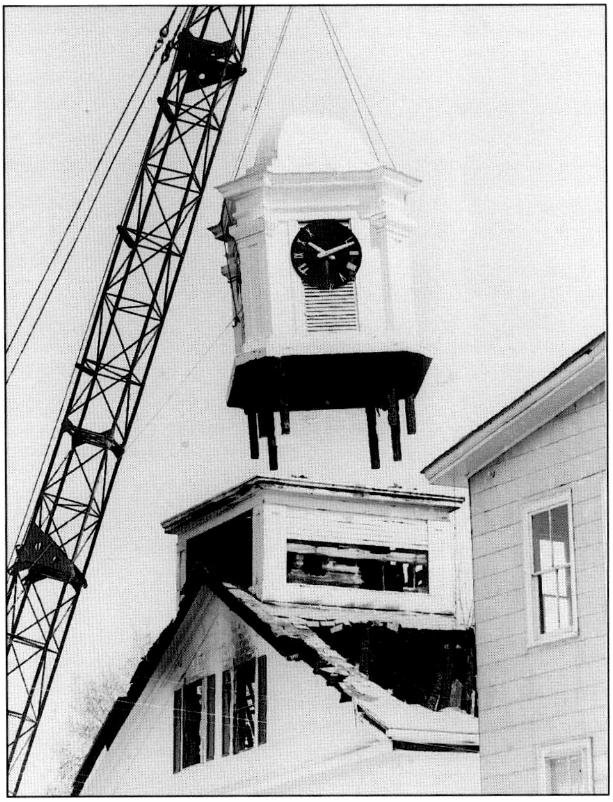

In 1981, disaster struck in the form of a destructive fire in the 143-year-old town hall. Here the belfry is carefully removed weeks after the blaze. A delay in construction had occurred while the town decided what to do about the building.

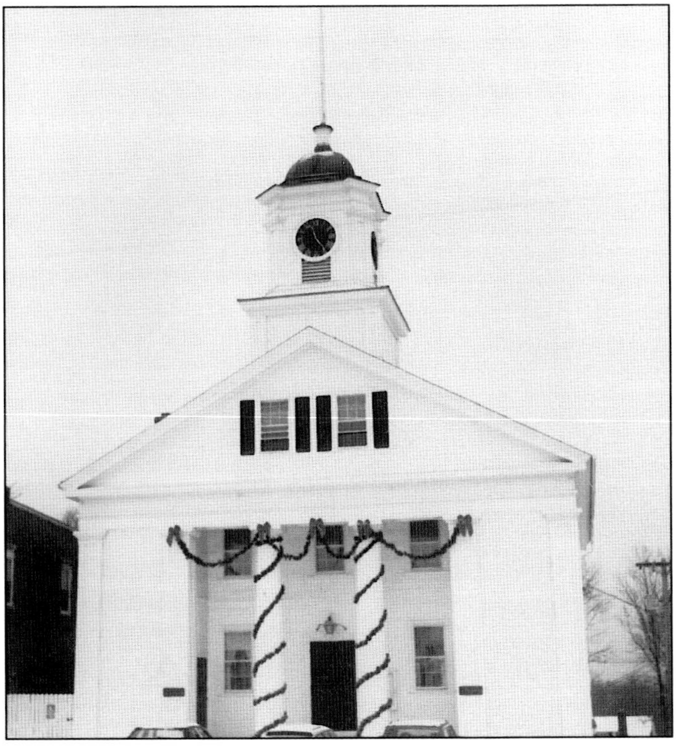

Through the efforts of the selectmen, a devoted restoration committee, and countless local artisans, our country's flag flew high above a lovingly rebuilt town hall and over our ever changing, but indestructible, Common.

Two

Businesses

When this town was first settled by those of English and Scottish ancestry, the principal daily work activity was farming. However, the rivers within Barre's boundaries fostered the growth of industry. There were the Burnshirt and Prince Rivers in the north part of town; from the east flowed the Ware River and the Connestow Brook; to the west were Silver, Moose, and Pine Hill Brooks; and near the center of town was Galloway Brook. Dams were built and businesses were established that subsequently flourished.

By 1835, there was a hat shop, a powder mill, a chair and cotton factory, three scythe and cabinet shops, five carriage manufacturers, four tanneries, four gristmills, six shingle shops, 13 sawmills, one copper pump shop, and one printing office. All of these shops were delineated on the Ainsworth map of that year. The flood of 1868 devastated many mills along the streams; some were never rebuilt.

Two major industries, the Charles G. Allen Co. and the Barre Wool Combing Co. Ltd., have bolstered the economy, brought new citizens to the town, and provided work close to home in Barre for the past century. Many small businesses pictured in these pages provided the amenities necessary for the people of Barre and its vicinity "to live the good life."

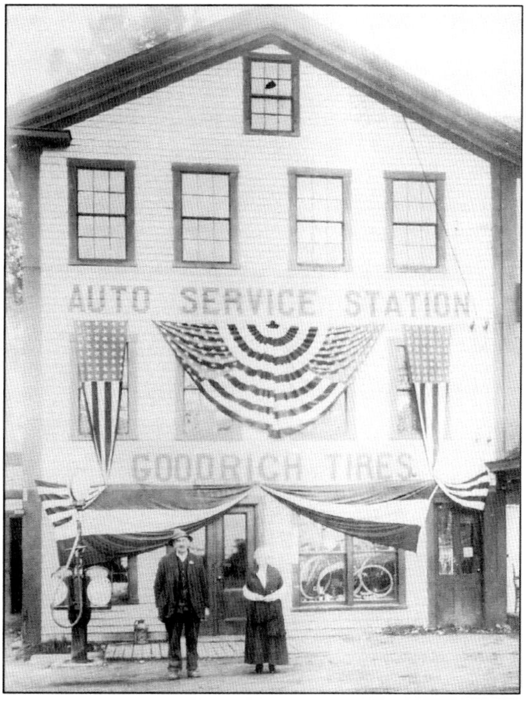

Rufus and Mary Dudley came to Barre with their son, Joseph Potter, in 1913. Joseph Potter was the son of Mary and stepson of Rufus Dudley. Rufus had the contract to build the dormers and finish the third floor of Barre High School. This is a photograph of their gas station in 1918, near the end of World War I. The station stood at the corner of James and Summer Streets. Mary's grandchildren, great-grandchildren, and great-great-grandchildren still live in and around Barre today.

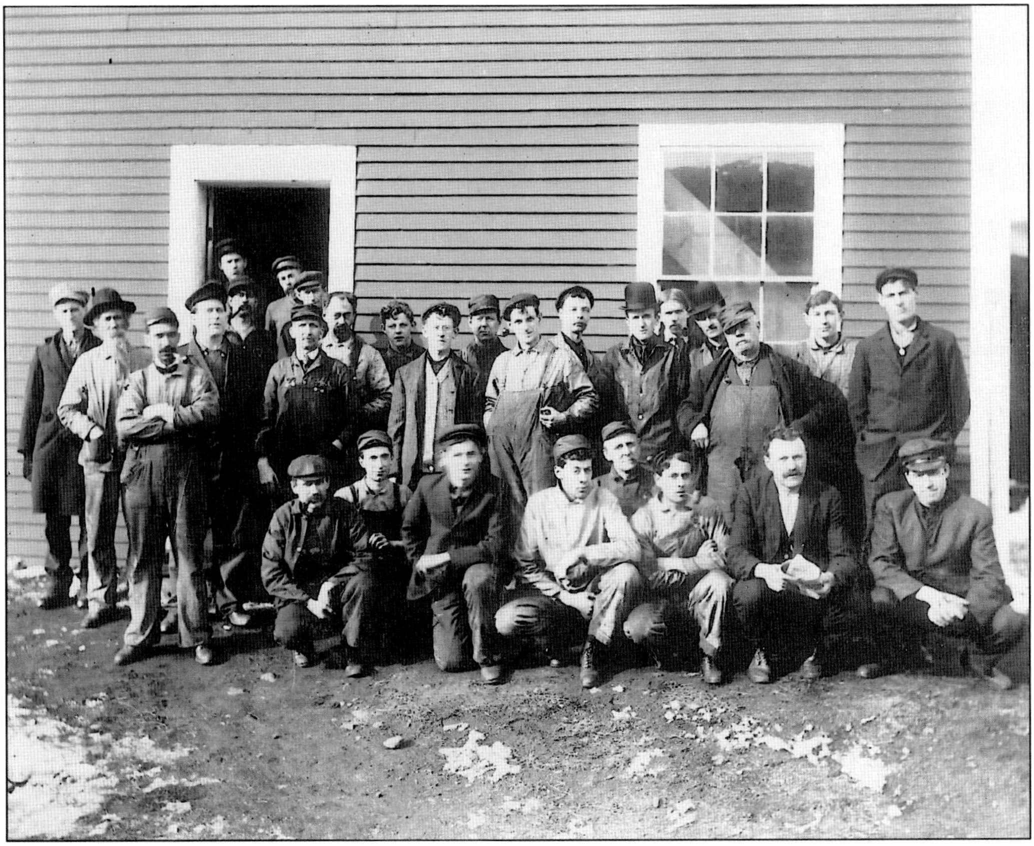

Ever since Dr. Charles G. Allen bought the water rights on the Prince River from his father-in-law, the company has provided employment for many of the residents of Barre and surrounding towns. Pictured here is the work force in the early 1900s.

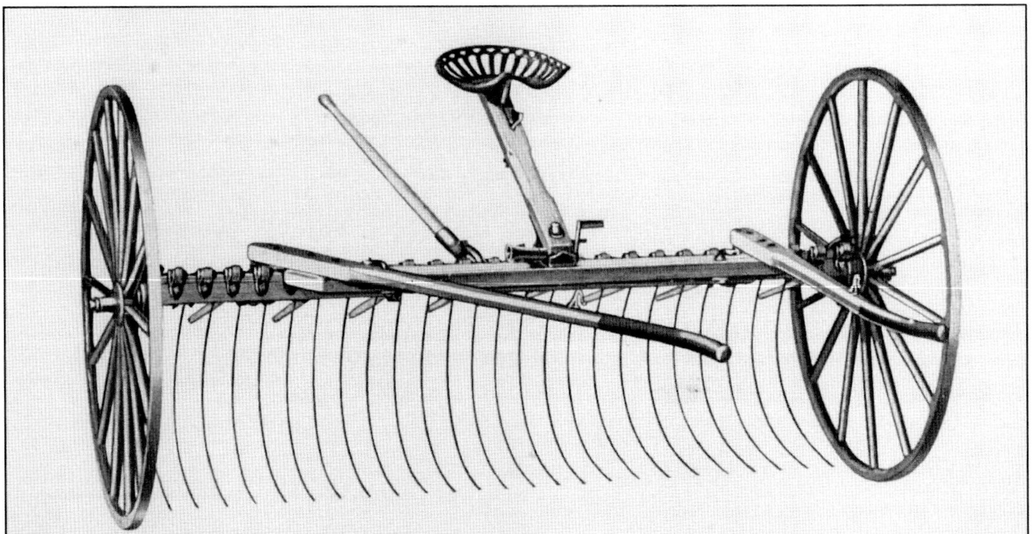

The Yankee Hay Rake, the first item the Chas. G. Allen Company manufactured, was assembled from 1874 to 1930.

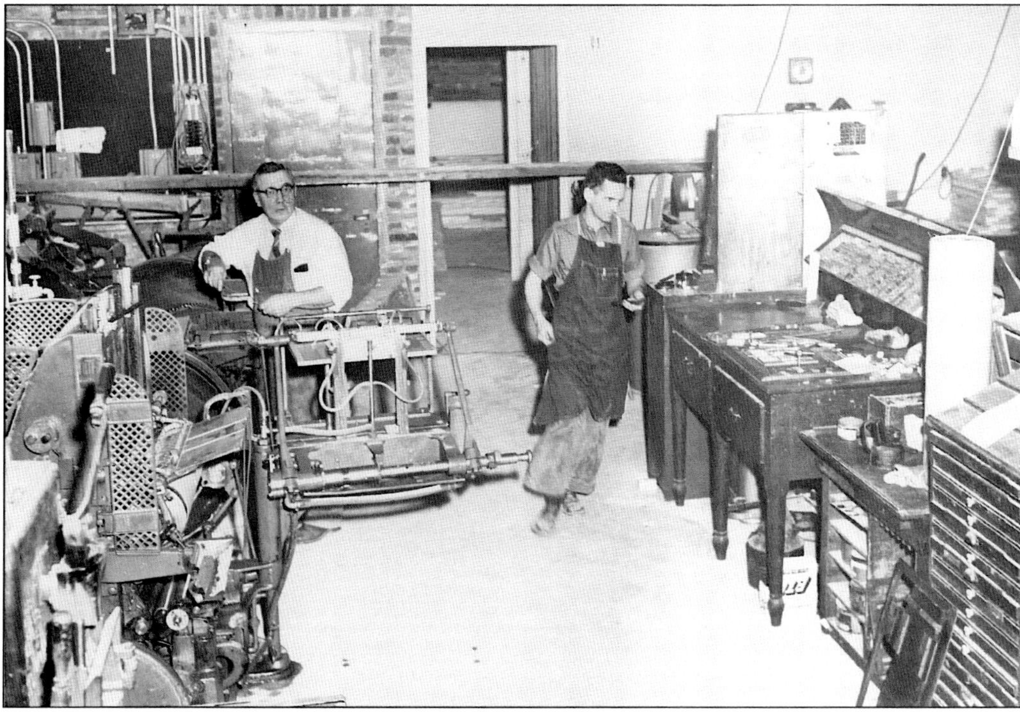

Gaetano D'Annolfo and Lewis Paquin were getting used to working in the new Barre Gazette building on South Street in November 1956.

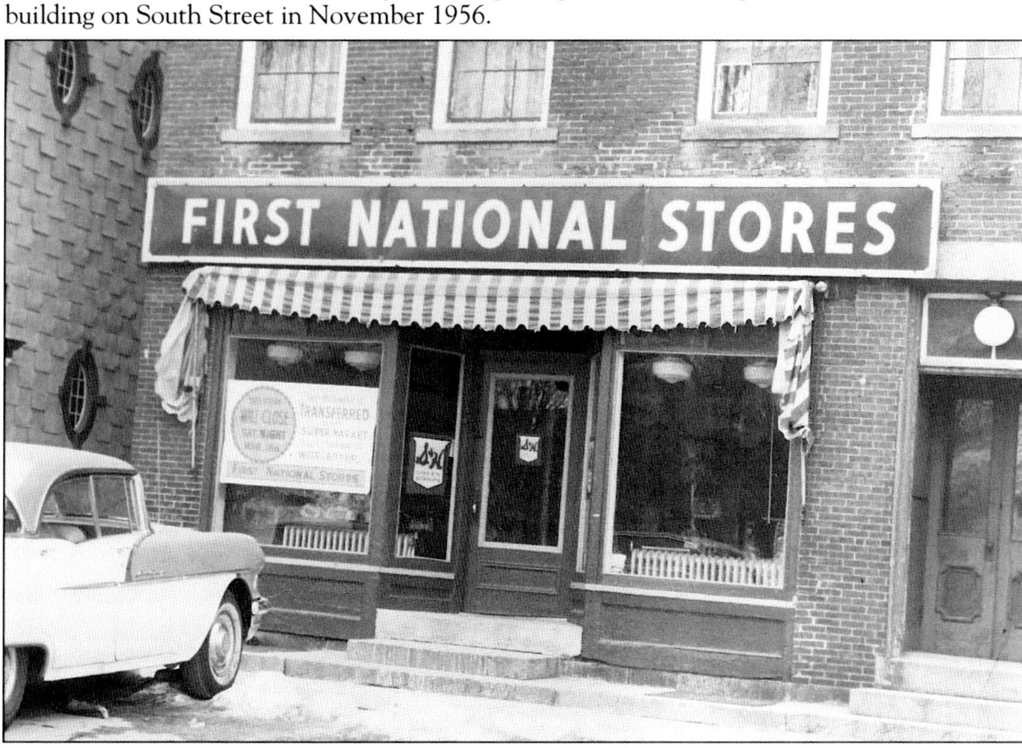

This First National storefront was a familiar sight to many Barre residents until the early 1960s, when it closed.

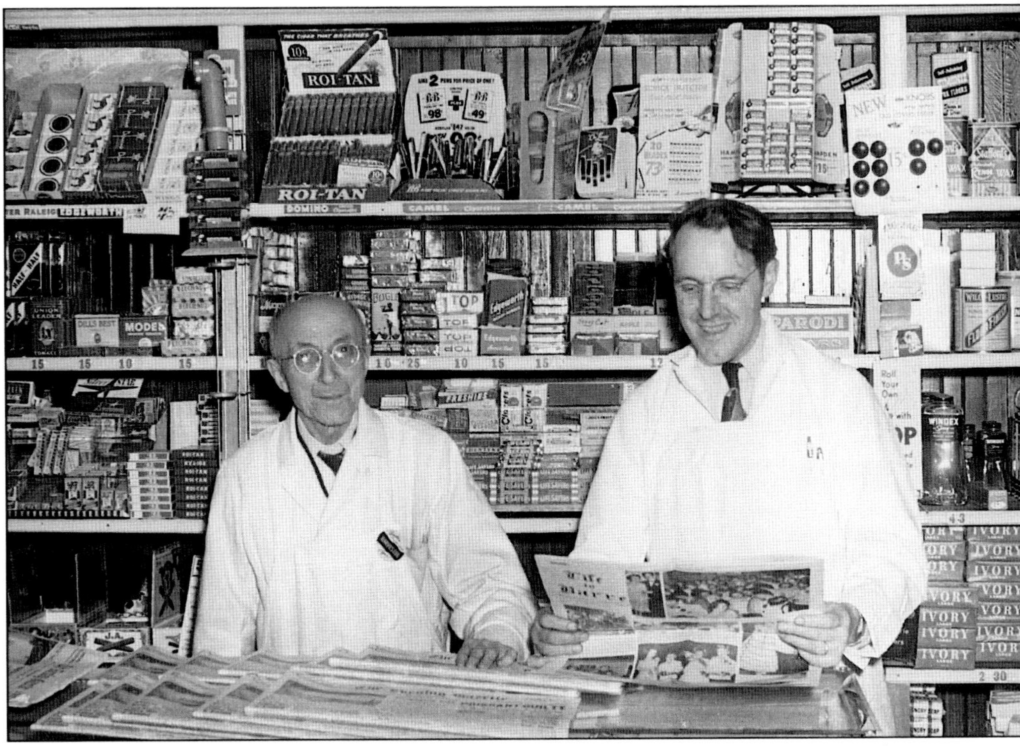

Former owner Onesime Ethier is shown with his son, Roland Ethier, proprietor of Ethier's Store in Barre Plains, c. 1938.

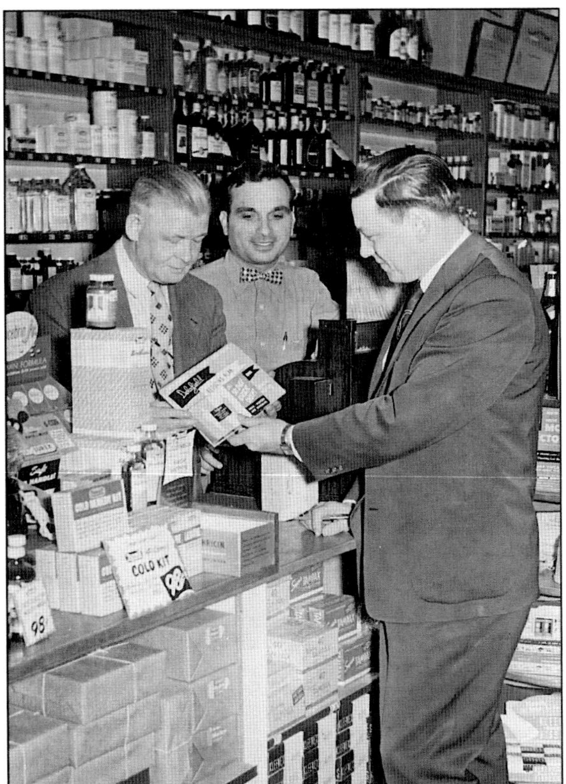

W. James McAndrew is in his South Barre drug store with employee Joseph Giarusso and customer Jerry McCabe.

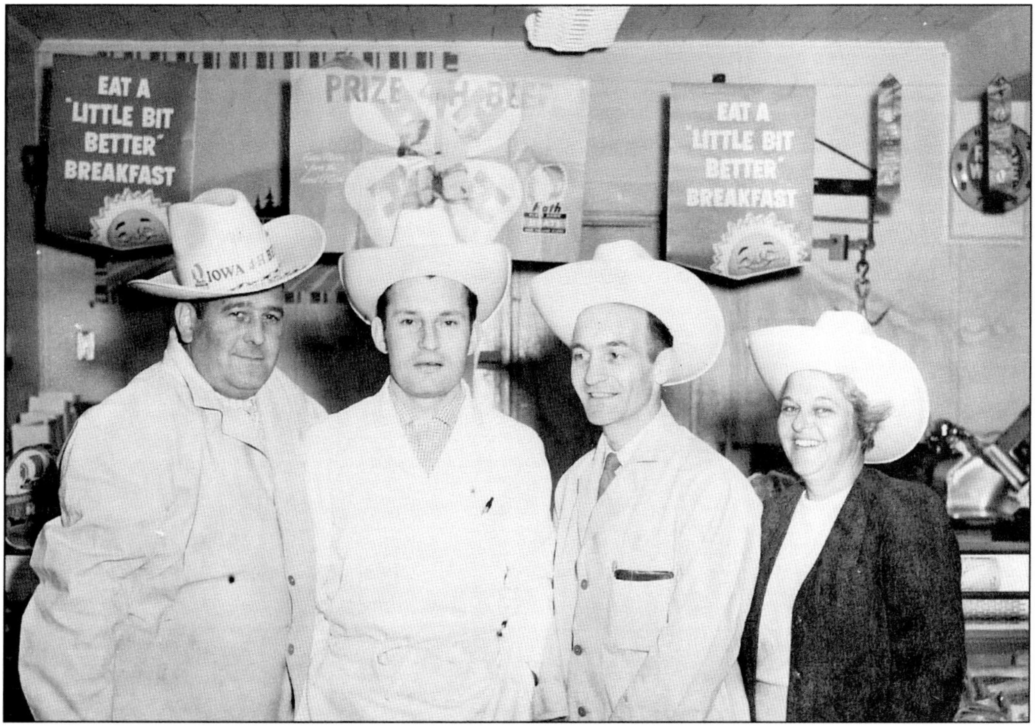

"Britton's 4H Beef Cowboys" posed with their 10-gallon hats in 1959. Shown here, from left to right, are Pat DiRuzza, George Janulevicus, and Dominic Franciose. Barbara Britton (far right) and her husband, Joe Britton, were proprietors of Britton's Market.

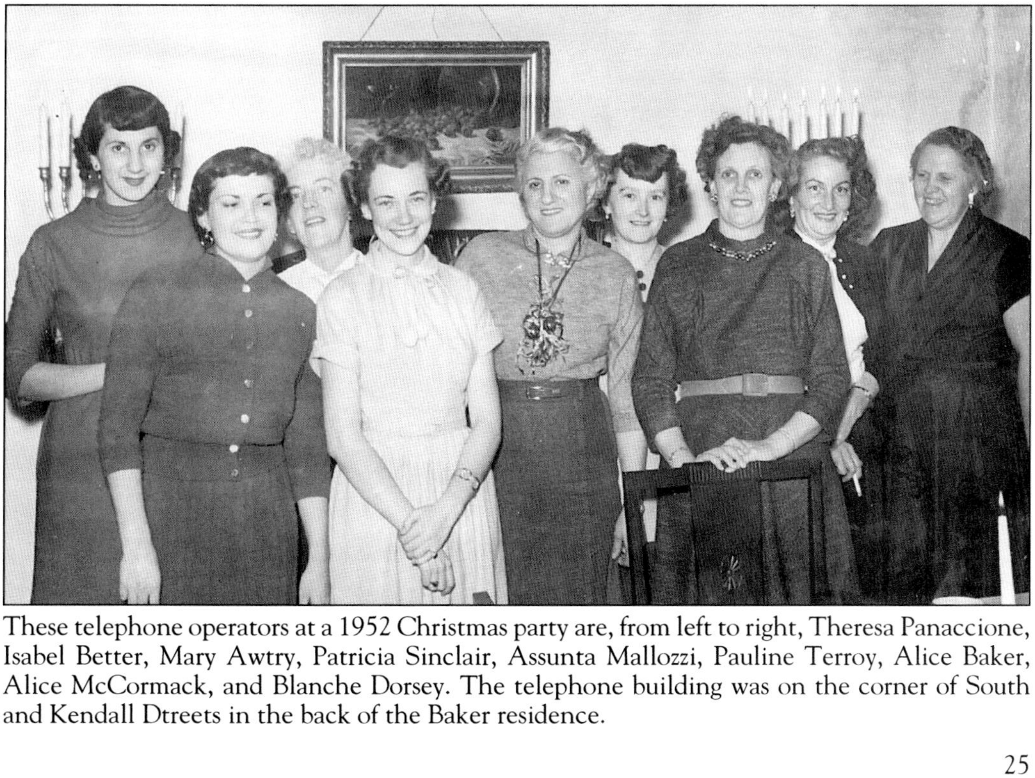

These telephone operators at a 1952 Christmas party are, from left to right, Theresa Panaccione, Isabel Better, Mary Awtry, Patricia Sinclair, Assunta Mallozzi, Pauline Terroy, Alice Baker, Alice McCormack, and Blanche Dorsey. The telephone building was on the corner of South and Kendall Dtreets in the back of the Baker residence.

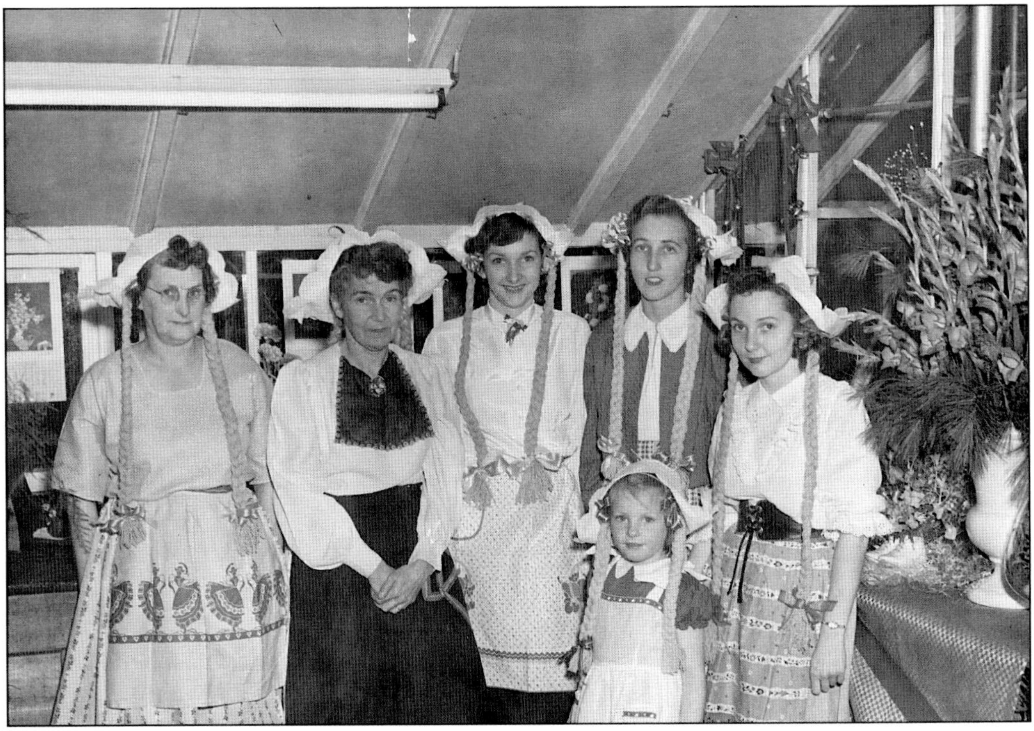

Pictured at the Easter Open House at Belcher's Florist are, from left to right, Laura Spinney, Viola Belcher, Lucille Belcher, Fay Dixson, Andrea Belcher, and Linda Spinney (front).

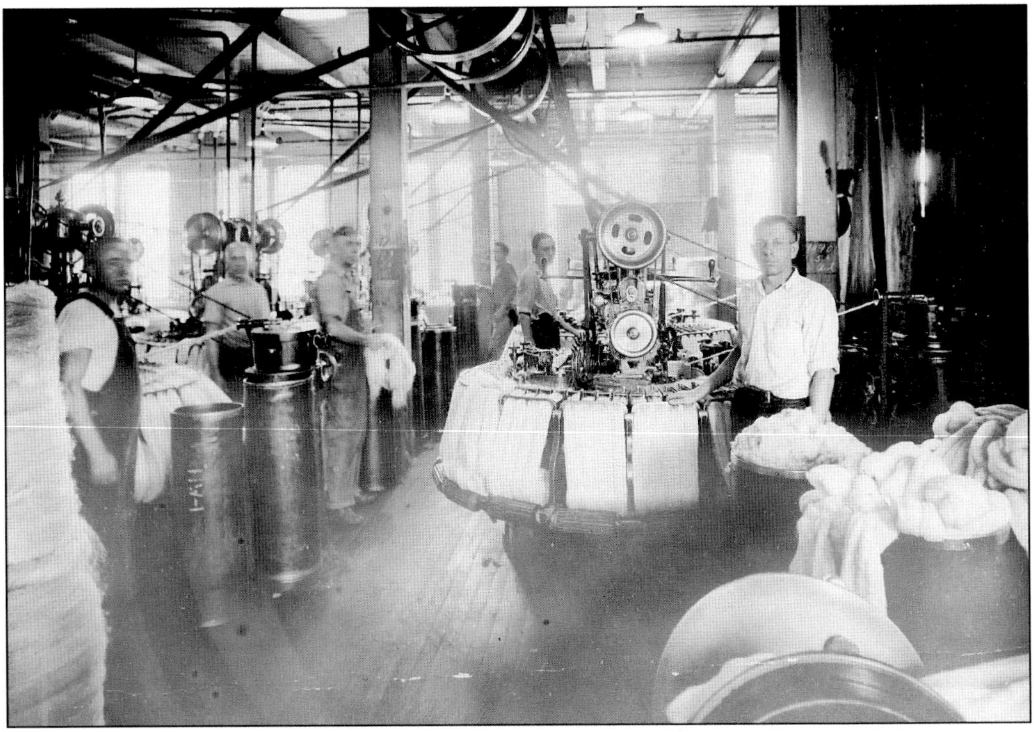

These employees worked for the Barre Wool Combing Co. Ltd.

Dorice Knight and Mrs. Iris Roan stand at the counter at the former Simenson's Store in 1954.

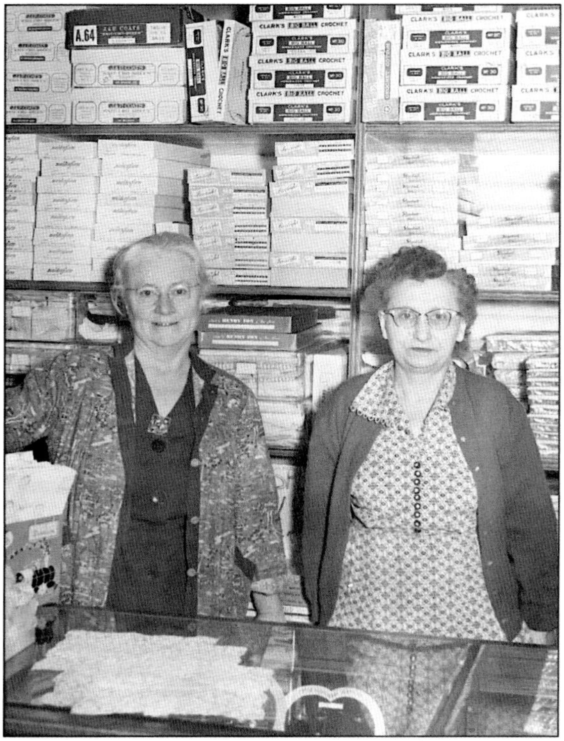

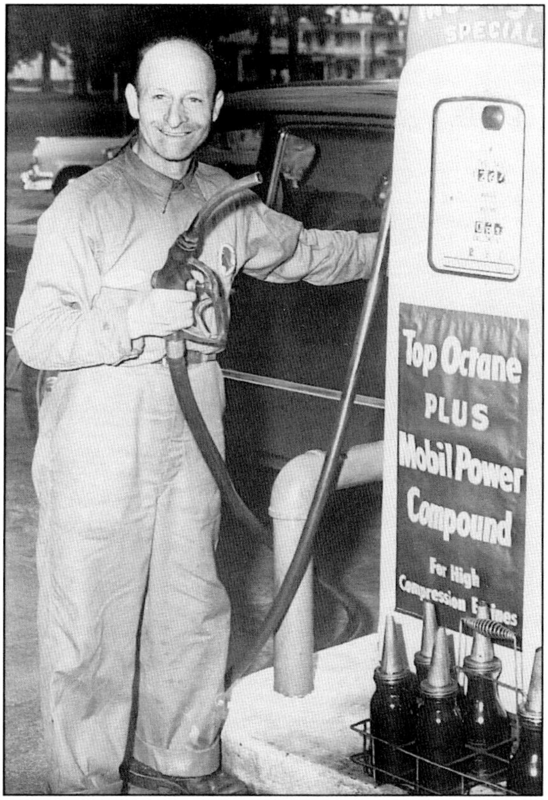

Employee Jimmy Rich always had a smile on his face when he filled a customer's gas tank at Beard's Garage. He is pictured here *c.* 1955.

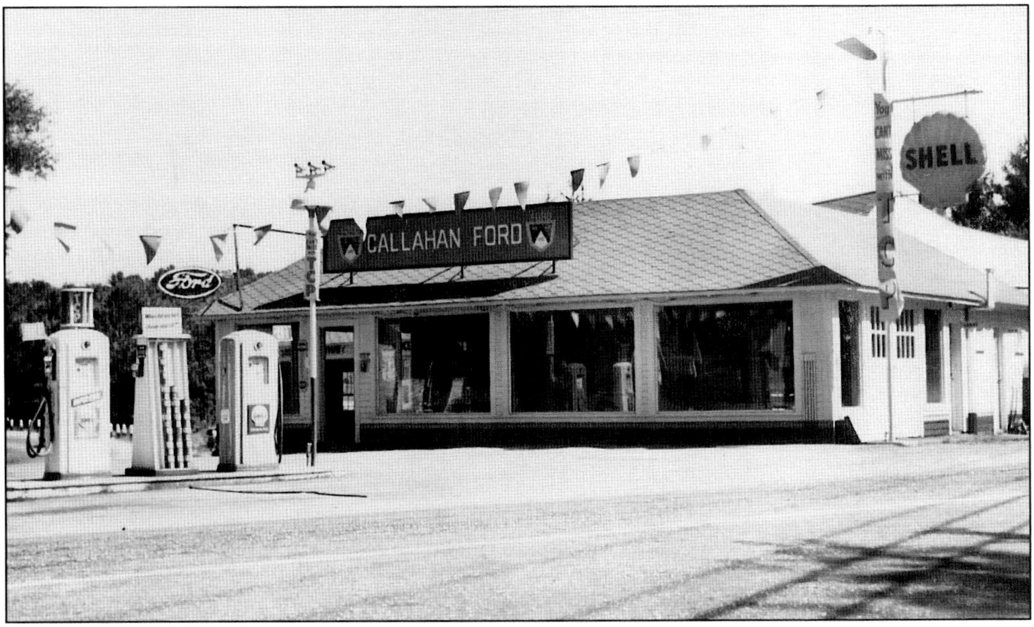

Callahan's Ford Garage served the needs of many in this convenient location on the corner of South Barre and Worcester Roads.

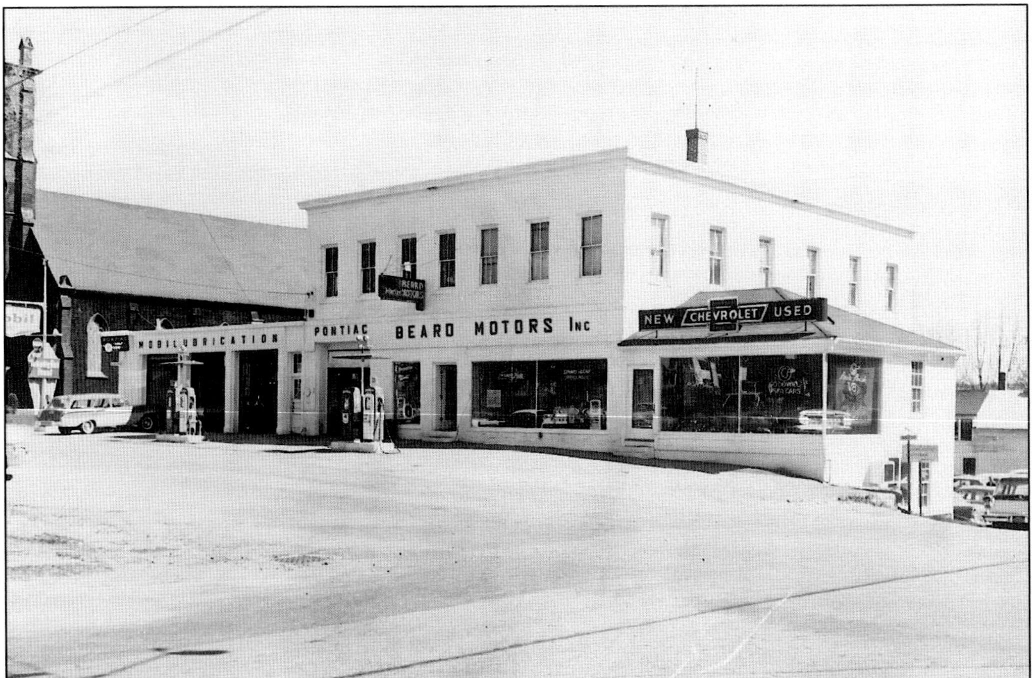

Beard's Garage was a dependable sales and service station in Barre.

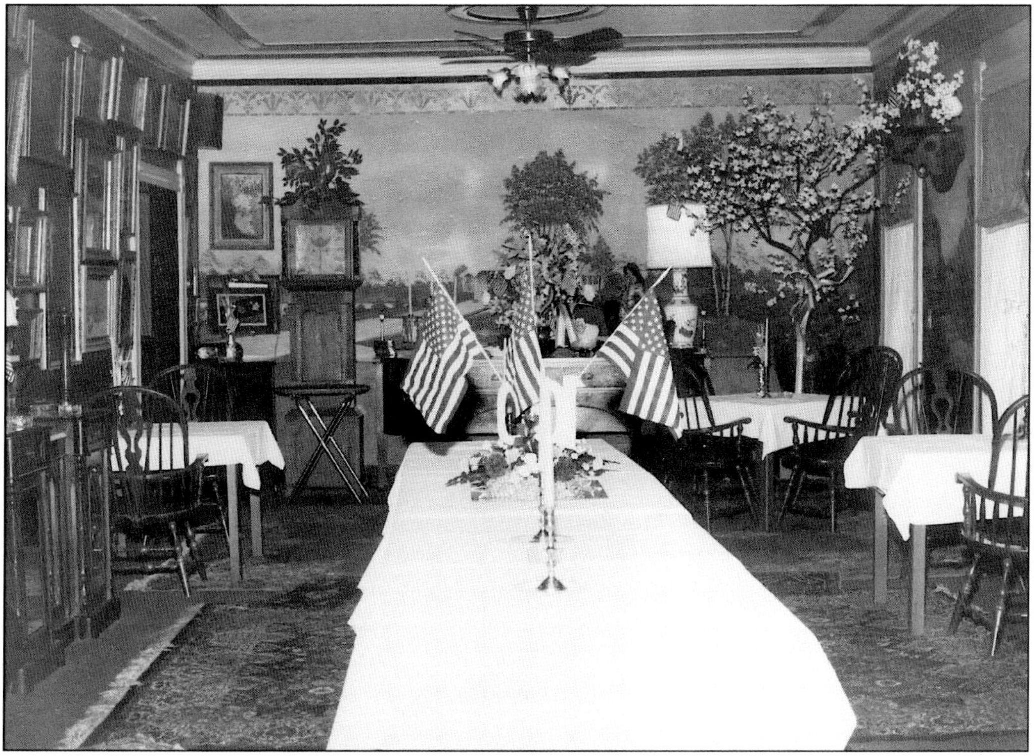

The Barre Room in the Hotel Barre was decorated to mark the centennial celebration of the hotel in 1989. The mural on the far wall depicted the covered bridge near East Barre Falls Dam.

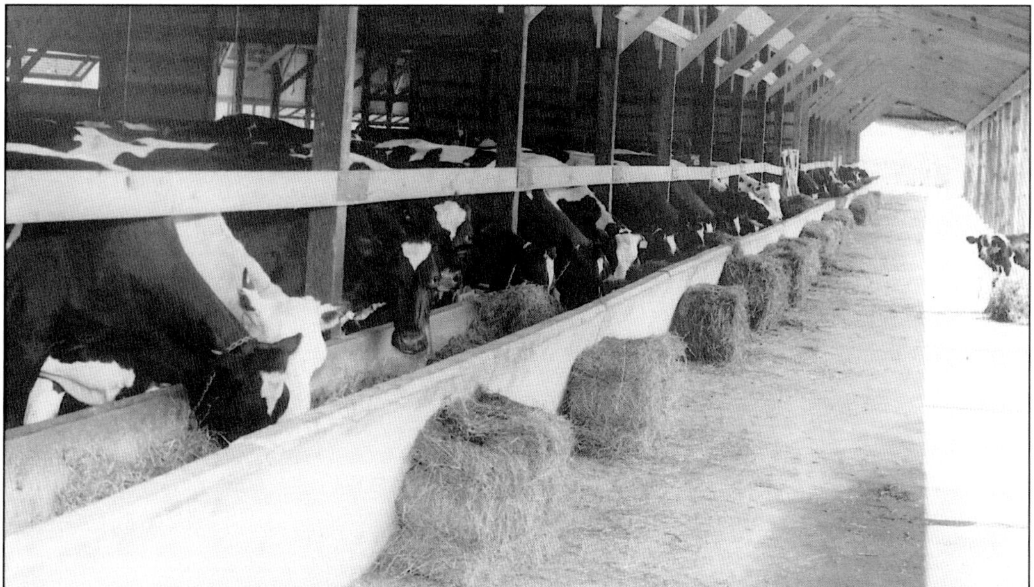

The Holstein cattle at Russell and Joan Chase's dairy farm in Barre Plains enjoy a peaceful noontime meal in 1983. One little calf stands in the sunlight by its bale of hay.

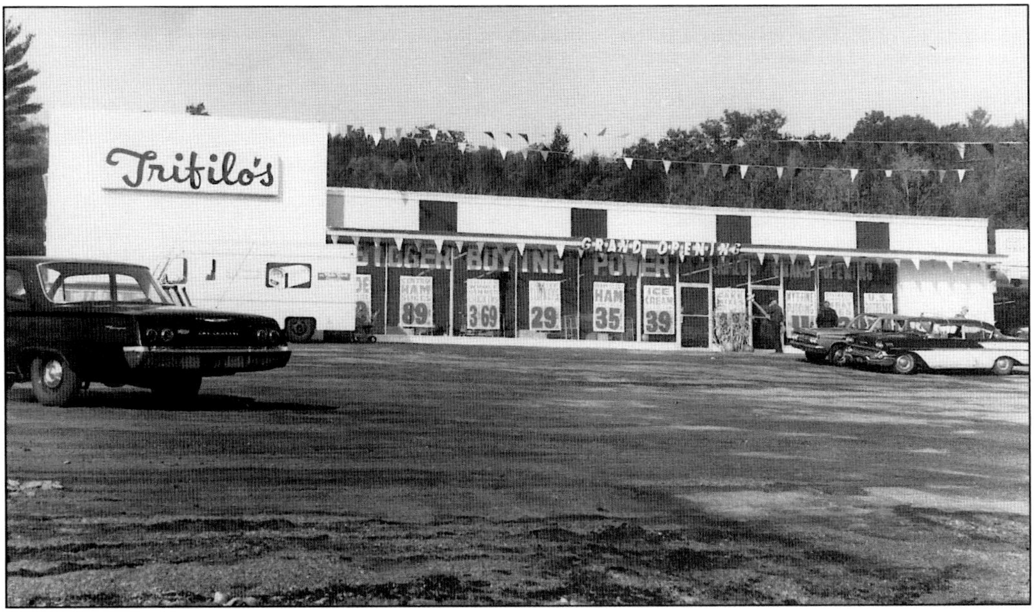

The gala opening of Trifilo's Super Market took place in 1964.

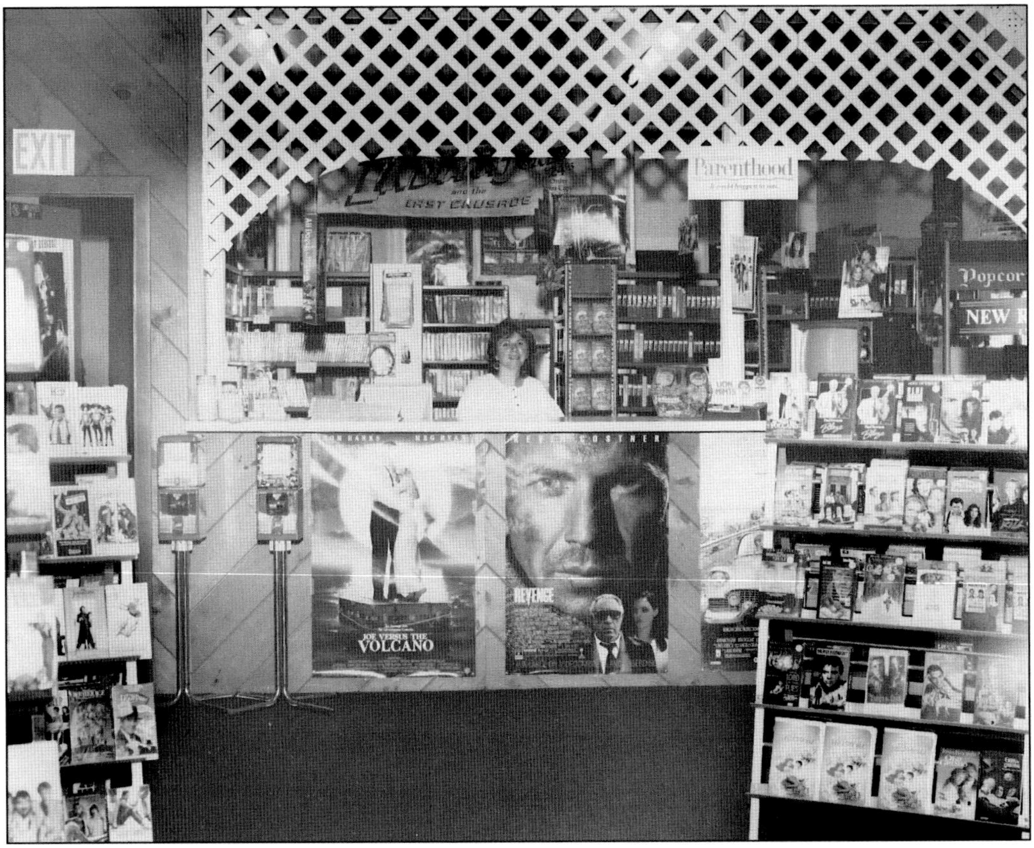

Uptown Video, a popular spot today, shows a facelift of the structure and many new videos in 1990.

Three

PAST TIMES: THE BEST AND THE WORST

Barre is not unlike many other villages and towns, which have seen the best of times and the worst of times. Over its long history, many such events have transpired and have been captured on film. The following is a sampling of pictures intended to preserve the flavor of some of those happenings.

"Mother Nature," in the form of floods, tornadoes, hurricanes, and sometimes fire has left an indelible mark on our lives and landscape. The tragedy of having one's business, home, school, or community damaged or destroyed by something beyond control cannot be measured monetarily. Loss of life because of outside circumstances exacts an even greater toll.

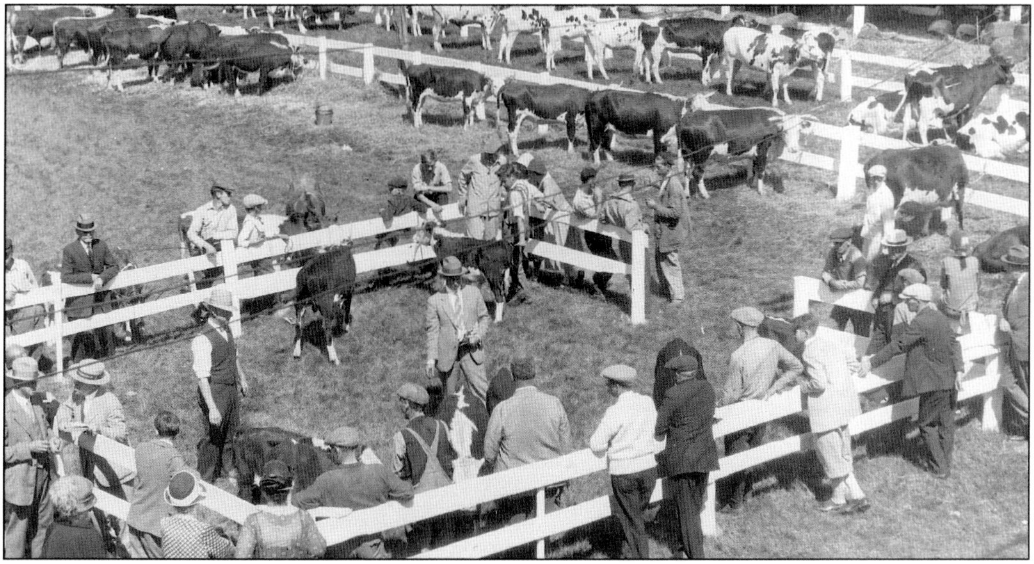

But Mother Nature also has a maternal side, which is manifested in the glorious way she blesses us with bountiful harvests and foliage. Nowhere was that better showcased than when the Barre Fair was in full swing. First held in 1833 on the Barre Common, it drew participants and viewers from around the county. Fast horse racing around the Common was part of the festivities, which eventually caused the fair to be held at what is now Felton Field. As this photograph shows, the viewing and judging of cattle was and is an integral part of the Barre Fair.

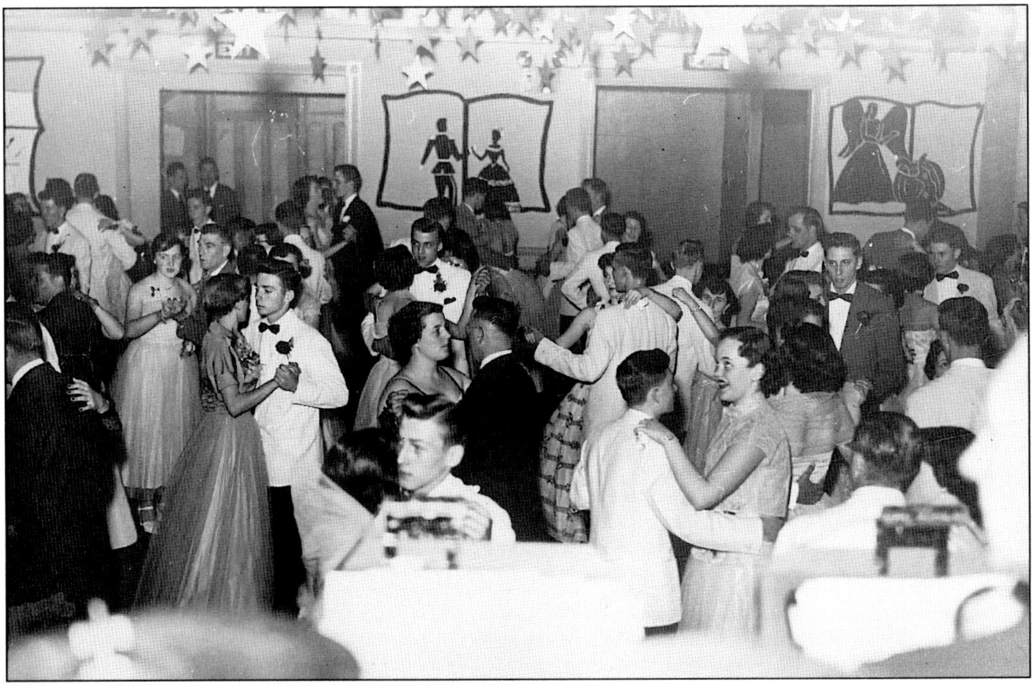

The very words FIRE! FIRE! strike the worst kind of fear in everyone. In the past, dances and other social events (above) were held in Williams Hall on the second floor.

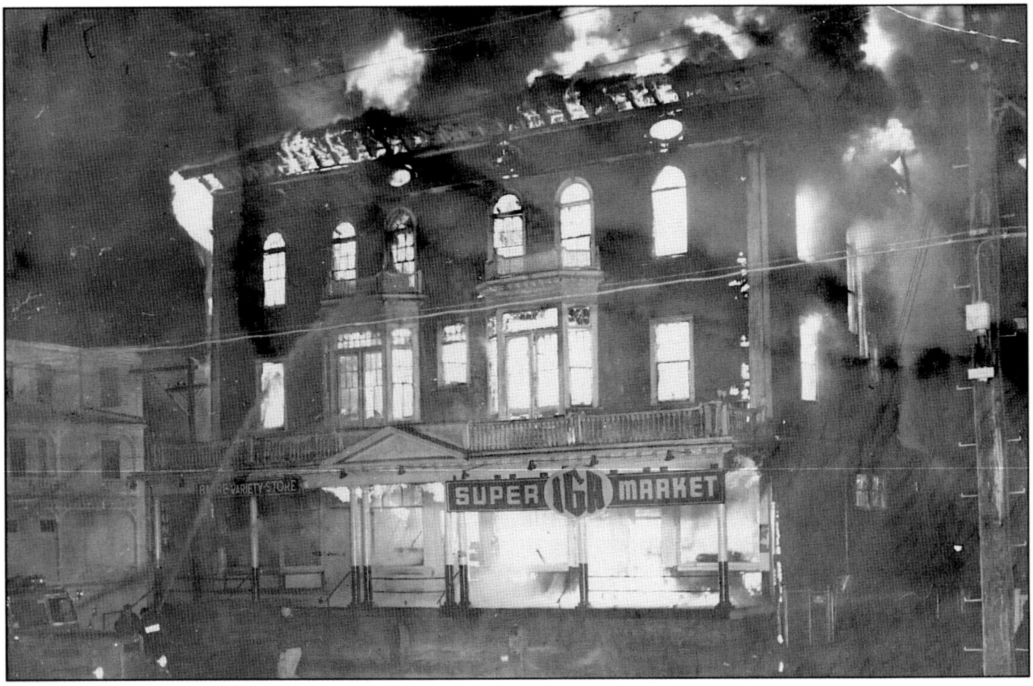

In the wee hours of the morning of November 8, 1956, the Williams Block, which housed the IGA Supermarket and a dry goods store, was engulfed with flames that brought complete destruction. Today, the empty lot next to the Barre Historical Society building is where that prominent establishment once stood.

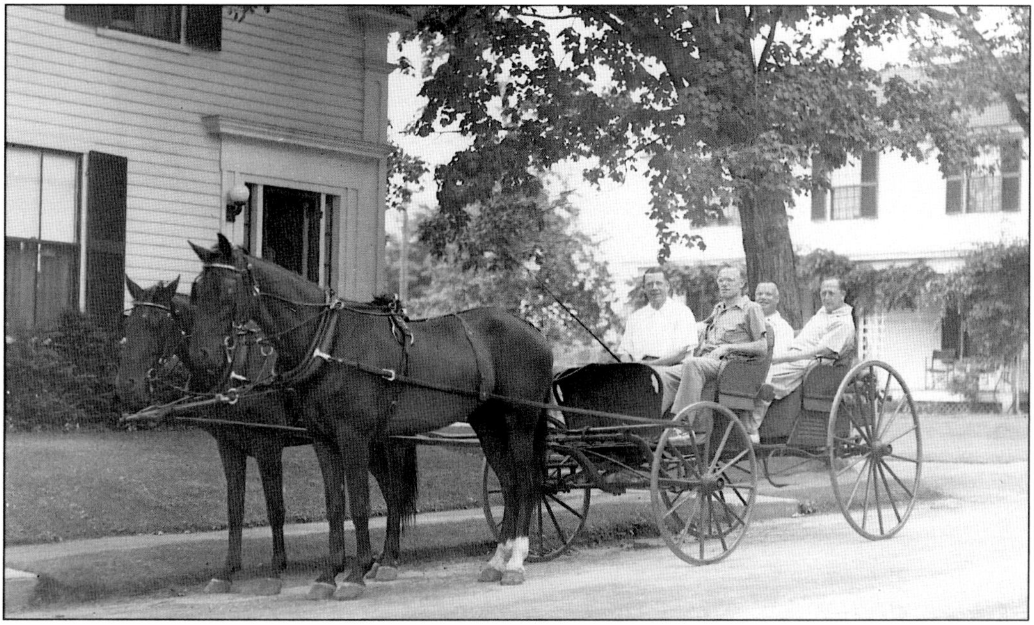

The history of the Chas. G. Allen Co. has been chronicled many times over the years. This pictorial narrative is intended to present the people who led the company during some of its most successful years, culminating with the winning of many awards for excellence during World War II. Seen here, from left to right in front of the Allen home on Union Street, are as follows: (front row) Charles G. Allen II and Charles G. Allen III; (back row) Dr. Bixby and Clarence Allen. The year was 1943, during gasoline rationing.

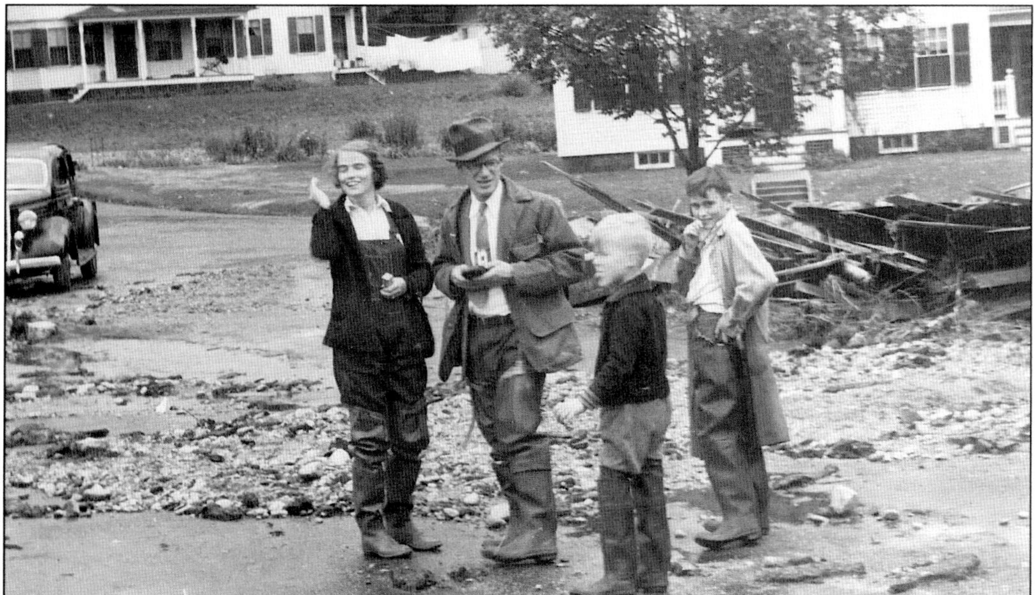

The mettle of the management of the Chas. G. Allen Co. was tested during the worst of times, such as the flood of September 1938. Shown surveying and photographing the damage at the junction of Christian Hill Road and Valley Road is Charles G. Allen III with Gladys Allen, Charles G. Allen IV, and Frank Amsden.

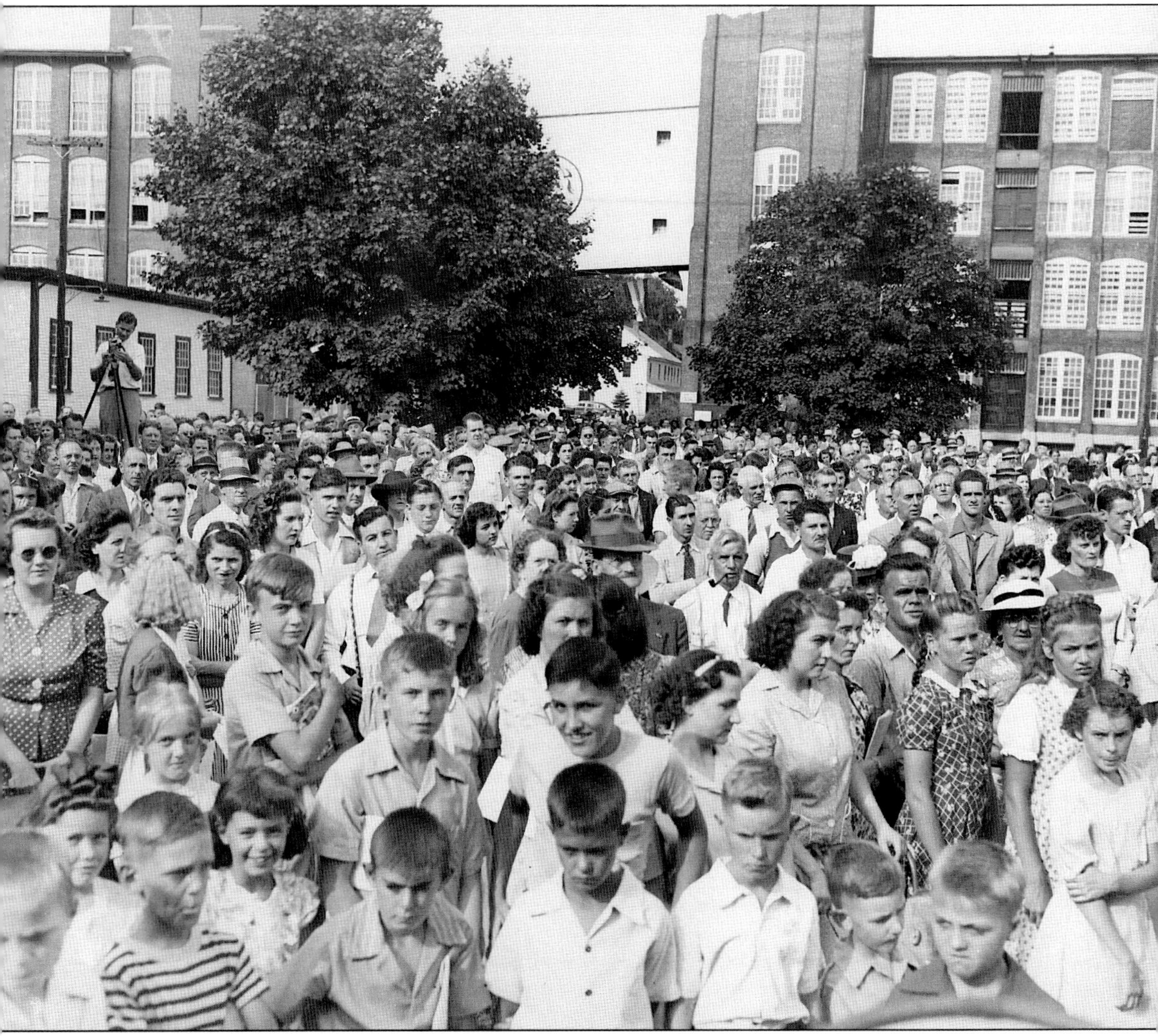

Not only was the Barre Wool Combing Co. Ltd. the largest employer in Barre, it was the largest establishment of its kind in the U.S. Founded in 1903 by Francis Willey (Lord Barnby) of England, Barre Wool produced wool top, which is used in making worsted yarns. Barre Wool also conducted excellent relations with the community and its employees. The photograph above was taken on July 22, 1943, when the coveted Army & Navy "E" citation was awarded for excellence in production during wartime. The families pictured here had sons and daughters in the U.S. armed forces and they worked hard to make certain there was an abundance of worsted clothing. Later, service award parties were an annual affair, and the whole town of Barre was invited to enjoy the games, food, and entertainment.

Interlaced with the good times, however, there were several very contentious episodes of labor strife, which those involved still remember. There were times when business was slow, and people experienced unemployment. However, the impact of Barre Wool on the community was generally positive until the company's demise in 1974.

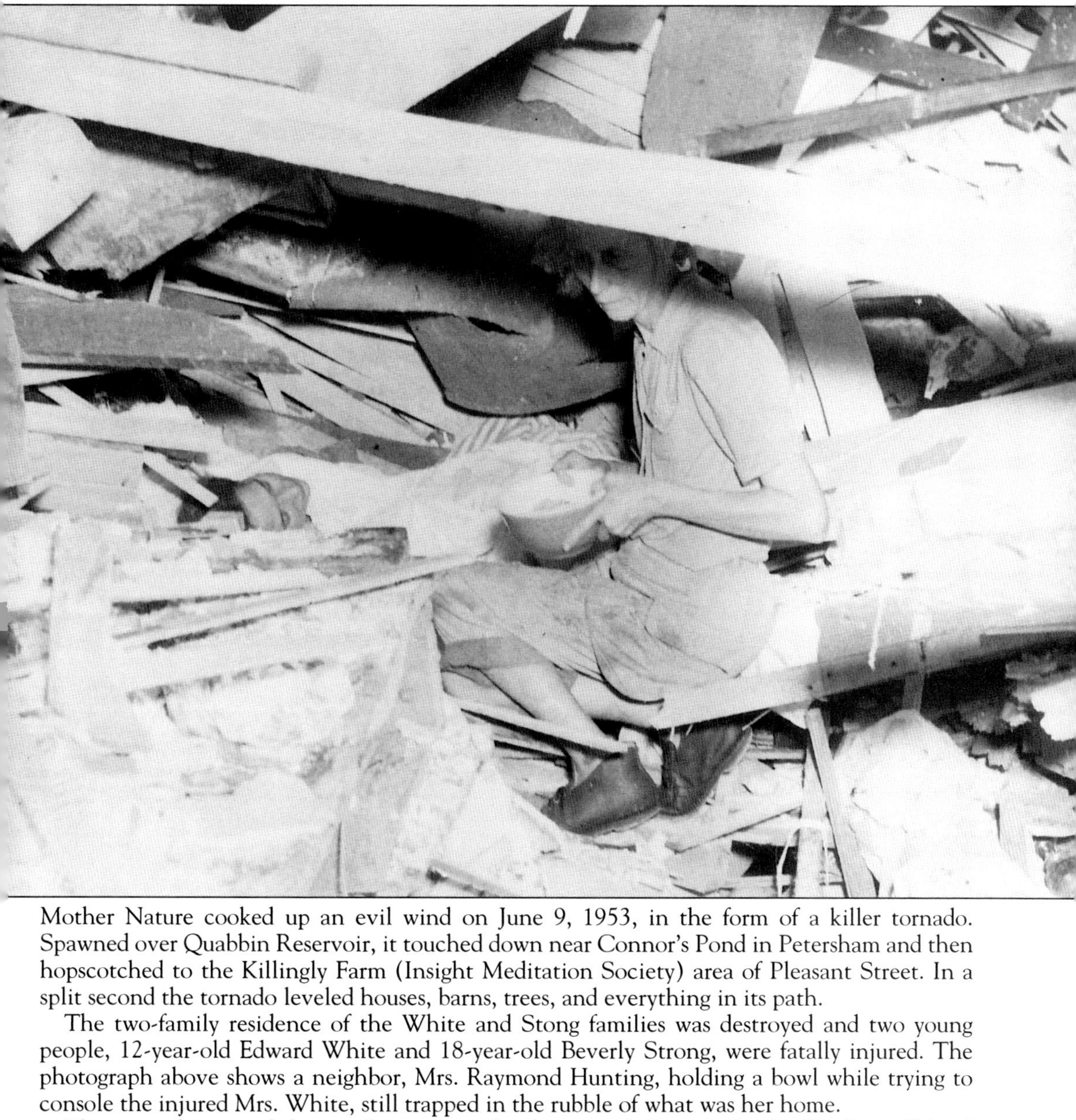

Mother Nature cooked up an evil wind on June 9, 1953, in the form of a killer tornado. Spawned over Quabbin Reservoir, it touched down near Connor's Pond in Petersham and then hopscotched to the Killingly Farm (Insight Meditation Society) area of Pleasant Street. In a split second the tornado leveled houses, barns, trees, and everything in its path.

The two-family residence of the White and Stong families was destroyed and two young people, 12-year-old Edward White and 18-year-old Beverly Strong, were fatally injured. The photograph above shows a neighbor, Mrs. Raymond Hunting, holding a bowl while trying to console the injured Mrs. White, still trapped in the rubble of what was her home.

The tornado caused heavy damage to the homes of George R. Guilford on School Street, Lyle Stratton on Pleasant Street, Lewis Paquin on Christian Hill Road, and to the Charles G. Allen Co. before spreading massive destruction and death in Rutland, Holden, Worcester, and Shrewsbury.

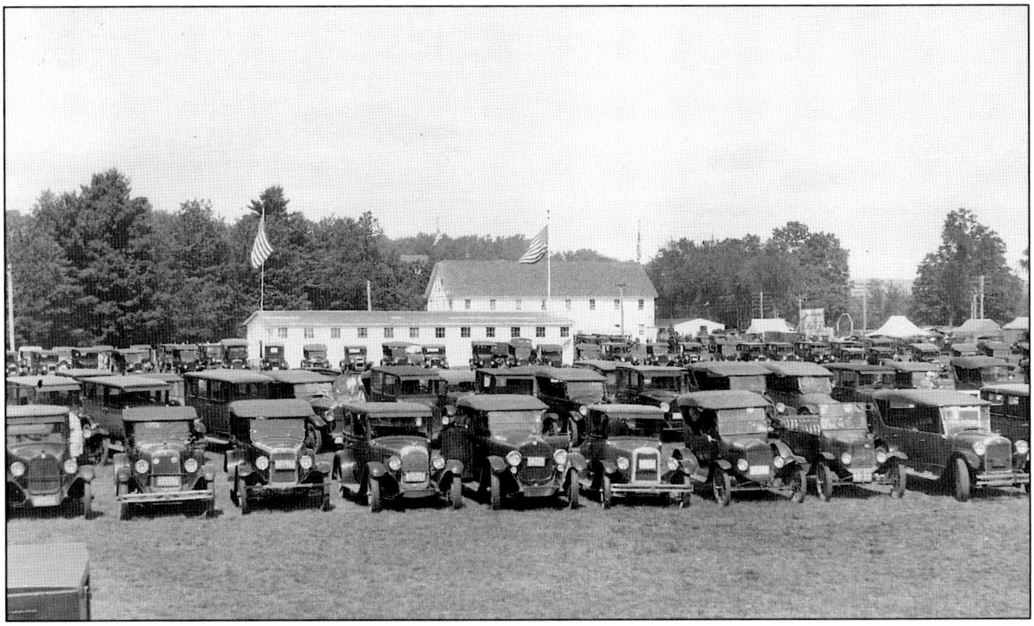

The 1920s were tumultuous years. Henry Ford had paved the way by making it possible for almost everyone to own an automobile. From miles around, people would flock to such events are the Barre Agricultural Fair, and a grand time was had by all. This photograph shows that a large portion of the field was taken just to park these wonderful machines.

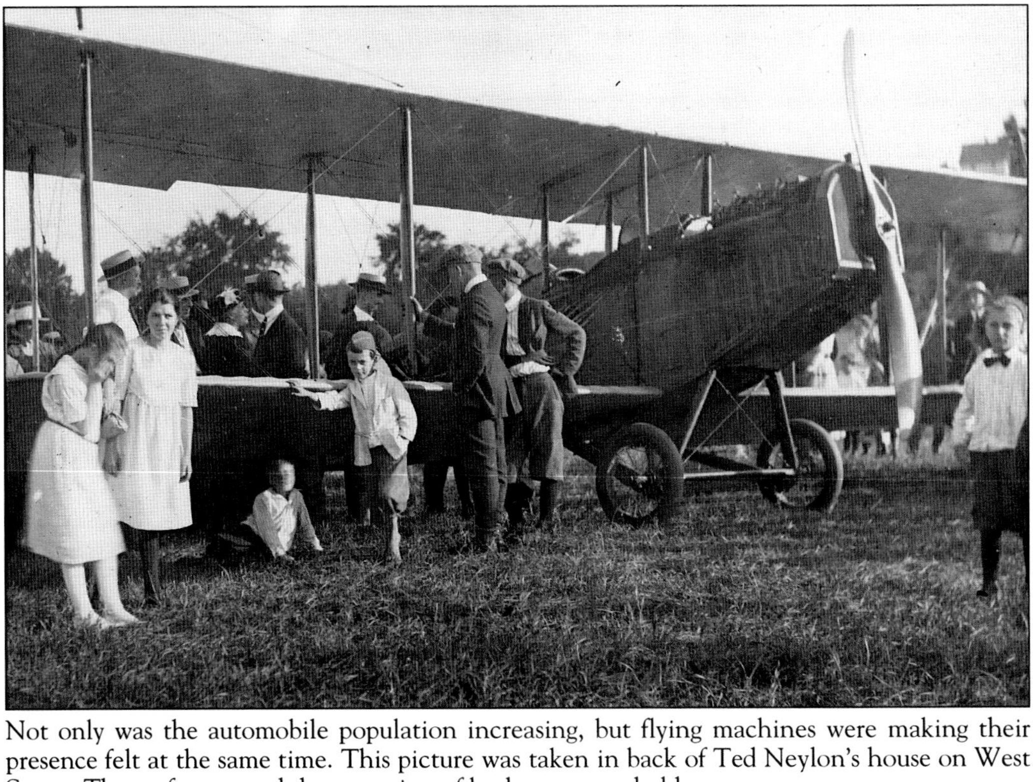

Not only was the automobile population increasing, but flying machines were making their presence felt at the same time. This picture was taken in back of Ted Neylon's house on West Street. The craft attracted the attention of both young and old.

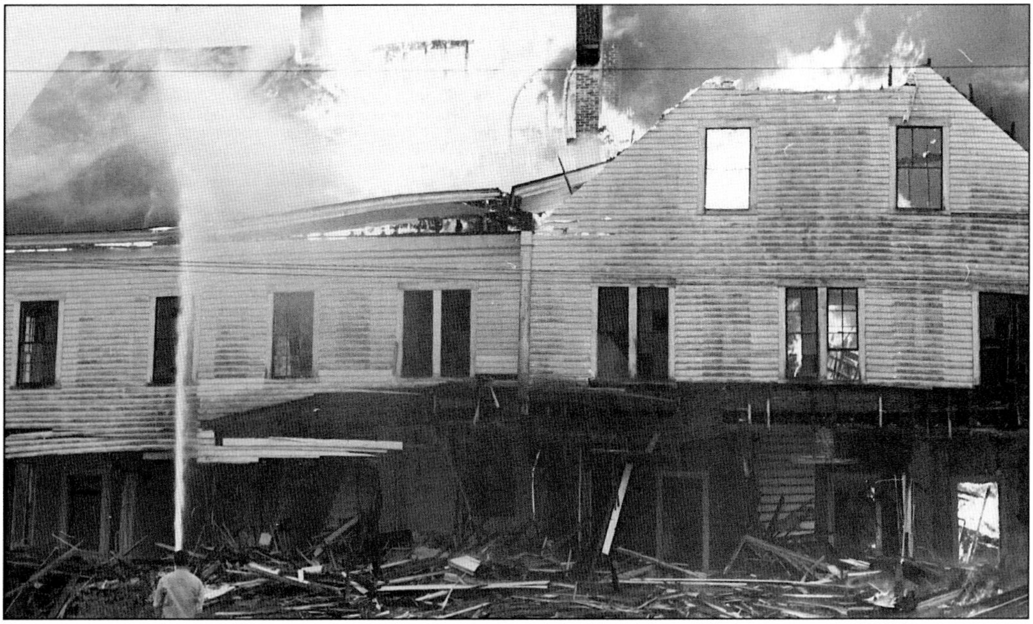

A spectacular "controlled" fire demolished the Barre Town Infirmary located on an isolated hilltop. There were 19 infirmary residents when its doors closed in December 1966. The state assumed the administration of public welfare from the town in 1968. A fire was the most useful way to remove this potential hazard.

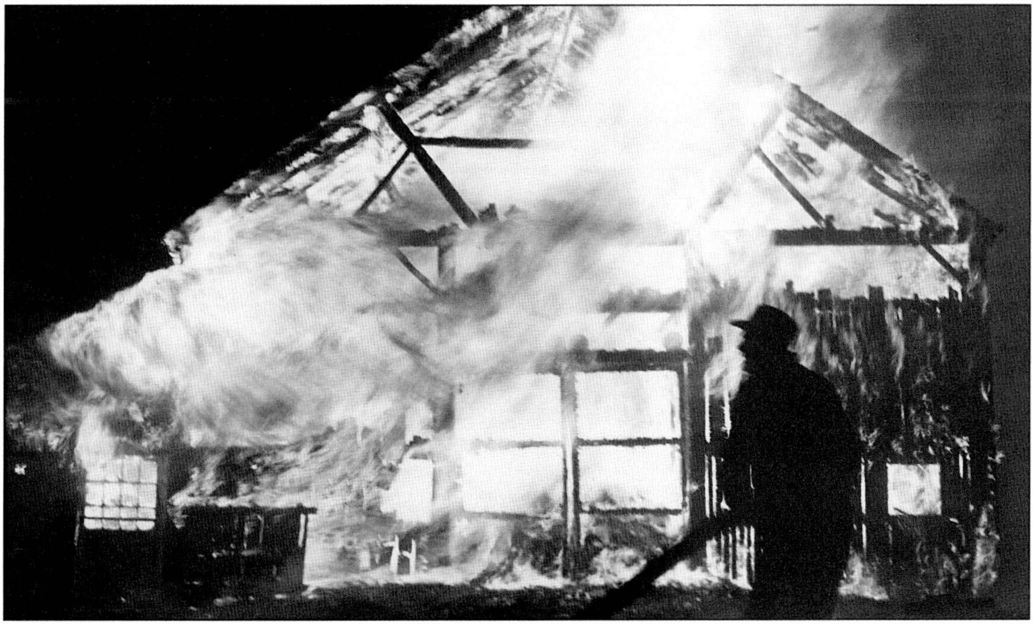

In the 1968 Barre Town Report, Fire Chief Harold E. (Had) Weeks laconically reports: "The Fire Department had a year that was fairly successful, in that, although we had some 73 calls, the overall was not too bad because the majority of them were small. We are still plagued by fires started by vandals, having one barn destroyed and about 12 fires in woodland." The Stetson Home barn, in 1958, and the Center School, in 1966, were other examples of Had Weeks' "plague."

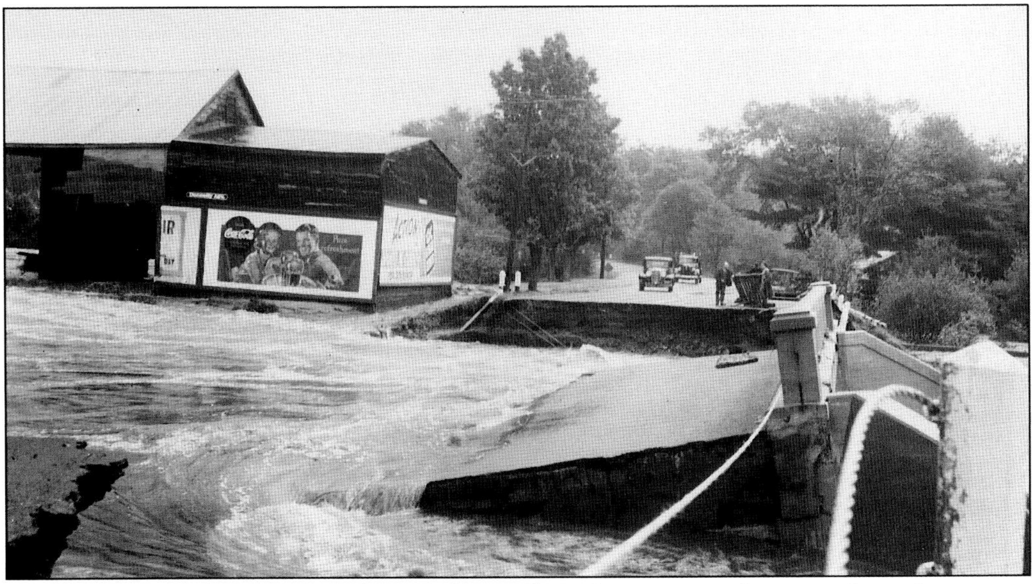

Torrential rains can cause great havoc when collected in rivers and sent crashing down upon man-made structures such as roads and houses. The above scene took place at the bridge on Worcester Road near the icehouse (now the location of Higgins' Energy) on September 21, 1938, just after the fierce hurricane.

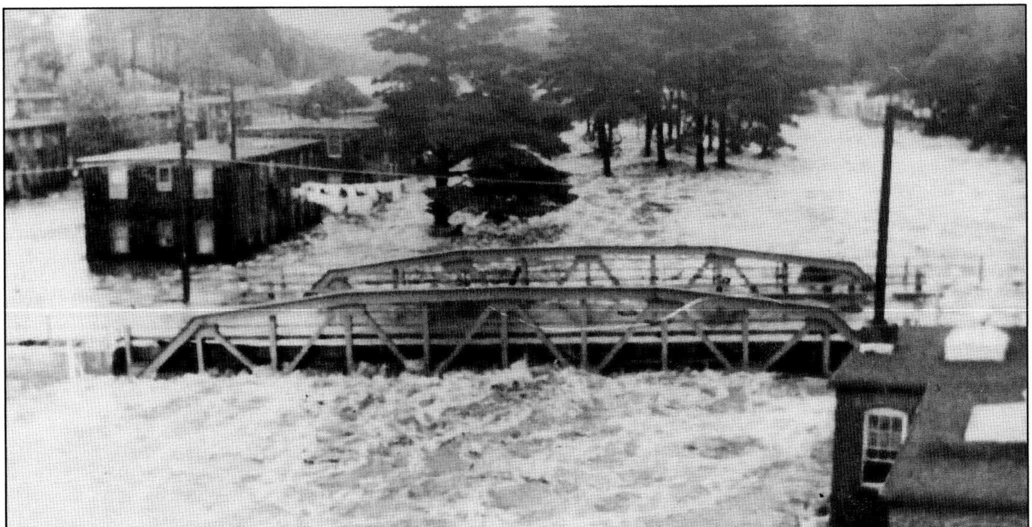

The next year, in March 1939, another flood of the Ware River occurred. This picture, taken from the roof of the Barre Wool Combing Co. Ltd., shows the bridge awash and the flooded houses on what used to be Ash Street. Note the clothes still "drying" on the clothesline.

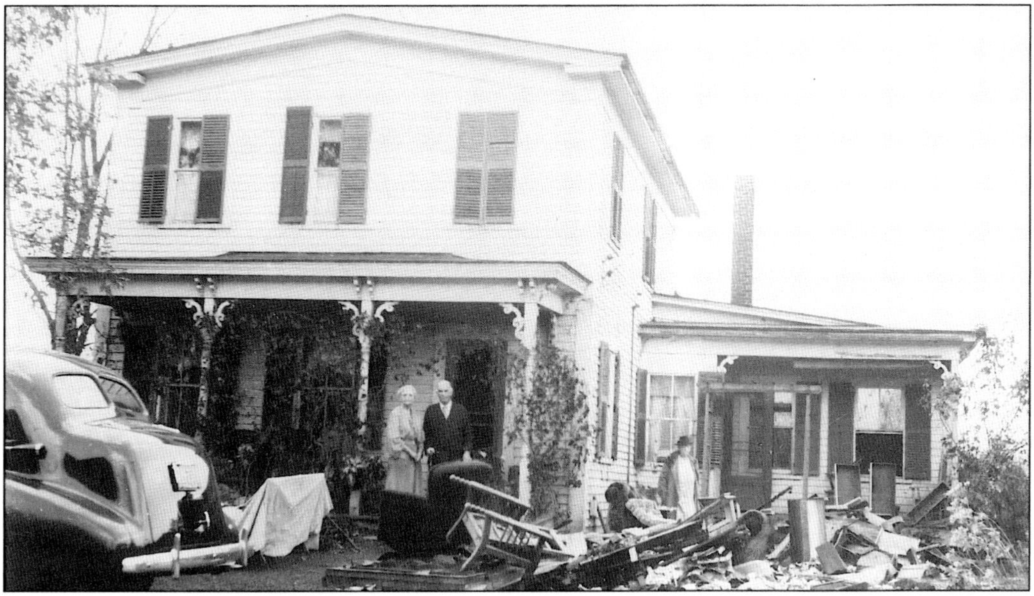

In this photograph, taken just after the 1938 hurricane and flood, children are looking out from the upper windows as occupants survey the damage. The water had risen 5 feet or more in the living room of this house at 46 Austin Street in Barre Plains.

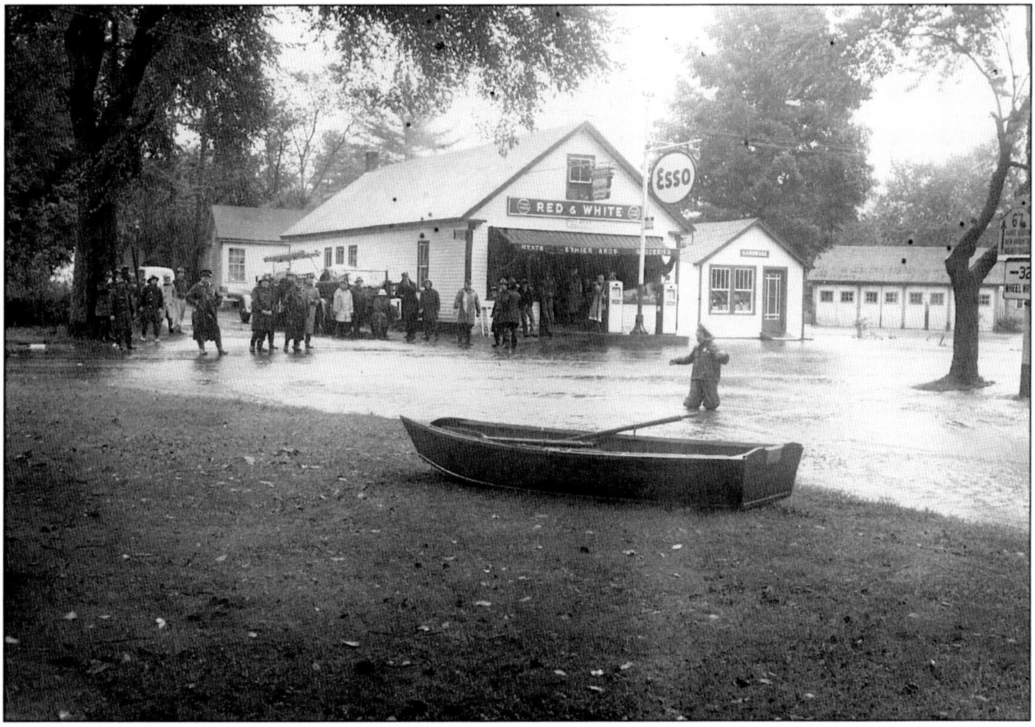

Barre Police Officer Joe Giarusso directs "traffic" at Ethier's Corner in Barre Plains. The occasion, the Flood of August 1955, prompted the need for flood control of the Ware River. The Army Corps of Engineers Flood Control Dam at East Barre Falls was dedicated on May 16, 1958.

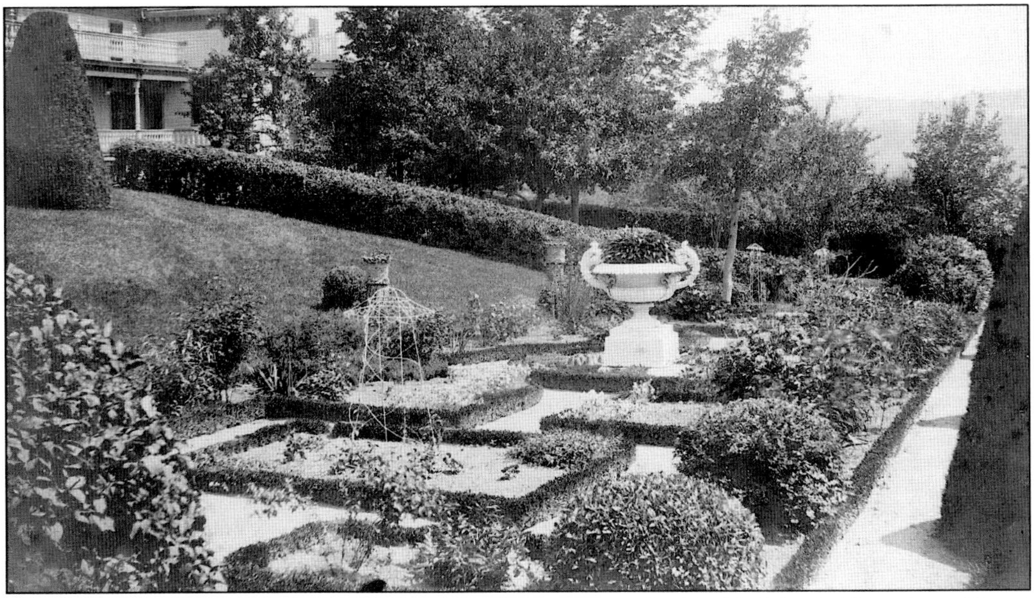

The marvelous grounds of Dr. George Brown's Institution for Feeble-Minded Youth on Broad Street (above), and the Central Park on Barre's Town Common (below) helped lift the spirits of residents and visitors alike. Even today, public-spirited citizens like Joe Pitisci and members of the Barre Business Association, spearheaded by Atty. Dan Kirkpatrick and Quabbin Regional High School students, plant and maintain beautiful gardens around the Common.

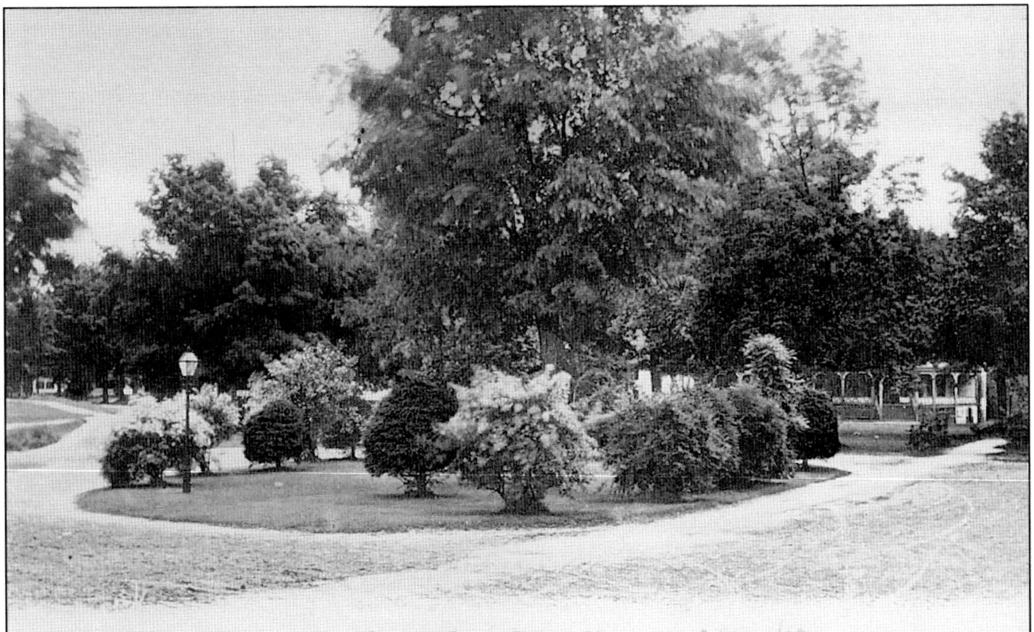

Four

MEMORIALS

Memorials can take many forms, from gravestones to large structures. Our stately library is a memorial to members of the Woods family, illustrious and philanthropic residents of Barre in the 19th century. Many memorials are to honor men and women who served our country in times of conflict. Others are just to show our appreciation for a life-long commitment to the community.

Since the Civil War, a succession of monuments has been placed in North Park as the nation and residents of Barre have been involved in tragic wars. For more than a century, an observance has taken place on Memorial Day where people assemble in the town center, not just to honor our former servicemen, but to show support for all the civic groups that march around the Common.

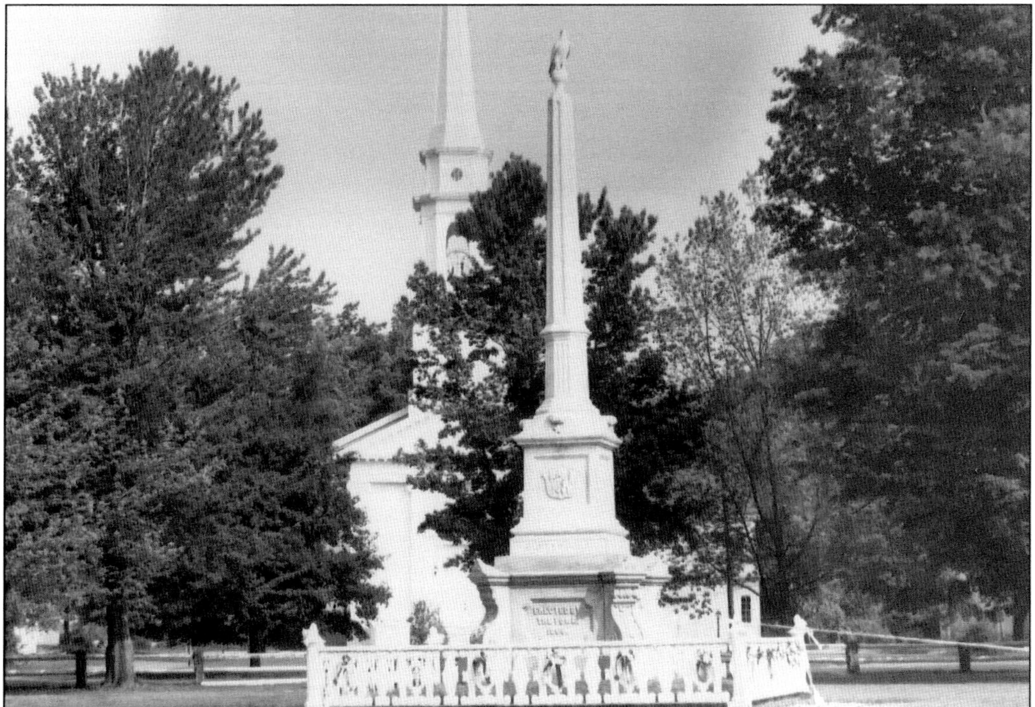

The centerpiece of North Park is the large granite shaft, which was erected in 1866 as a tribute to those from Barre who served in the Civil War.

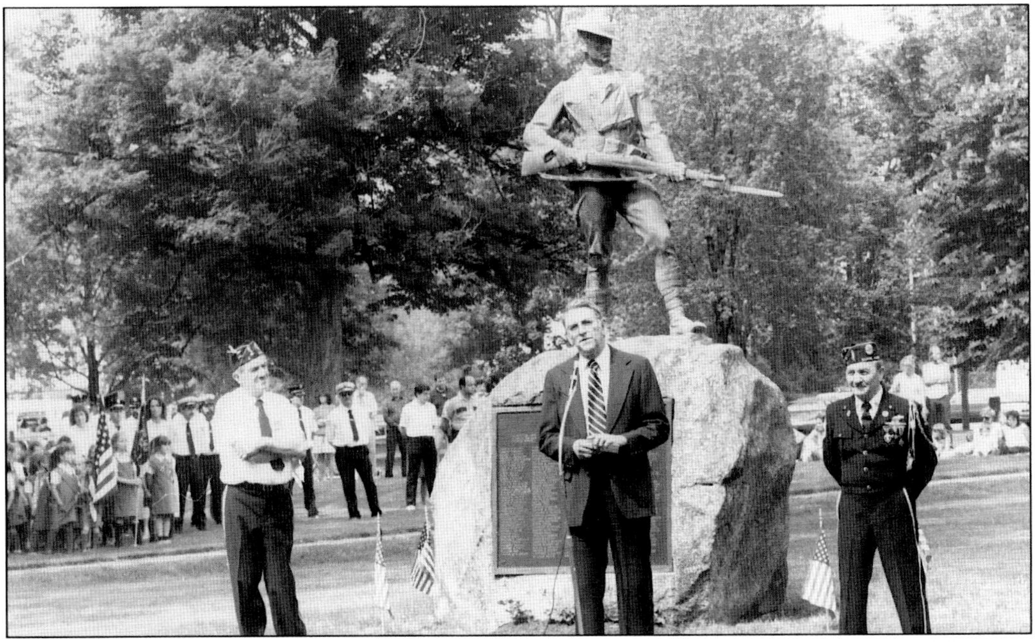

Speakers at Memorial Day exercises are escorted to the microphone near the World War I monument, a doughboy perched on a Barre boulder. Karl Witt and Dominic Franciose have brought Albert Clark, front and center, to salute the Civil War dead.

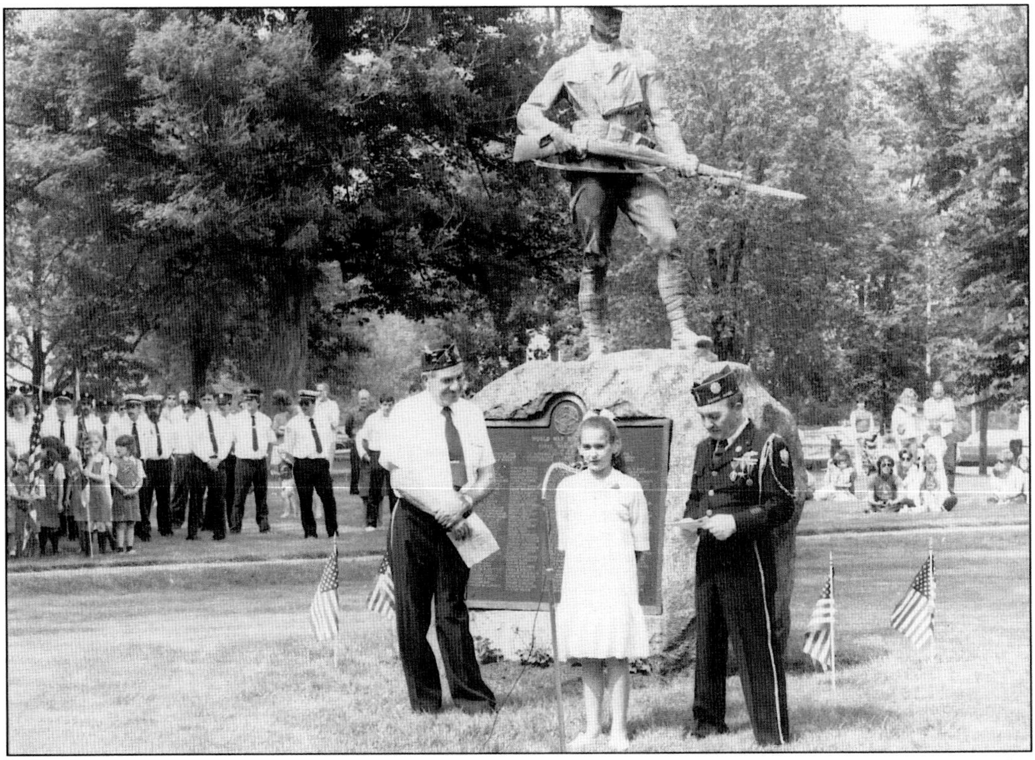

Another annual element of the exercises is the recitation of Lincoln's Gettysburg Address by a local student.

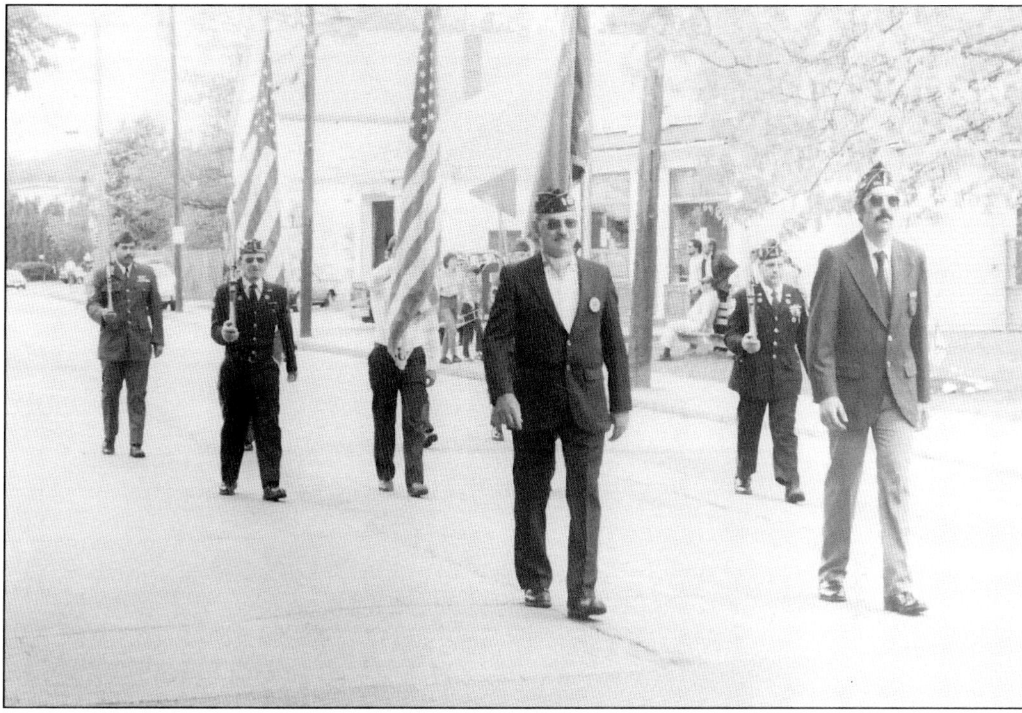

Legionnaires march to morning exercises in South Barre, Memorial Day, 1987.

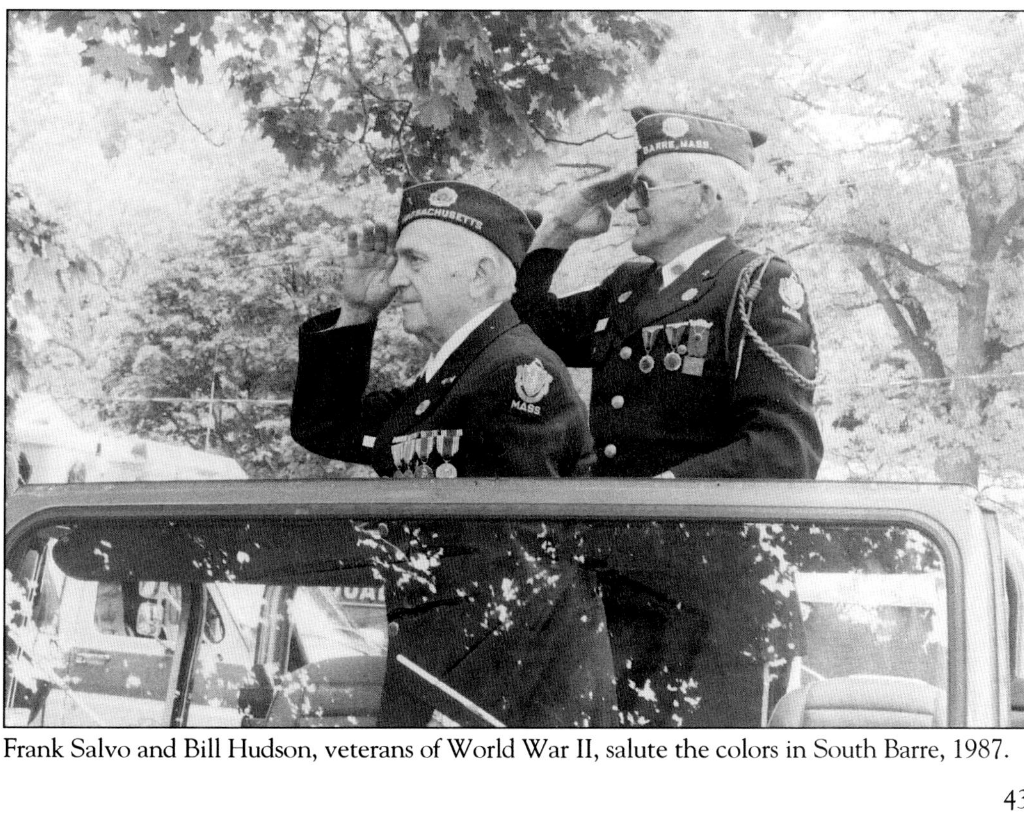

Frank Salvo and Bill Hudson, veterans of World War II, salute the colors in South Barre, 1987.

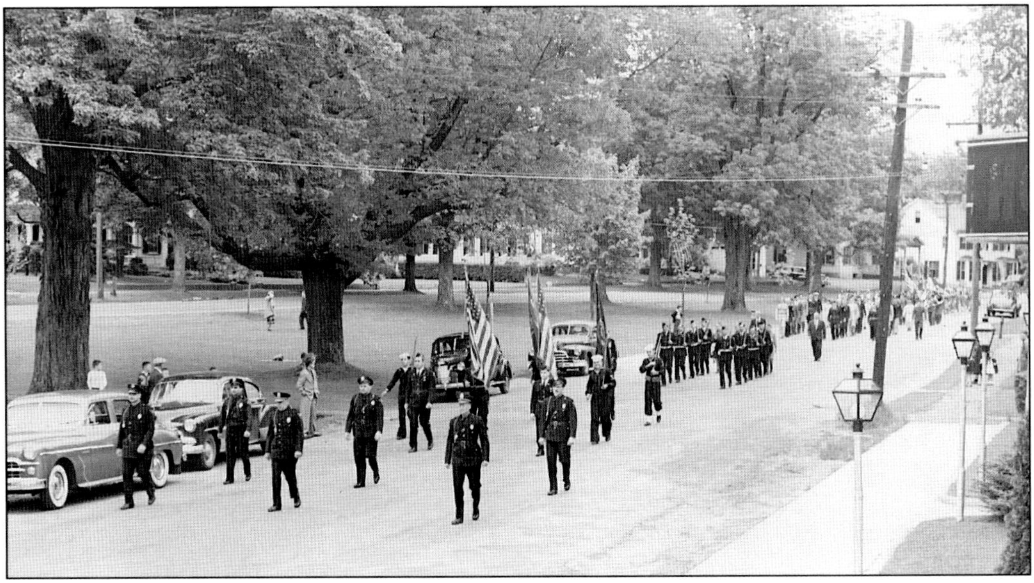

Local police officers lead the parade past the Hotel Barre, 1953.

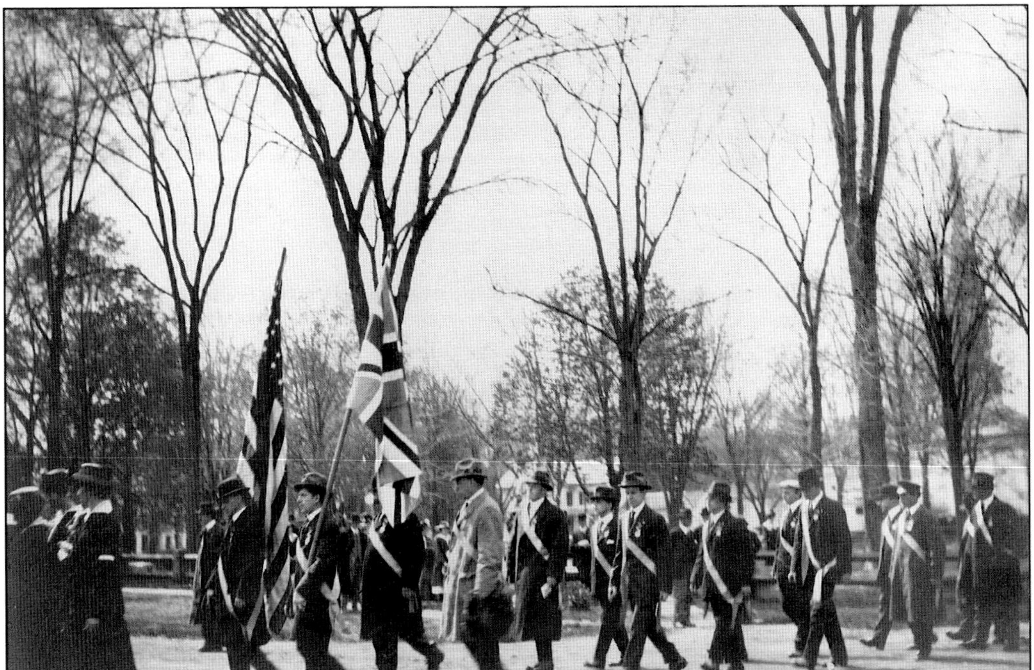

Among the groups recognized in 1917 by their World War I participation was the Sons of St. George, a men's group of the Episcopal Church. They are carrying the flag of an ally, Great Britain.

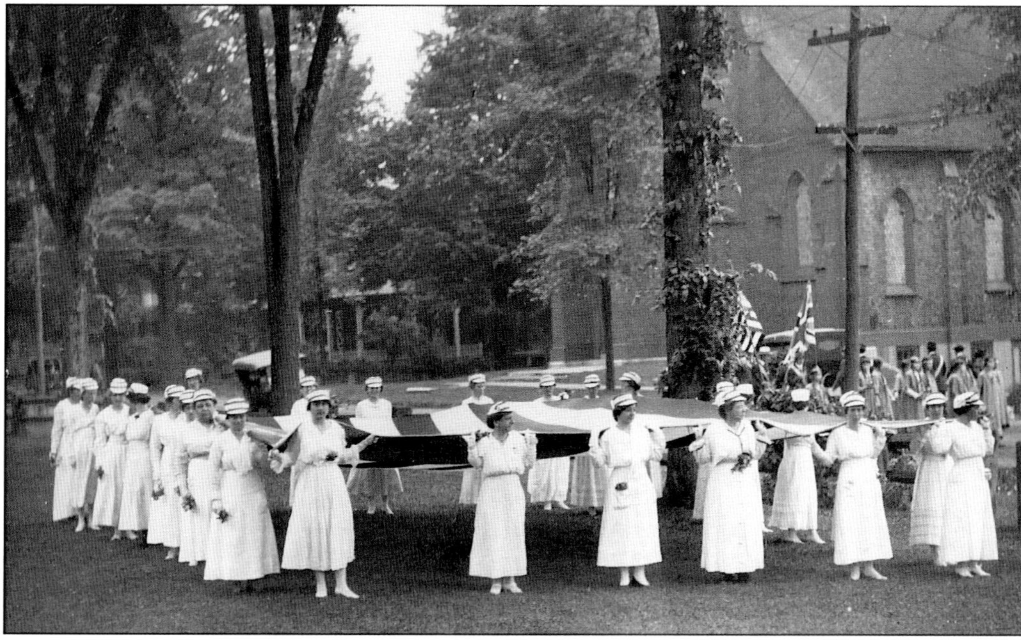

The American Legion posts have had their auxiliaries for many decades. During the 1918 observances, the Ladies of the Grand Army of the Republic showed their patriotism by carrying a large flag.

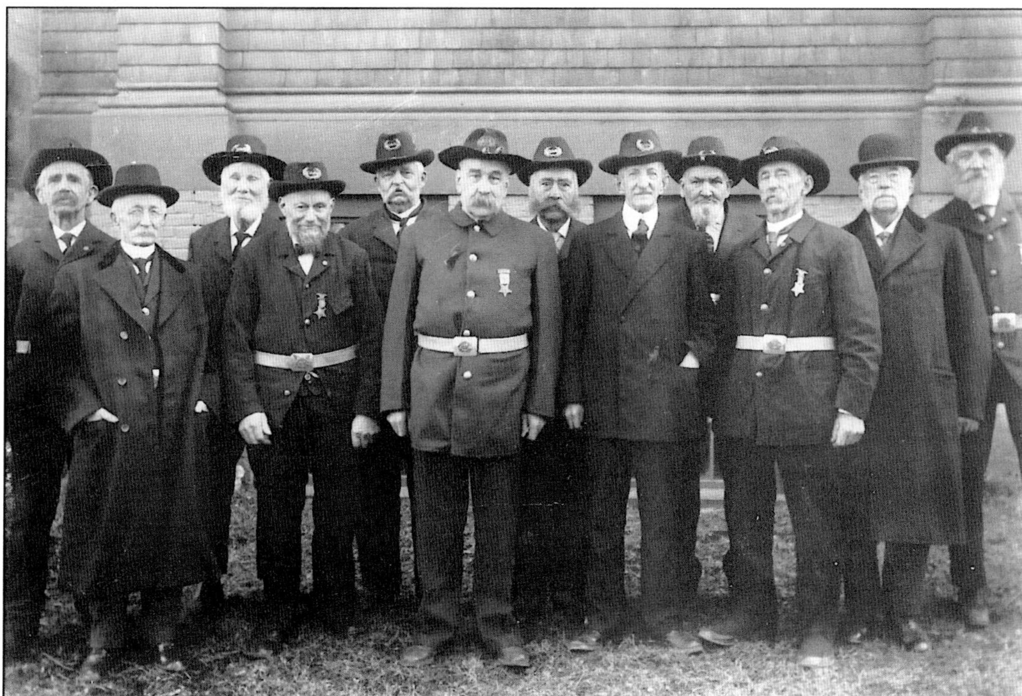

After the mammoth war between the states, veterans formed an organization to commemorate the conflict. Nearly 20 years passed before Barre men secured a charter for a post named after Lt. Col. Samuel F. Woods, who died of his wounds in 1864. These survivors marched in 1915.

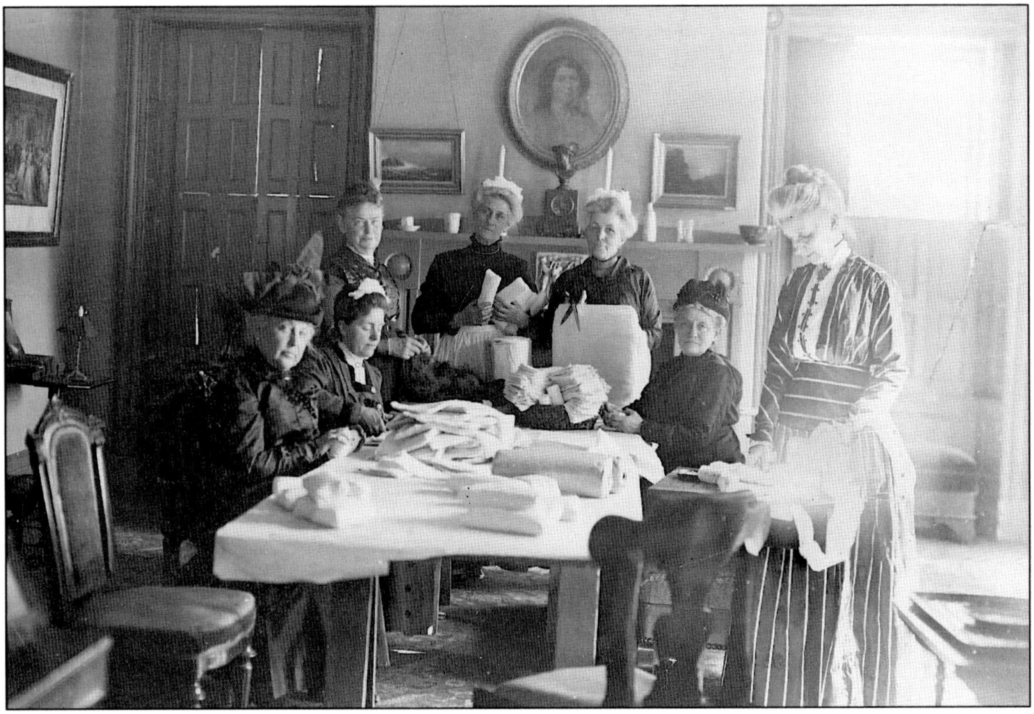

The American Red Cross, started by Central Massachusetts native Clara Barton, had its first great test in World War I. These ladies are one of the many work parties here in Barre who aided in the relief effort.

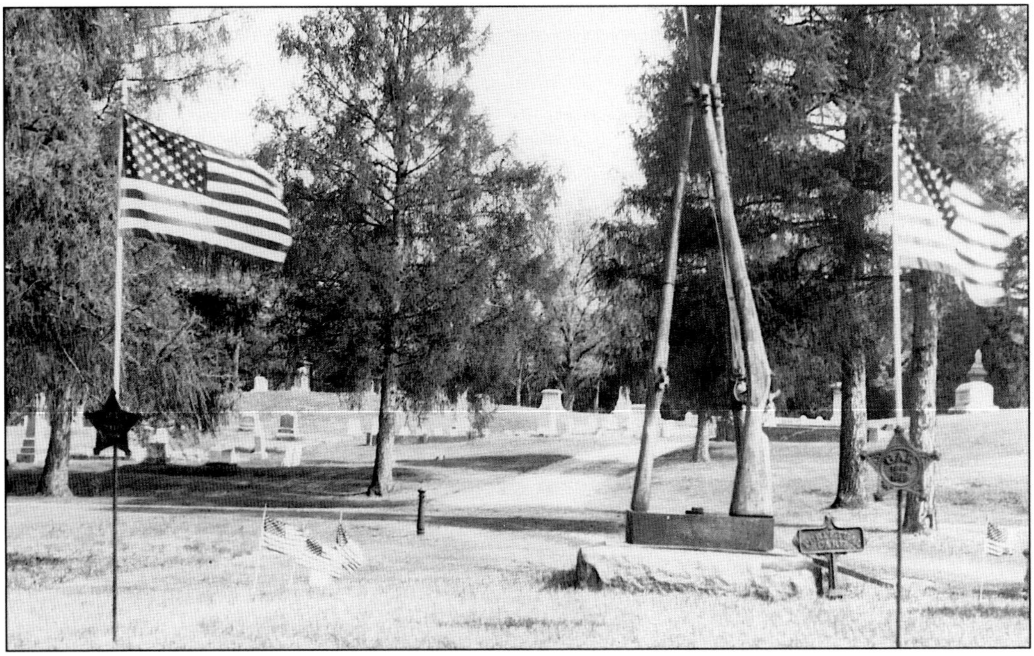

As it became the custom to have short exercises in Glen Valley Cemetery annually on Memorial Day, a monument in the form of three "stacked" rifles was placed there. The sculpture was made by a firm in Chicopee out of bronze and mounted on a granite base.

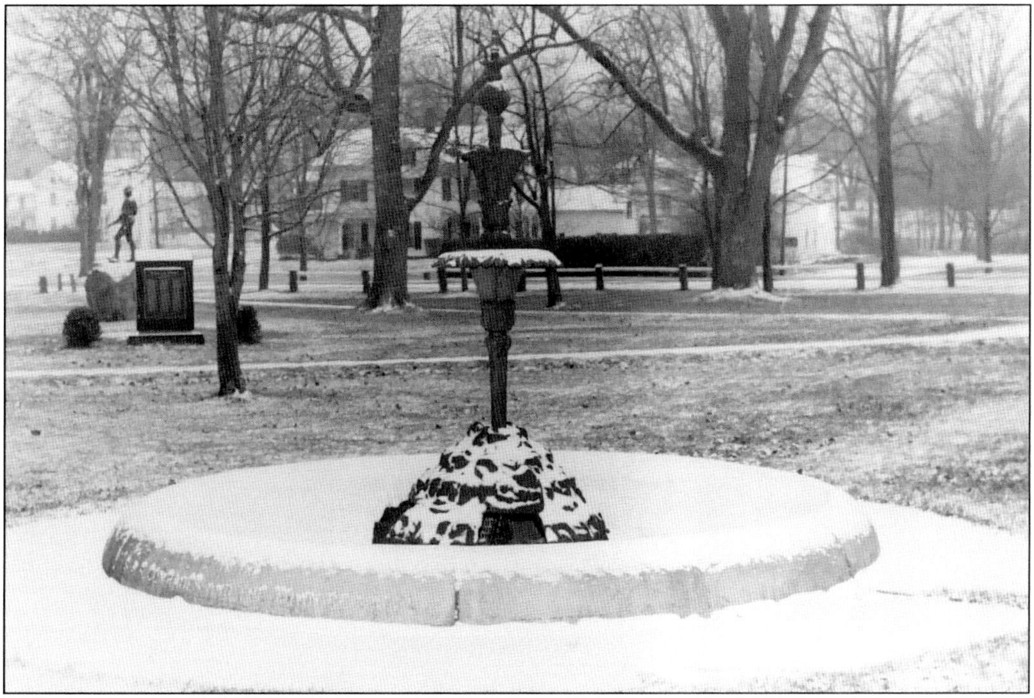

More than 40 years after the Civil War, a Barre woman donated a fountain for North Park in memory of her brother, James R. Brown, and "his comrades." Manufactured by the Mott Iron Works of New York City, it sits on a round base made of granite from Fitzwilliam, New Hampshire.

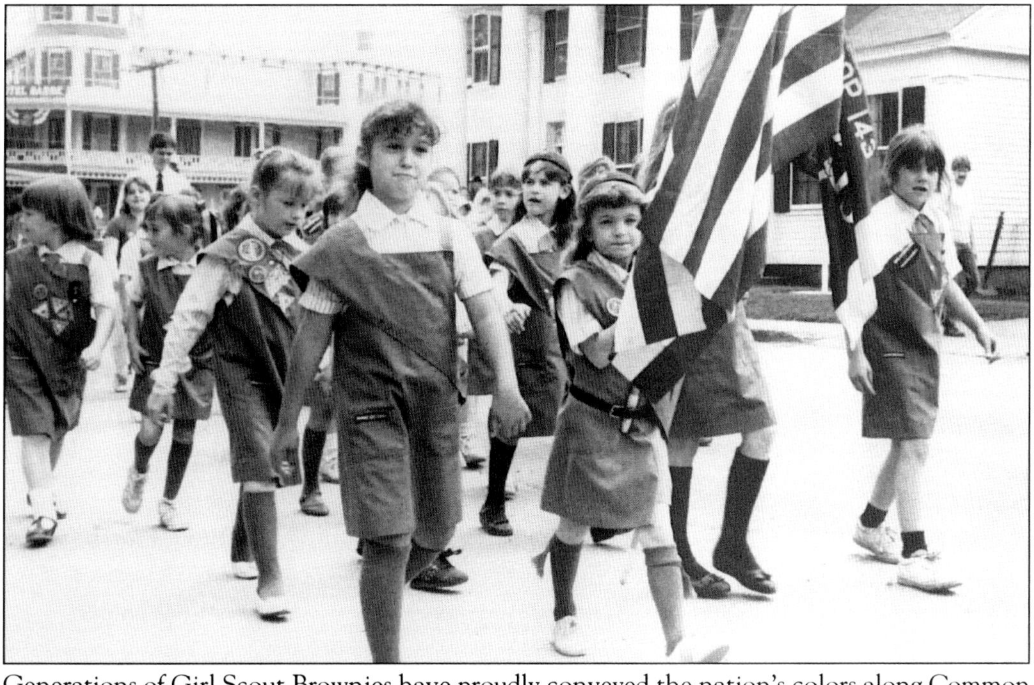

Generations of Girl Scout Brownies have proudly conveyed the nation's colors along Common Street on Memorial Day, despite sidewalk distractions.

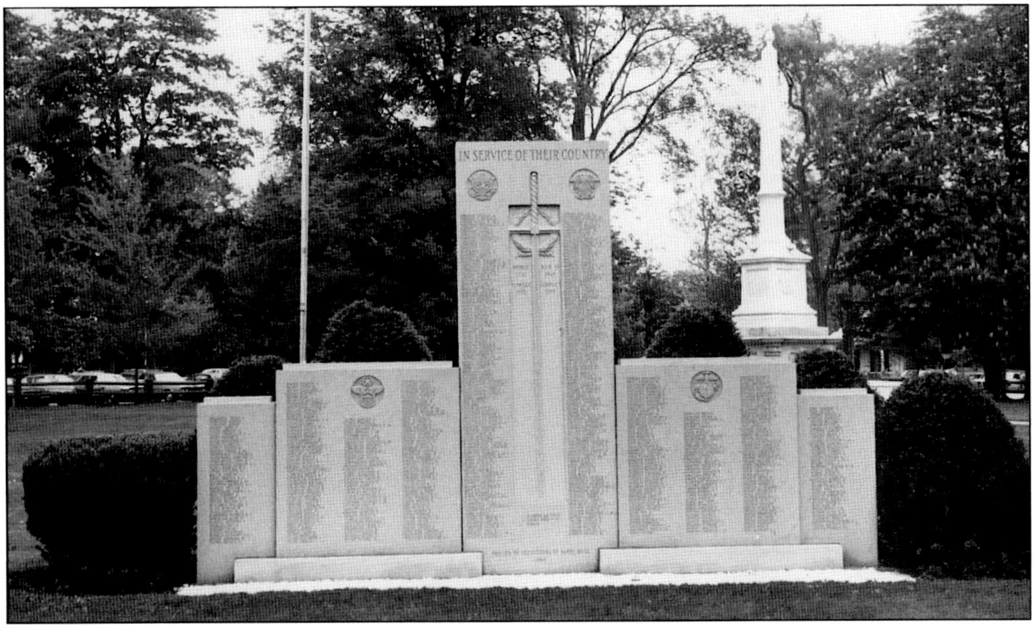

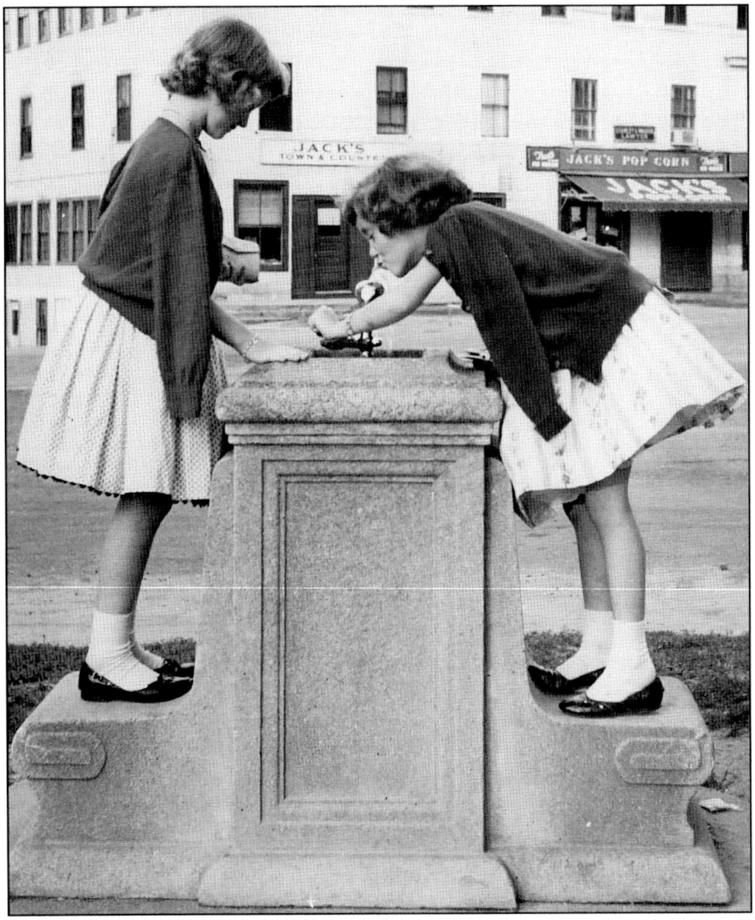

One large granite monument lists the names of Barre residents who served in World War II and the Korean War.

Dr. Walter Bates was a town physician for many decades, dedicating his life to the care of Barre's citizens. Here a pair of young girls gets a cooling drink from the fountain on the Common erected by grateful citizens in Bates memory.

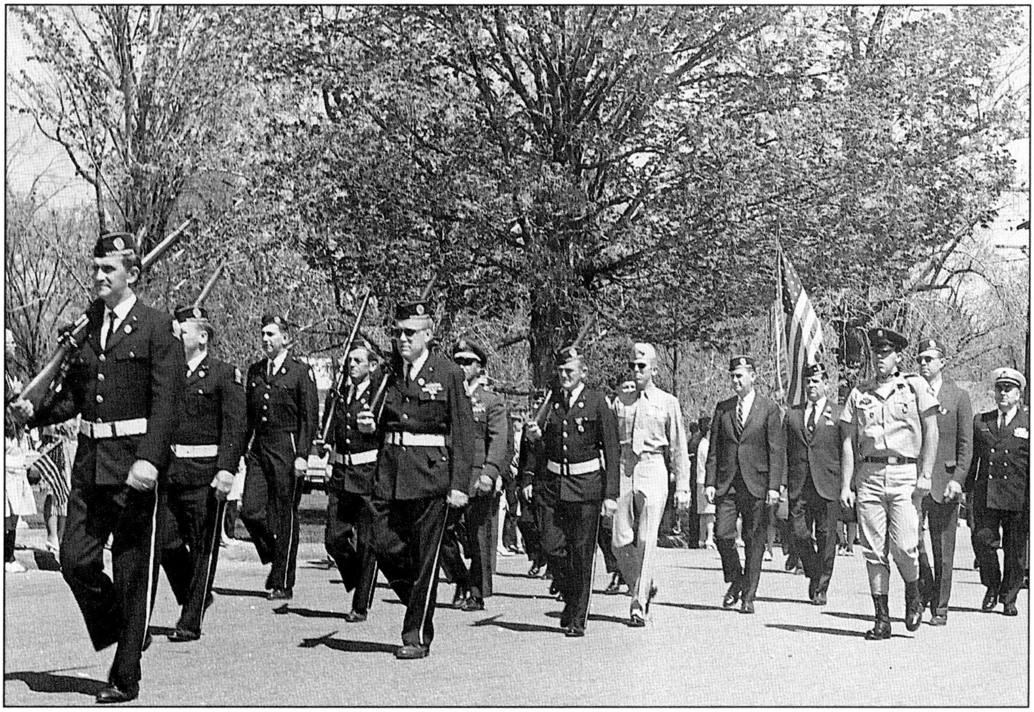

Veterans step out on Exchange Street in 1967 for Barre's Memorial Day parade.

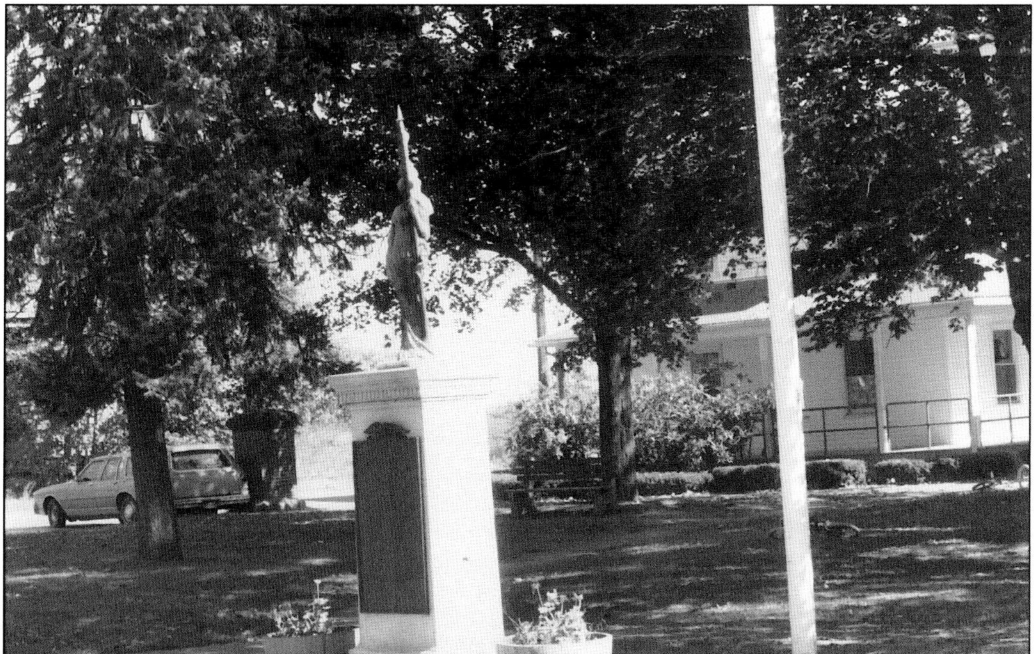

In the square in front of the former Hotel Blythe, a special monument recognizes those who served in World War I from South Barre and Barre Plains.

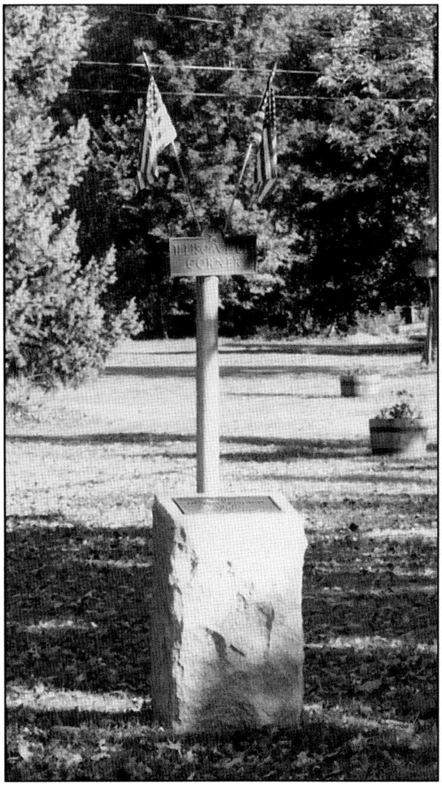

In Barre Plains, individual monuments, at the corners of the triangular green, are dedicated to fallen heroes Staff Sgt. Thomas W. Power, Sgt. Joseph A. Illiscavitch, and Pfc. Francis R. Sinclair.

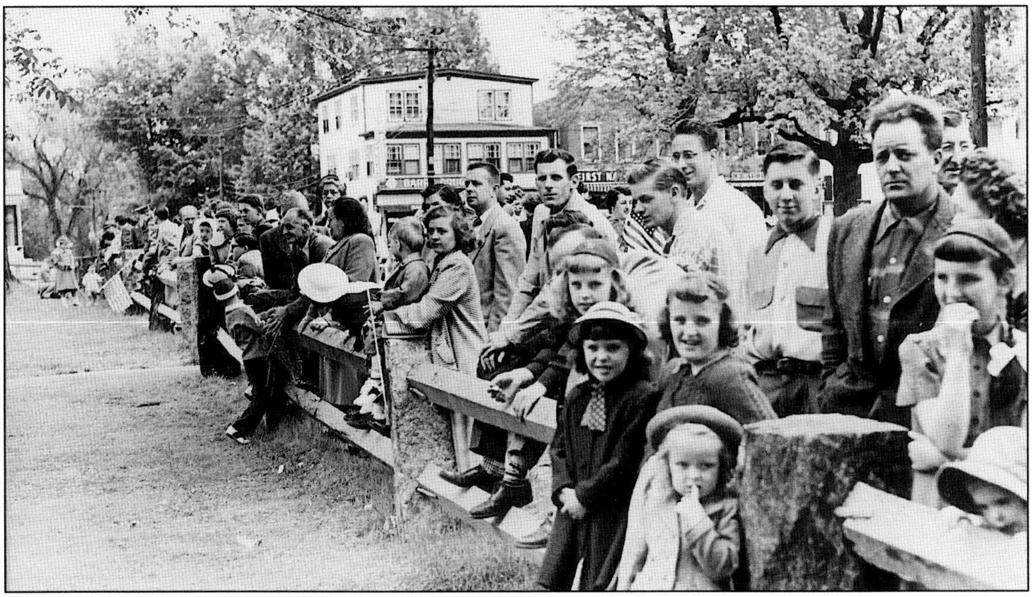

The best memorial of all is the throng of people who show their respect and sympathy each year by attending the several Memorial Day exercises in different parts of town.

Five

EDUCATION

"As very early in our history it has been seen that our fathers recognized the importance of education, and provided for the support of the schools as the basis of our prosperity and safety as a community—and as along the progress of the century we have kept up with the progress of the times—so to-day we appreciate our school system, honor all connected with its administration as holdings in their hands the future of the town." This is a quote from "A Memorial of the One Hundredth Anniversary of the Incorporation of the Town of Barre," 1884. Although a little more than 100 years have passed, our priorities in education have not changed very much. The three R's—reading, writing and 'rithmetic—are still priorities, but now we have added courses in Chinese, poetry, NJROTC, cultural anthropology, computers and related technology, multicultural exposures, and honors programs. Students are bused from the four neighboring communities to our newly reconstructed Quabbin Regional Middle/High School.

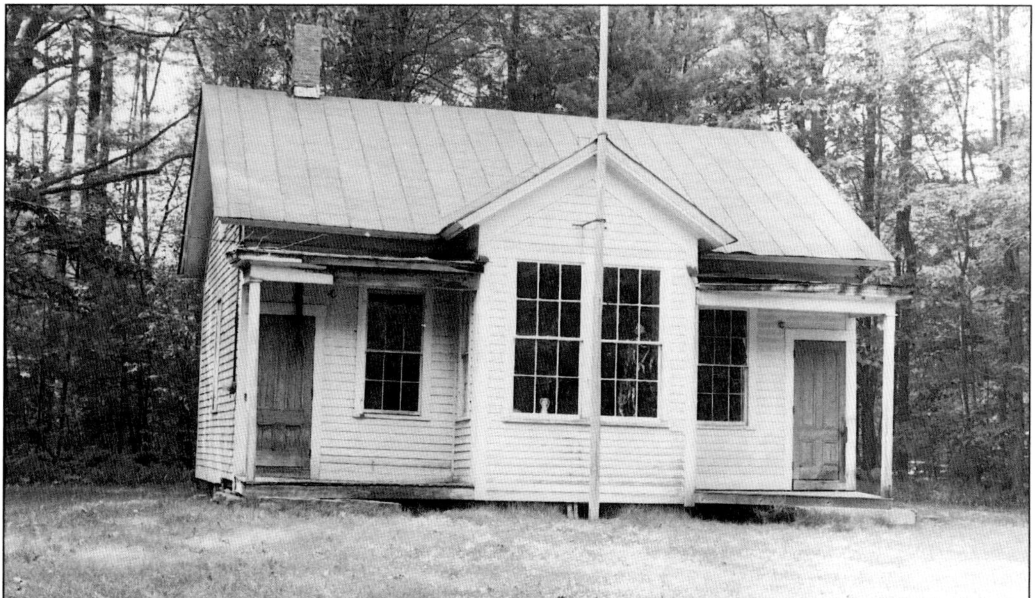

This school building, built in 1883, served as the schoolhouse for the No. 4 School District until 1930. The Town of Barre deeded the property to former students in 1937. Since then, it has been used as a community center. It was listed on the National Register of Historic Places in 1988, and is shown here during renovations in 1998.

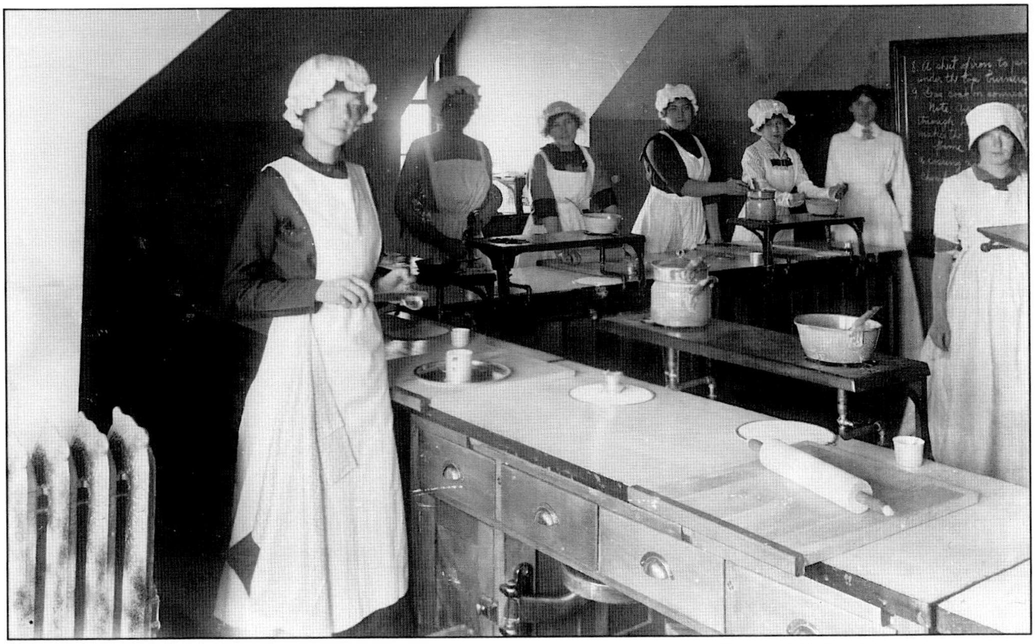

In this glimpse of a turn-of-the-century classroom at the former Barre High School, one sees white caps and starched aprons firmly in place; these young students learned the proper kitchen etiquette in domestic arts classes. Most students would bring their lunch pails, but some students could purchase their lunch for a few pennies. Welsh rabbit was a typical meal. M. Hunt is pictured third from the right.

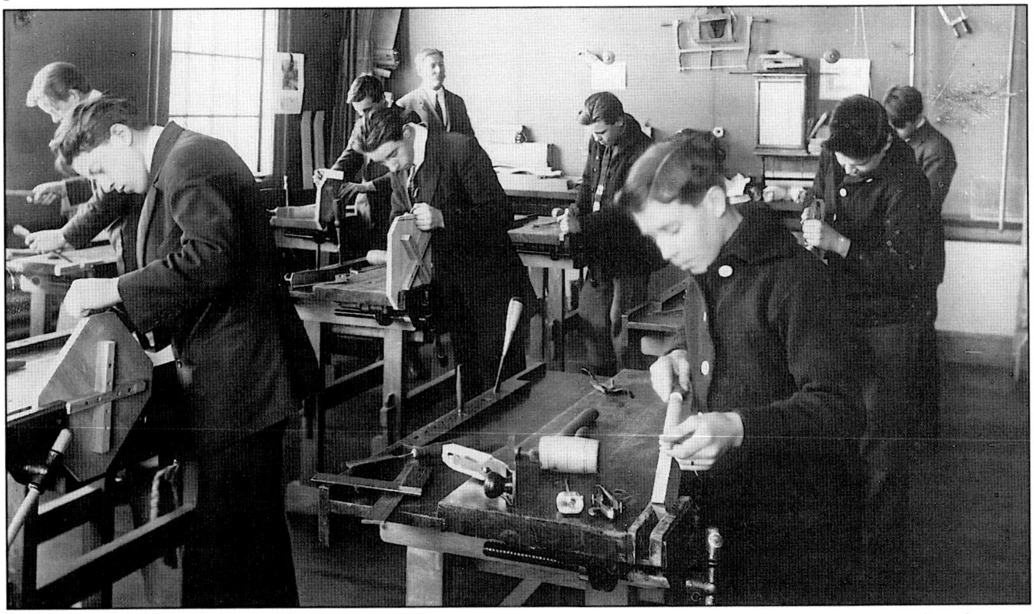

Shown here are some handsomely dressed students in a manual training class at the former Barre High School in the early 1920s. On the left is Joe Fleming; Harry Bruce, the teacher, is in the background. Mr. Bruce was very methodical in his training. He instructed his students in the use of all hand tools. In 1922–23, there was some controversy about converting to power tools. How things have changed!

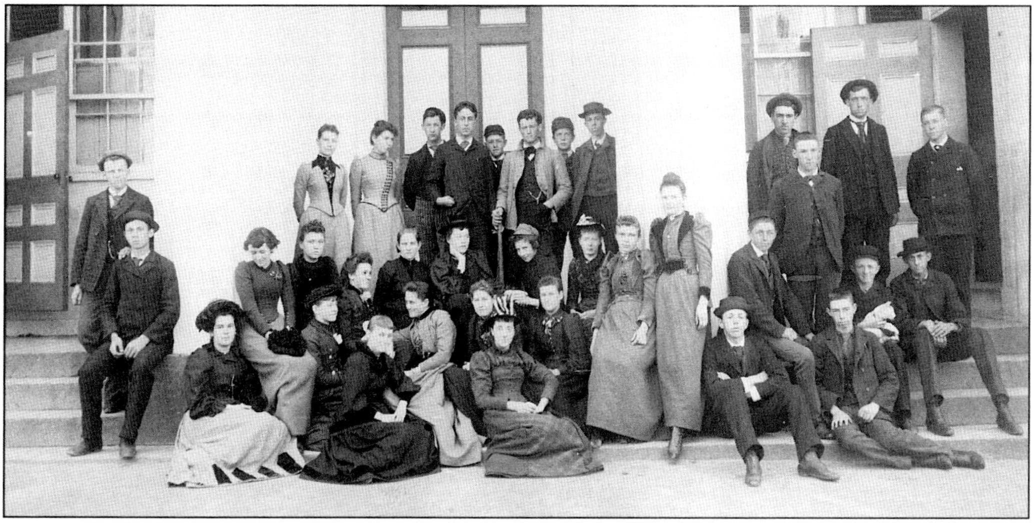

In 1892–93, Barre High School was in session at the Barre Town House. Shown here, from left to right, are as follows: (front row) Grace Ball, Mary Kenney, Mary Allen, Maude Johnson, Carrie MacCullar, Harry Irish, Charles Harwood, Ray Underwood, and ? Sibley; (middle row) Charles Hemenway, Charles Bassett, Ida Crossley, Elsie Spooner, Ella Cole, May Ross, Bessie Bruce, Bertha Bailey, Louise Barry, Henry Walker, May Smith, and Maude Smith; (back row) Miss Andrews, Miss True, Harold Brooks, Clarence Brooks, Clarence Stone, C. Walker, Arthur Sawyer, Arthur Bassett, unidentified, Clarence Deane, and Charles Allen.

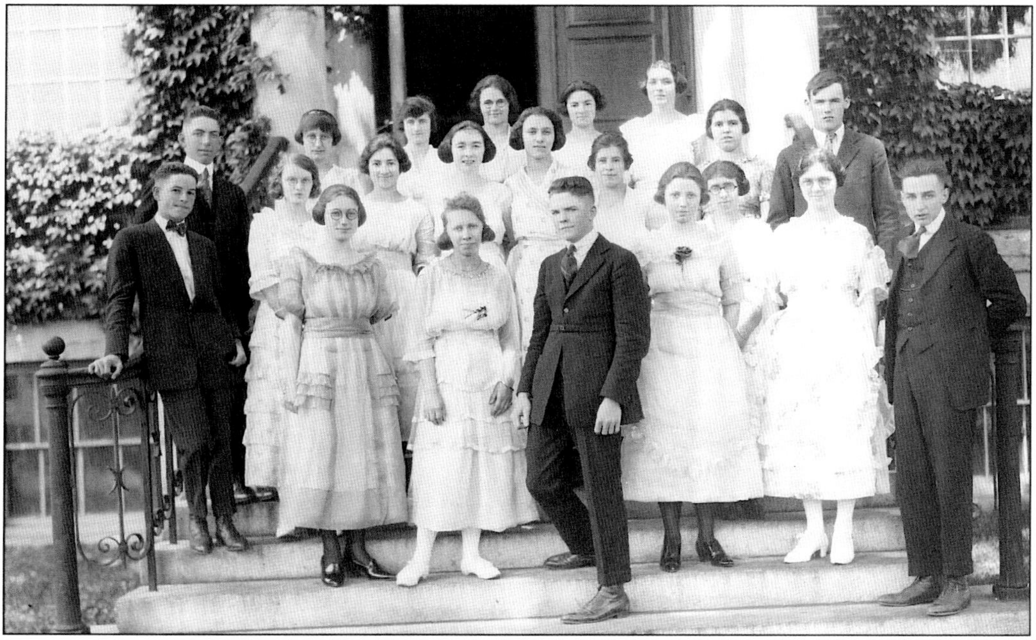

Shown at this graduation of Barre High School in 1920, from right to left, are as follows: (front row) Barbara Allen, Eleana Wassel, Edward Gaffney, Evelyn Brown, Miriam Ellsworth, and Chester Harper; (middle row) Armand Gariepy, Gladys Flagg, Marian Hunt, Reina Carberry, Elizabeth Williams, Jeannette Gariepy, Mary Murphy, and Robert Udall; (back row) George Porter, Bertha Pratt, Mildred Paquin, Ellen Valuzki, Madeline Hunt, Mary Neylon, and Olive Ricketts. Many young men of this age were home working on the farms.

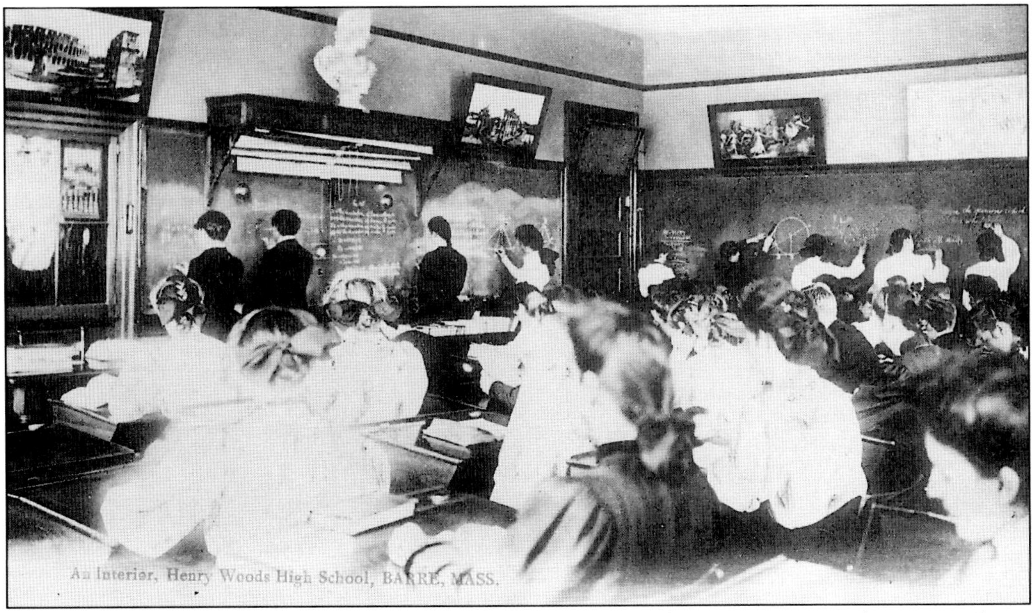

The interior rooms of the old Barre High School, such as the Junior Room, have now been stripped of their character. Gone are the Roman photographs, the busts, the pull-down charts, the maps, the blackboards, the fixed desks, and the young ladies with bows in their hair. Instead, the rooms have been converted to municipal offices and for use by the regional school administration; dormers were also added.

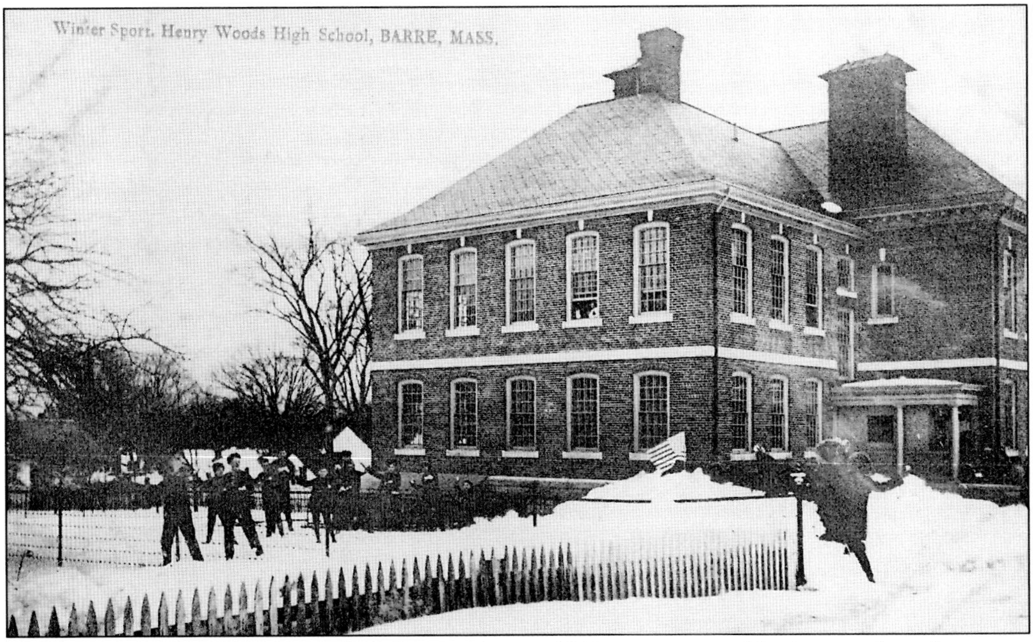

This picture of the Henry Woods School, taken *c*. 1910, is recognizable despite the subsequent addition of a third floor. One chimney, the windows, a portico, and the granite blocks are still the same. Indeed, one can still find 14 of these blocks inscribed with the year of each graduating class from 1901 through 1914. The area where the boys are playing in the snow is now a parking area.

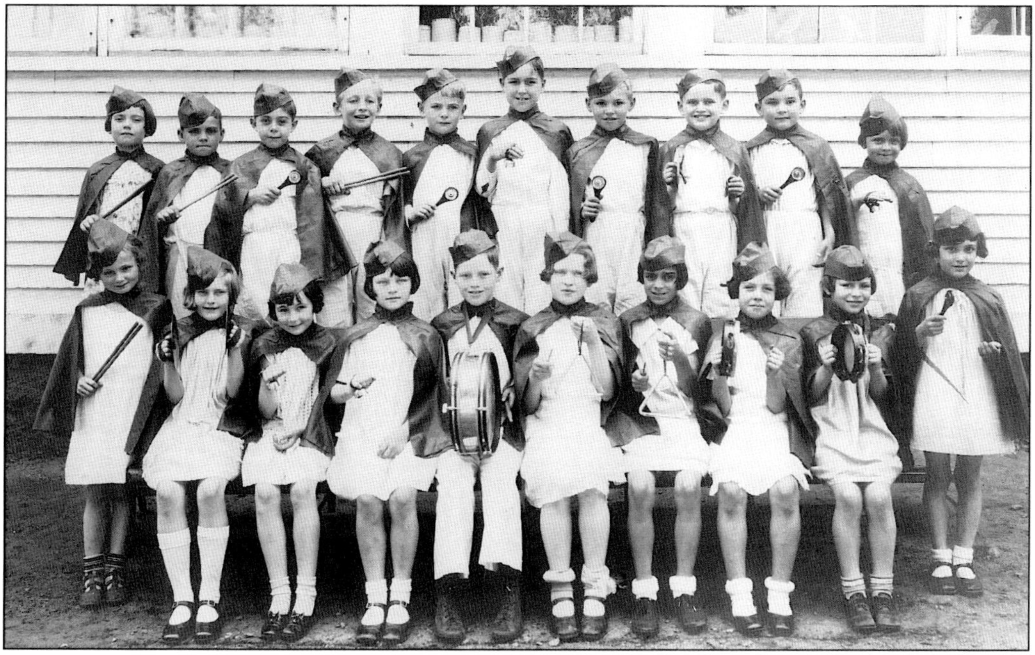

Members of the Barre Center School Toy Band from Helen Carey Murphy's second grade, in 1928-29, can be seen, from left to right, as follows: (front row) Elizabeth Brown, Lucille Bordeaux, Elizabeth Healy, Elaine Johnson, Arthur Charlton, Eve Stone, Lillian Brown, Alice Tolman, Florence Marshall, and Bernice Roberts; (back row) Aseneth Rice, Sammy Bullard, George Fisk, Fenton Carruth, unidentified, Harold Blake, Bob Better, Lewis Paquin, Bobby Crooks, and Alma Keddy. Barre is fortunate to have such a musical community, largely because of our schools and the Sunday bandstand concerts.

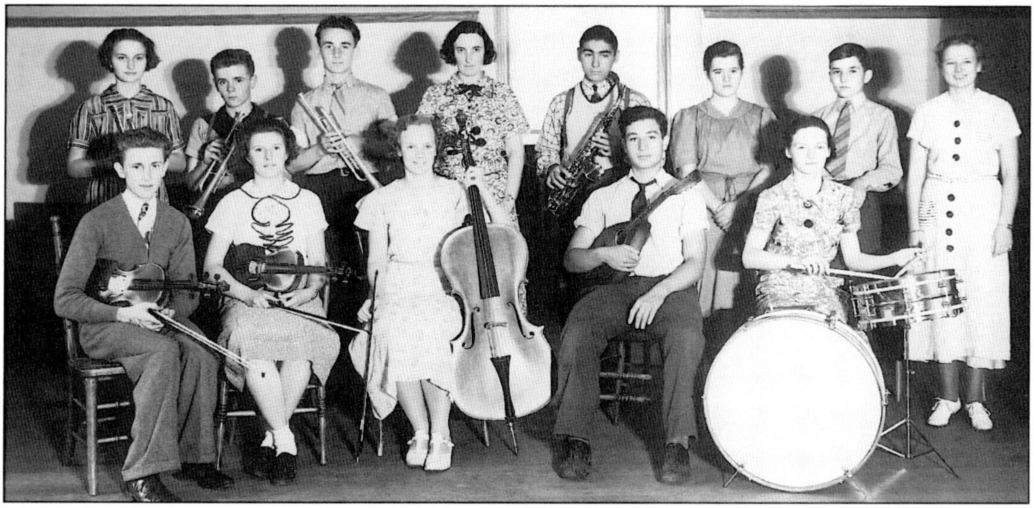

The next best thing to a walk back in time is a keepsake memory through photographs. Shown here is a group of musical enthusiasts, *c.* 1937. The seated violinist is Onesime Ethier. The others, from left to right, are as follows: (front row) unidentified, Bernice Sluckis, Susanne Paull, unidentified, and Elaine Johnson; (back row) Mary Crowley, Bud Green, Arthur Peck, Helen Chase (the music supervisor for nearly 30 years), Nick Mallozzi, Yvonne Agar, Bobby Crooks, and Janice Ackerman.

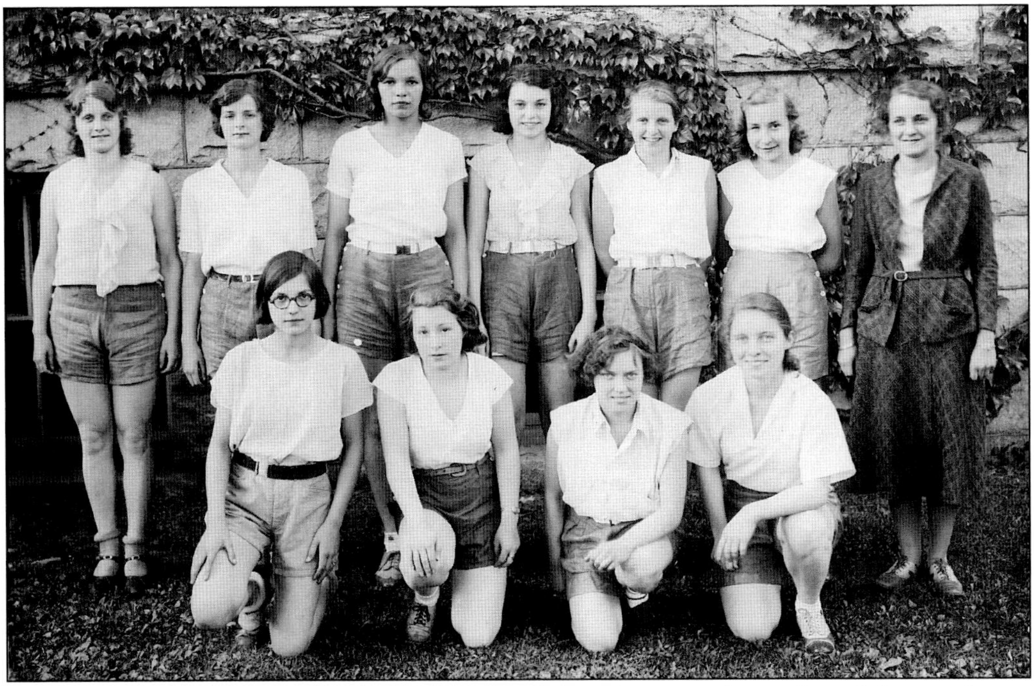

The Barre High School 1933 Girls Track Team can be seen above, from left to right, as follows: (kneeling) Antoinette Franciose, Marie Wring, Esther Cashman, and Mary Taylor; (standing) Lillian Sundberg, Betty Church, Blodgie Savickas, Alice Flynn, Frances Loughman, Lillian Whippee, and Elsie Nightingale.

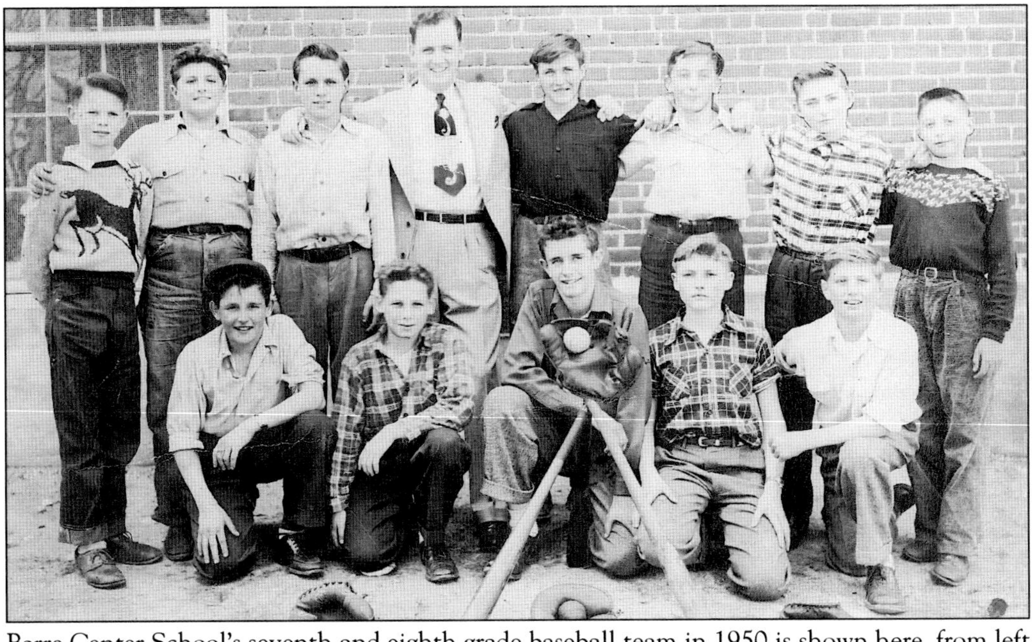

Barre Center School's seventh and eighth grade baseball team in 1950 is shown here, from left to right, as follows: (front row) Dick Parkinson, Dick Gariepy, Bill Gorman, Richard Wine, and Douglas Panaccione; (back row) Douglas Bryant, Joe Panaccione, Charlie Nicholson, John Hodgen (teacher), Arthur Sheldon, Glen Dickson, Clark Bordeaux, and Roger Varnot.

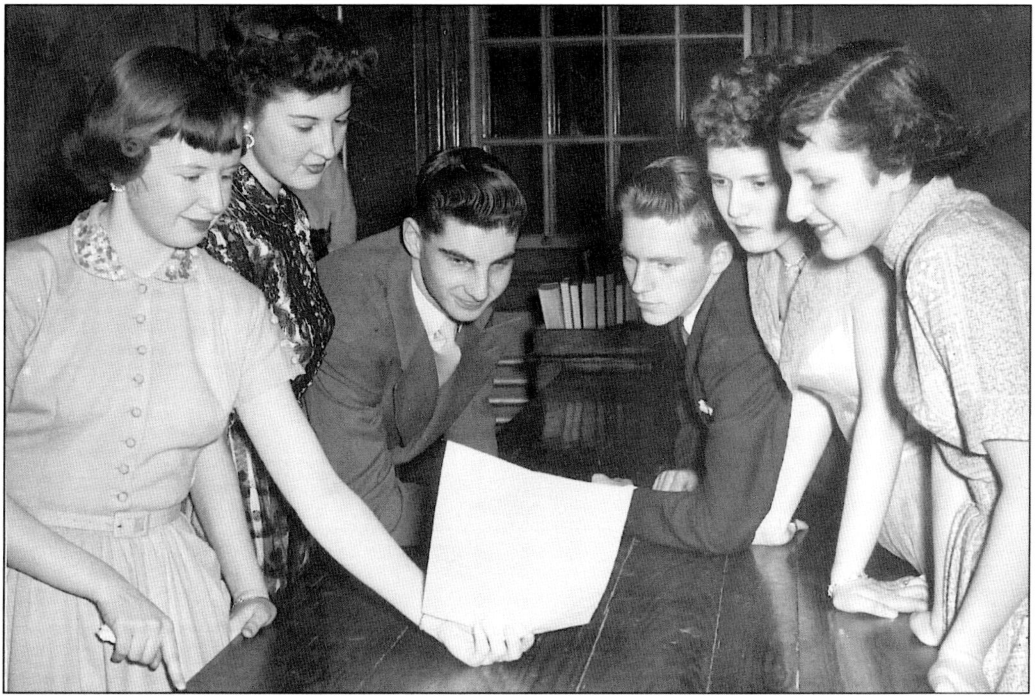

The prize speakers of the Barre High School in 1951 were, from left to right, Jeanne McAndrew, Nadine Stewart, Ralph Lincoln, George Mennard, June Mucha, and Mary Ann Molion. The annual oratorio contest sponsored by the Barre Woman's Club was held in the Barre High School Auditorium. All of the contestants chose interesting and varied speeches. Their spectacular delivery was the result of many weeks of preparation and practice.

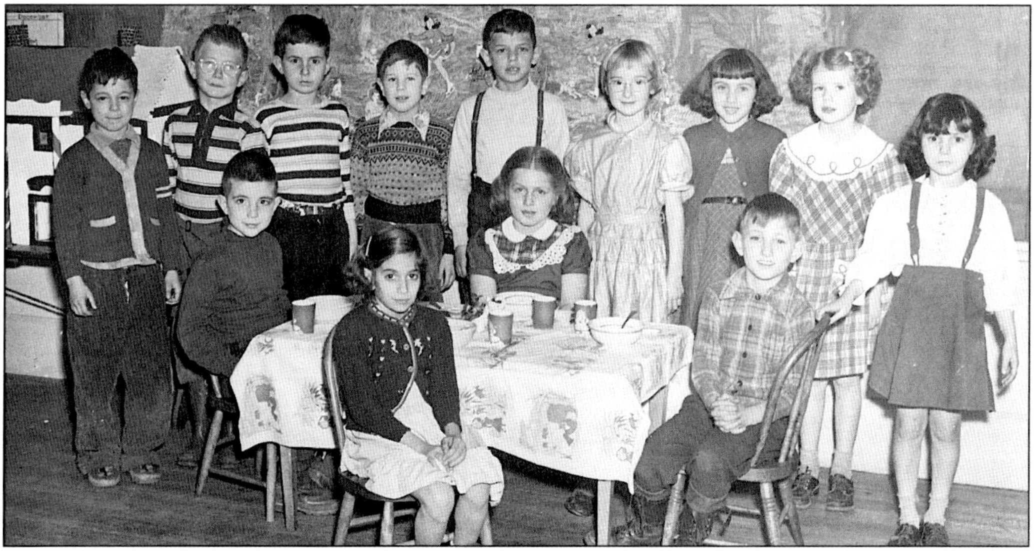

These children practice a project on table manners at the High Plains School in 1953. Seen here, from left to right, are as follows: (sitting) Peter Phipps, Josephine Trifilo, Carolyn Tetreault, and Angelo Salvadore; (standing) Richard Lamacchia, Alfred Whippee, Robert Stevens, John Lamacchia, Billy Valardi, Elaine Raffier, Jeanne Petracone, Barbara Whigham, and Lorraine Stevens.

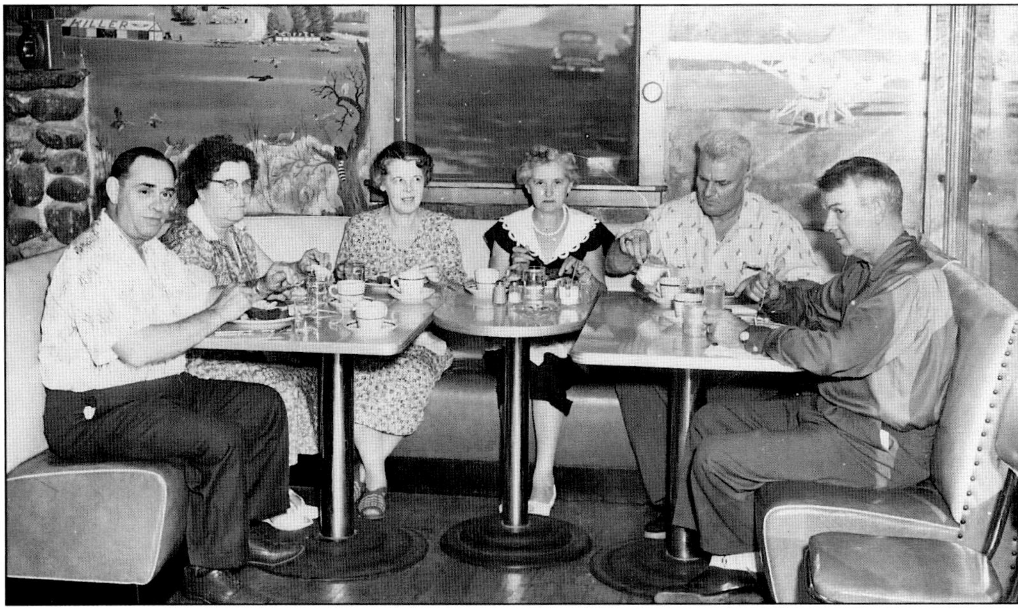

These folks gather at Hiller Airport in 1956 for a Stetson Home for Boys reunion. Seen here, from left to right, are Mr. Elmer Young, Mrs. Elmer Young, Mrs. Frank Lovering, Mrs. Ethan Clark, Mr. Ethan Clark, and Mr. Frank Lovering. Note the hand-painted murals on the wall behind them.

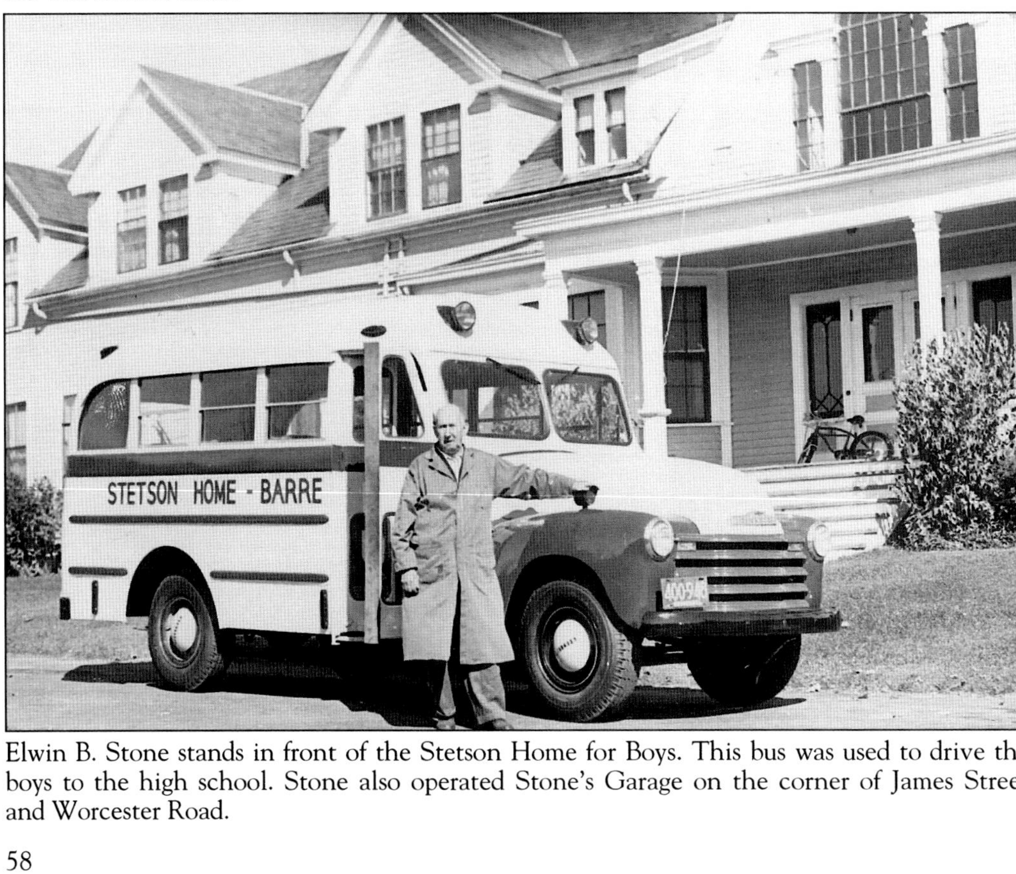

Elwin B. Stone stands in front of the Stetson Home for Boys. This bus was used to drive the boys to the high school. Stone also operated Stone's Garage on the corner of James Street and Worcester Road.

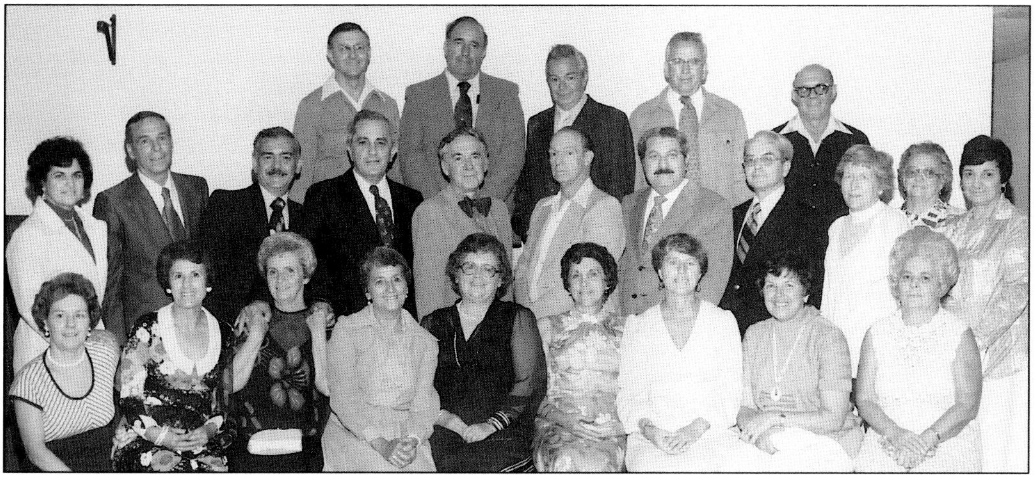

The Class of 1942 Barre High School Reunion took place at the Coldbrook Country Club in 1977. From left to right are as follows: (front row) Betty (Terroy) Spinney, Lucy (Petracone) Trifilo, Myrtle (Keddy) Dwelly, Josephine (Puliafico) Locantore, Victoria (Awtry) Hopkins, Nancy (Coppolino) Gravel, Marian (Rukstelis) Paskov, Margaret (Better) Harnois, and Rose (Rossi) Sottile; (middle row) Lucy (Gulino) Franciose, Roy Spinney, Guy D'Annolfo, Edward Powers, Robert Rice, George Wrin, James Chilleri, Roger Skelly, Viola (Stone) Hopkins, Mabel (Tucker) Casault, and Angie (Di Fonzo) Andrukonis; (back row) Fred Bechan, Wilbur Blake, Leonard Marshall, Howard Dean, and Charles Casault.

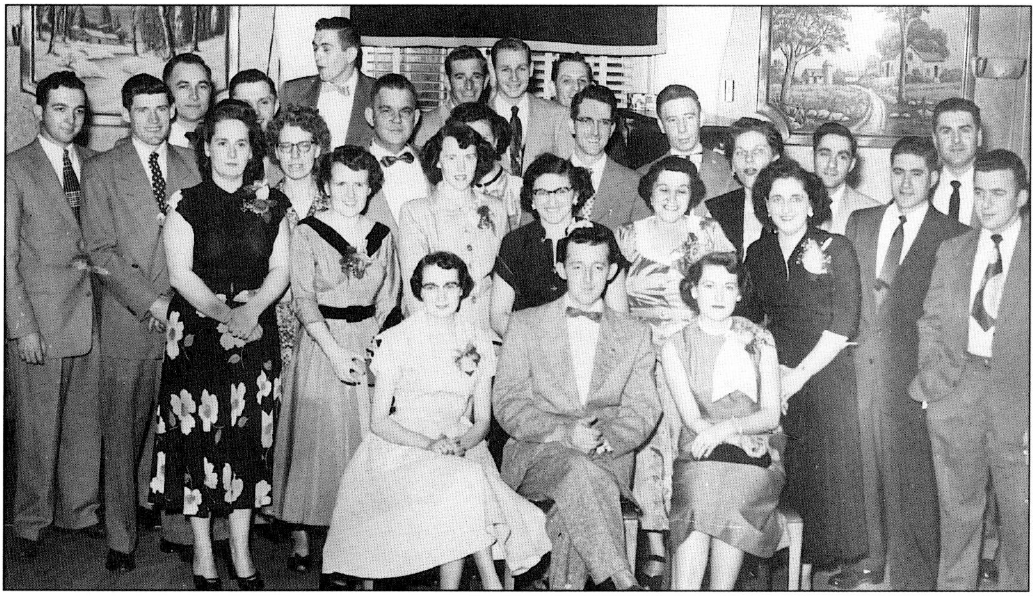

The Barre High School Class of 1943 Reunion was held in the Cotillion Room at the Hotel Barre. Note the beautiful murals in the background. Seen here, from left to right, are as follows: (front row) Rose Puliafico, Rev. Kenneth Lindsey, and Audrey Bordeaux; (second row) Ruth Jean Byram, Margaret Tobin, Shirley Stevens, Grace Tomasello, Frances Spasaro, Doris Newcomb, Matthew Trifilo, and Linda D'Annolfo; (third row) Philip Dwelly, Albert Kamarauskas, Edmund Andrukonis, Arlene Howe, John Wytrwal, unidentified, Ward Brown, Walter Rice, Bernice Martin, Sebastian Sottile, and George Mirabile; (back row) Francis Sokol, Harold Dorsey, Alan Macintosh, and Keith Roberts.

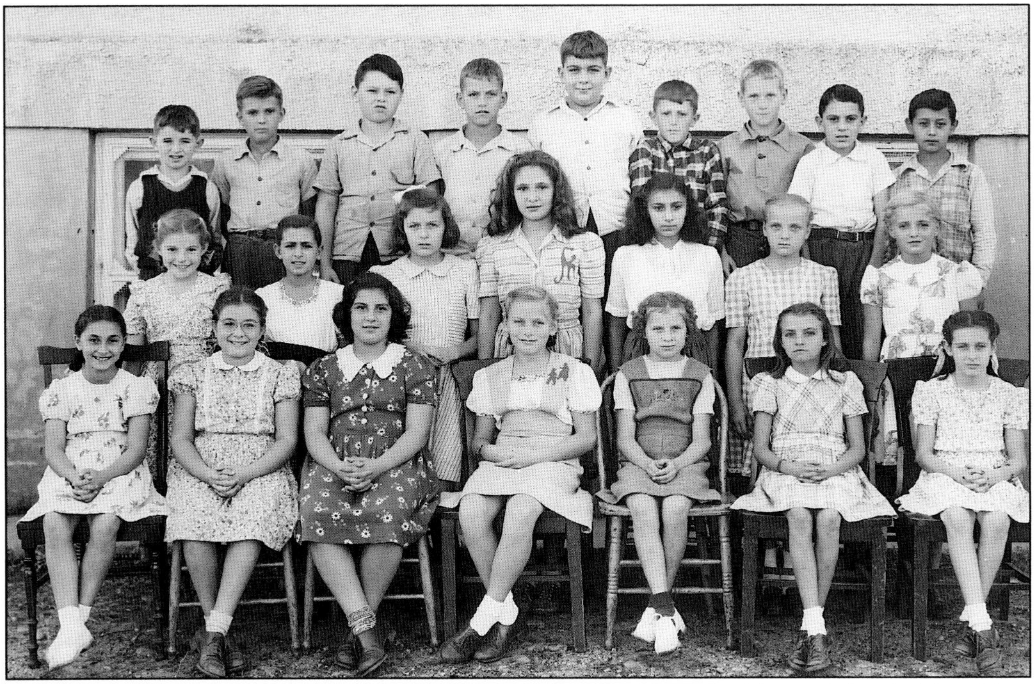

This 1946–47 class picture shows the fifth grade of the High Plains School (the Class of 1954). They are, from left to right, as follows: (front row) Sylvia Cornacchia, Mary Coppolino, Louise Tancredi, Audrey Gawthrop, Joanne Janulevicus, Anne Rotondo, and Mary Ward; (middle row) Audrey Sample, Pauline Sidoti, Stella Crawford, Adeline DiNatale, Antoinette Cionci, Polly Puchalsky, and Carol Stevenson; (back row) Wayne Cauvin, Karl Bussard, Steve Savasoriskas, unidentified, Joseph Pereshino, Jimmy Scott, John Robinson, Bobby Moran, and Francis Puliafico.

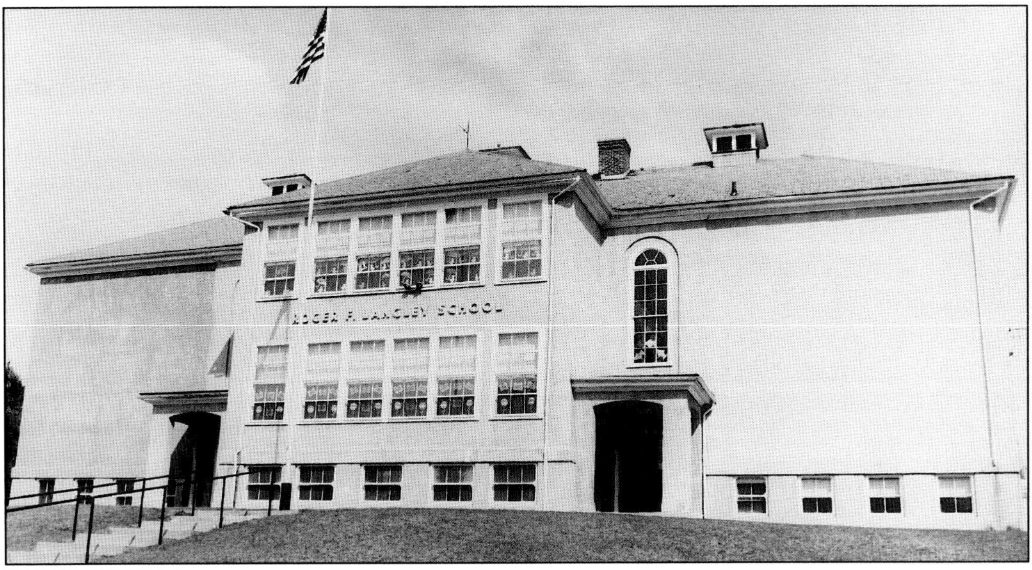

The High Plains School, later known as the Roger Langley School, is shown here in 1987 with its additions. The windows of the building always were media for the children's imaginative and creative decorations. The building was demolished in 1997.

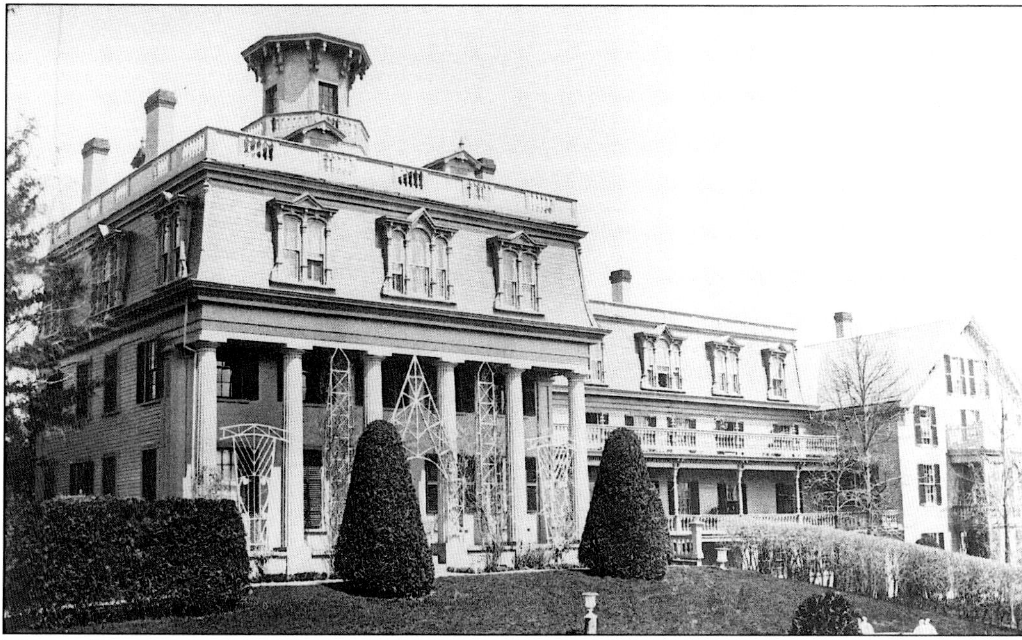

This well-maintained building was the Central Division of Elm Hill, run by Dr. George Brown and begun in 1848. "The aim was to furnish the best means of educating and training that class of children and youth who, from varied mental infirmities, are not amenable to ordinary modes of school life, and are generally termed feeble-minded."

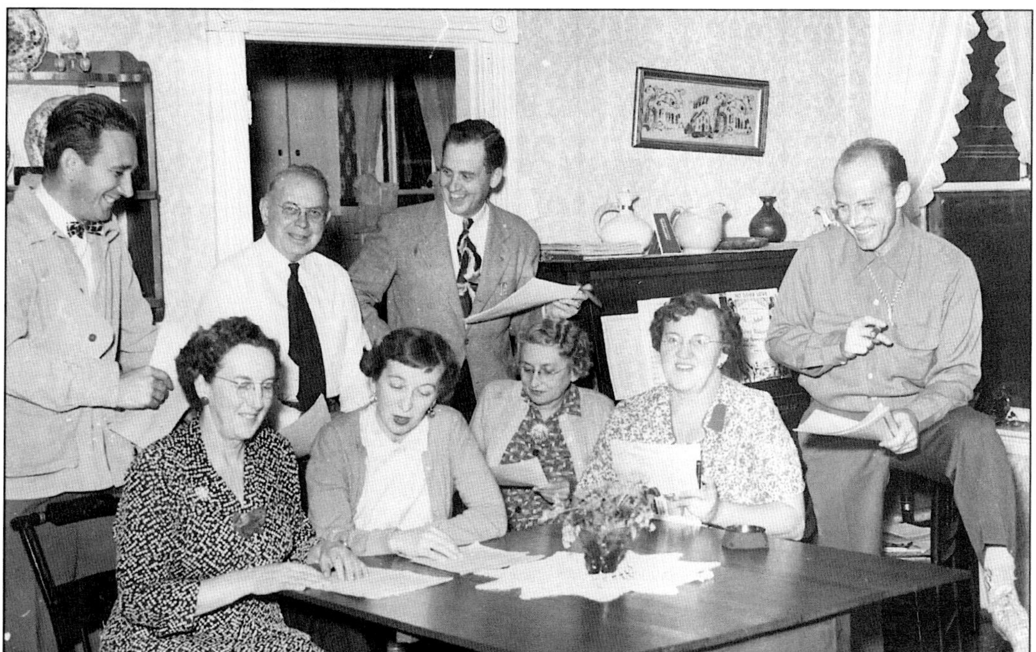

This 1959 rehearsal of the Teachers Club production *The Ruggles Lane Record Shop* took placeat the Smith's home. From left to right are as follows: (sitting) Helen Chase, Catherine Corbett, Lila Smith, and Teresa Miller; (standing) Paul Flynn, Martin Smith, John Hodgen, and George Mennard.

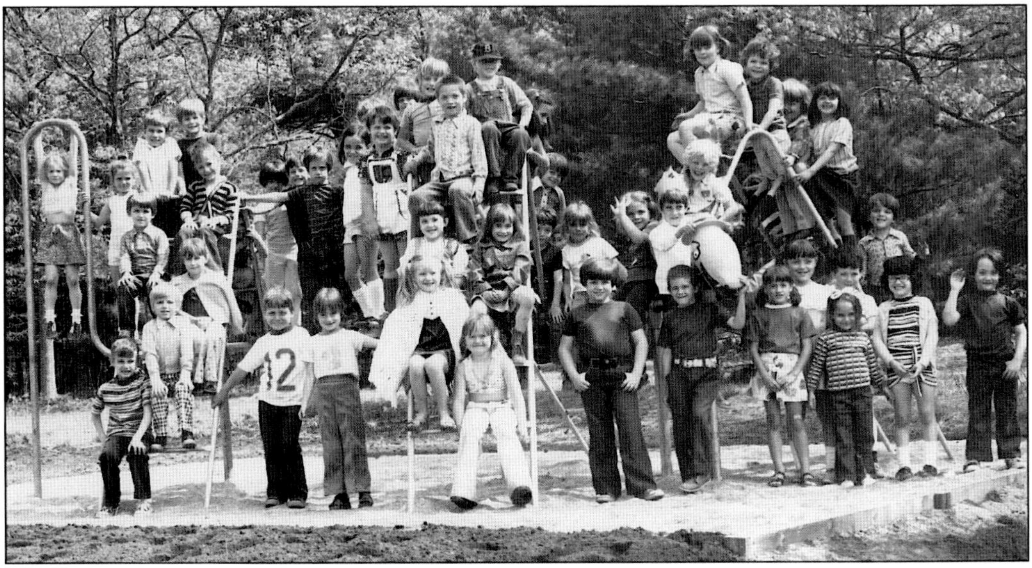

Second graders at the Roger Langley School show their excitement over the new jungle gym in 1975.

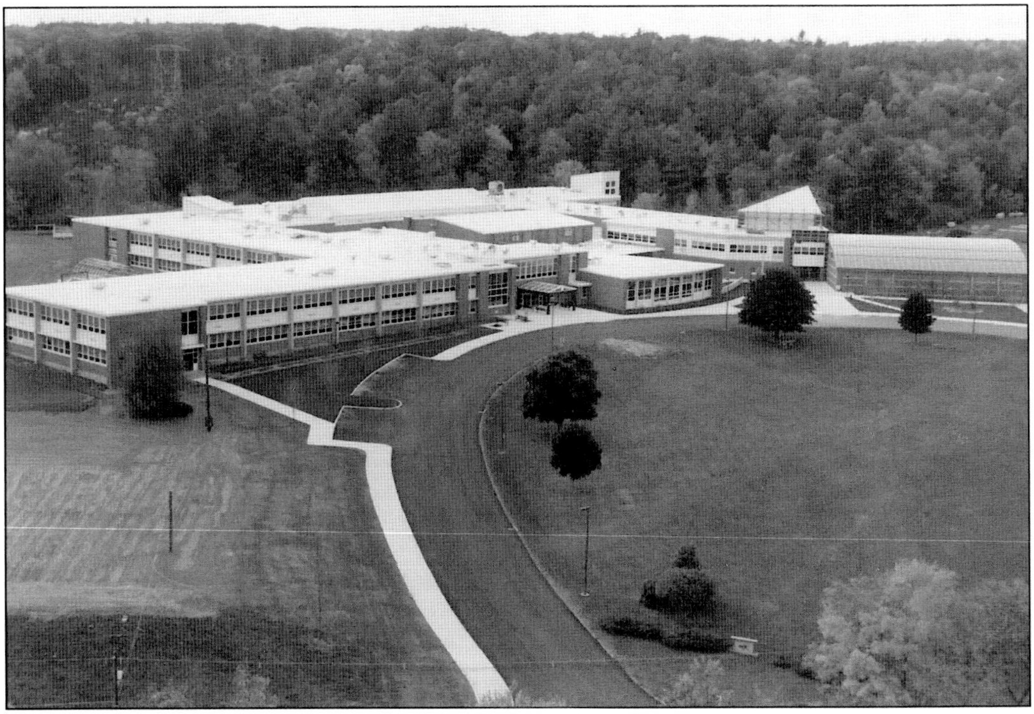

The Quabbin Regional Middle/School High School is shown here upon completion, 1998. The school, which can accommodate approximately 1,800 students, was originally built in 1967 to house 900 students. In 1998, renovations were completed so it now has two separate areas for the high school and middle school, two gymnasiums, and a three-level atrium above the cafeteria area.

Six

FAITH AND WORSHIP

Even before our first settlers arrived in Barre, generous lands had been designated for a place of worship as well as the home of an "orthodox minister." For more than a century, there was one established church for which all citizens were assessed. But as the population increased, beliefs diversified, religious taxation was abolished, and other churches were built.

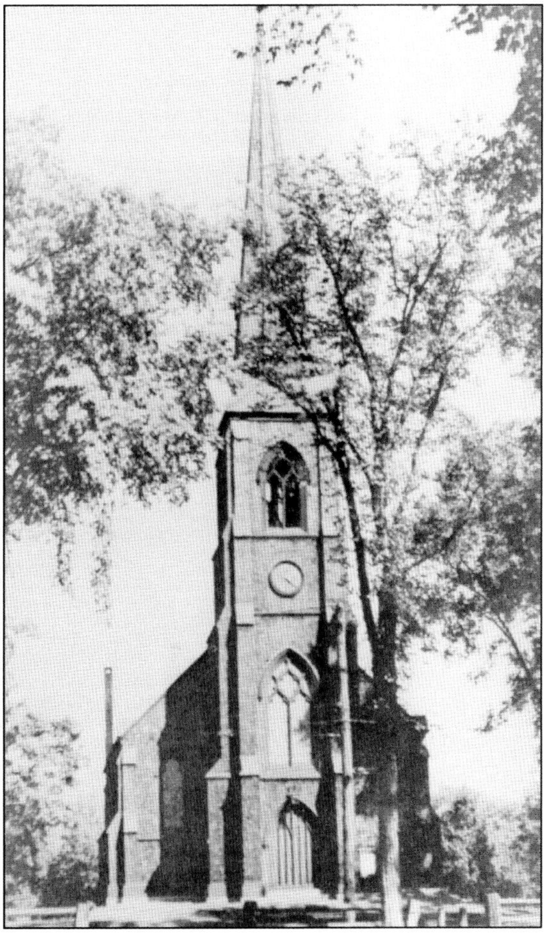

Spanning the years 1849 to 1968, the handsome, brown-shingled First Parish Church Unitarian guarded North Common. Actually, it was the parishioners' third meetinghouse, built after a controversial change from Orthodox Congregationalism to Unitarianism, but it was always called "The First Parish." Its graceful tower held a Paul Revere Bell as well as the town clock.

Over time, storms ravaged the structure and membership diminished, so the First Parish Church finally closed and was razed in 1968. The Parish Community presented both the bell and clock to Barre as a loan. They were installed in the Barre Town Hall belfry, from whence they continue to serve citizens melodiously.

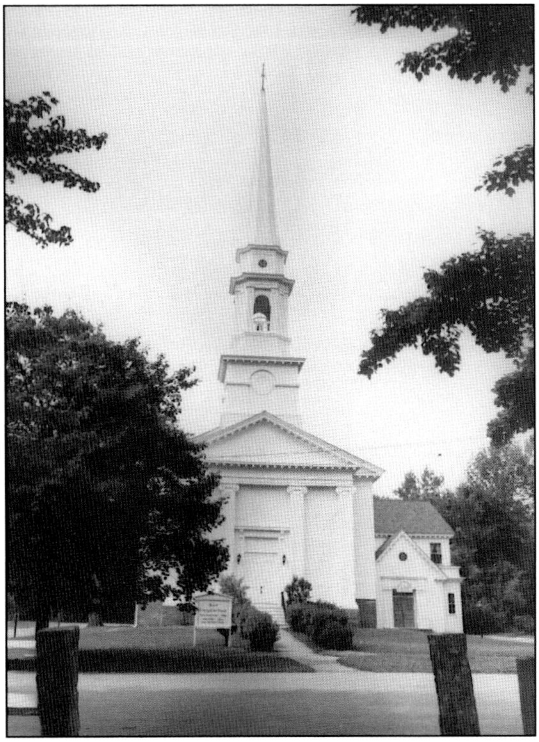

The Congregational Church adorns the North Common with grand dignity. It is the second meetinghouse, erected by the Evangelical Congregational Society in 1849, to meet the needs of a burgeoning parish. Like the neighboring First Parish Church across the street, it also rings a Revere Bell from its tower. Joseph Revere, the son of Paul, cast this one.

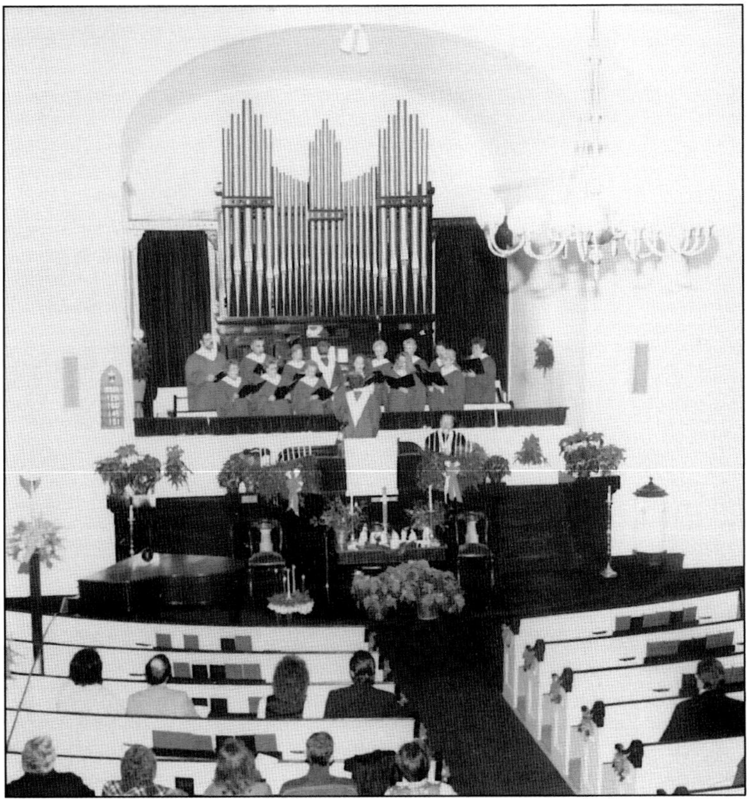

Taken from the balcony of the church in 1993, this photograph captures the spirit of the Christmas Eve service. We see the robed choir and the Nativity Creche amid holy day decorations and reverent parishioners.

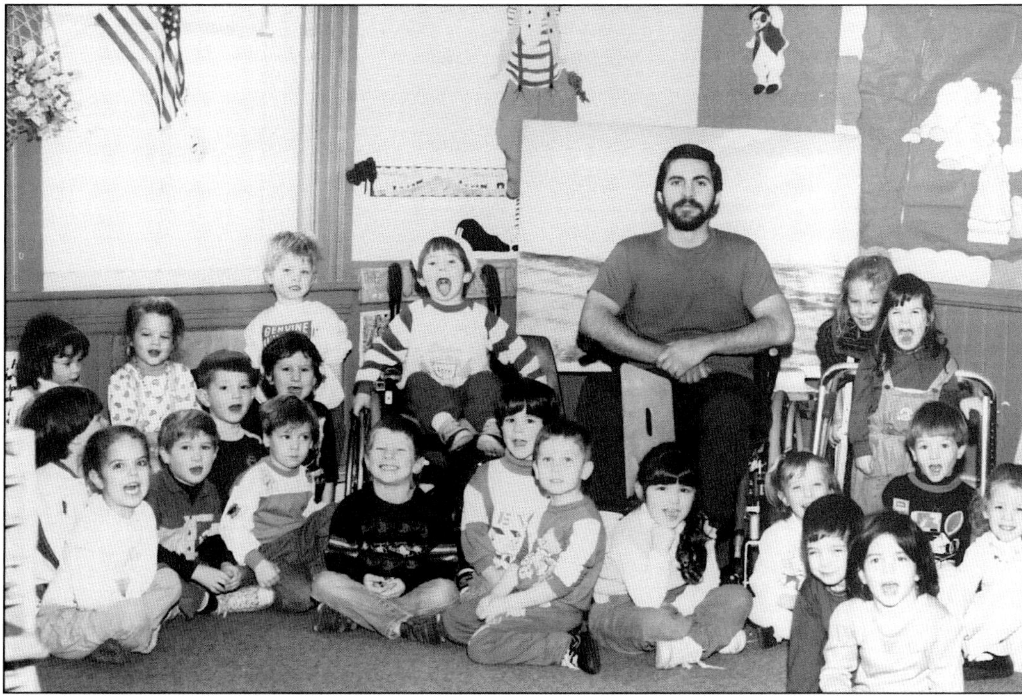

In 1991, these cheery tots enrolled in the Christian preschool at the Congregational Church spent a fortnight learning how handicapped persons (school friends and neighbors perhaps) manage to cope with their disabilities.

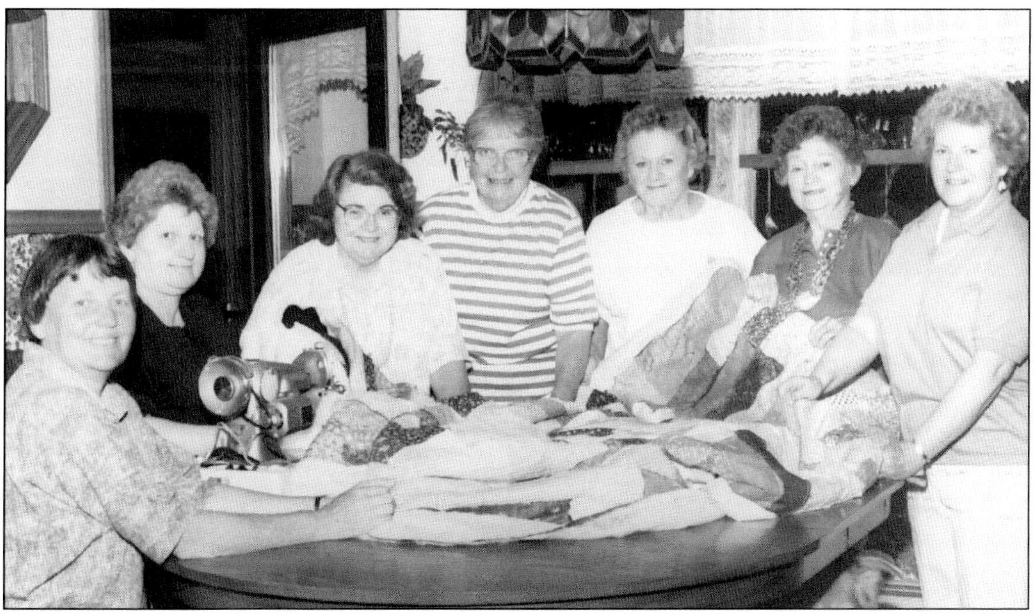

Many committees work through the year to benefit their Congregational Church. Posing for a photograph in 1995 is a group from the Women's Fellowship, which yearly designs, cuts, and stitches a quilt to be raffled in the fall. Gathered around the sewing machine are several capable stitchers who made a reversible topsy-turvy quilt—Carole Gariepy, Betty Snyder, Shirley Lewis, Peg Trask, Bessie Difley, and Hazel Wyman.

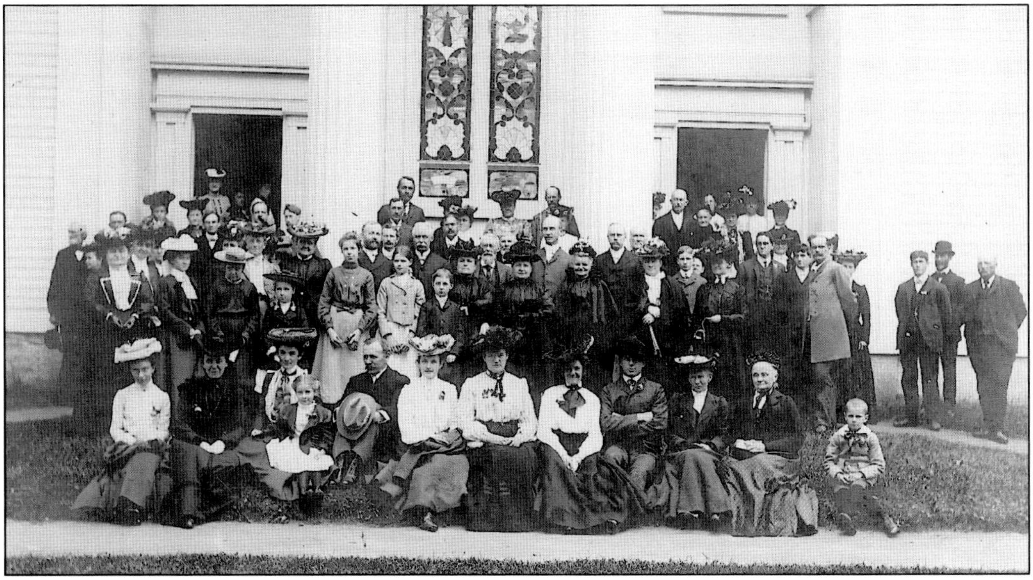

In the summer of 1903, parishioners gathered in front of the Methodist Episcopal Church to be photographed. The building was actually erected by Universalists. They disbanded within a few years and sold the building to the Methodist Society, who rededicated the 11-year-old church in September 1851. This congregation flourished on the South Common for a century and a quarter before closing in 1979. The fine building continues to be the focus of activity, having been purchased immediately by the Golden Age Club, who then conveyed ownership to the Barre Players, which works diligently for its preservation.

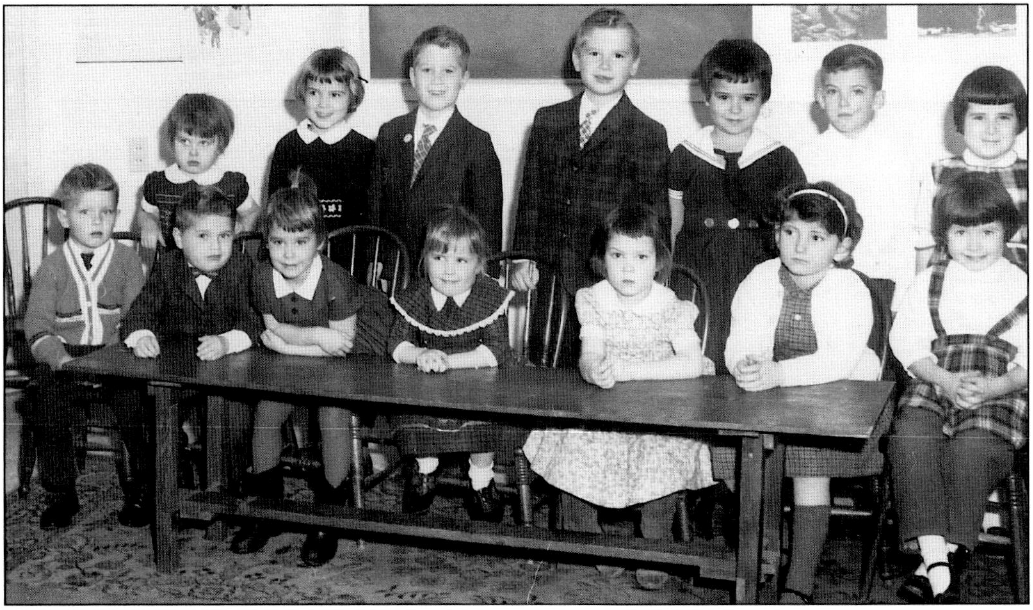

Probably in 1966, these bright well-scrubbed children were in the primary Sunday school at the Methodist Church. They are, from left to right, as follows: (sitting) Richard Mankin, Eric Trurin, Shelley Berthiaume, Jodi Paquin, Leona Flagg, Cyril Lagare, and Colleen Dixon; (standing) Janet Flagg, Carol Warfield, Duane Kustra, Richard Kustra, Cynthia Berthiaume, Alan Flagg, and Denise Shank.

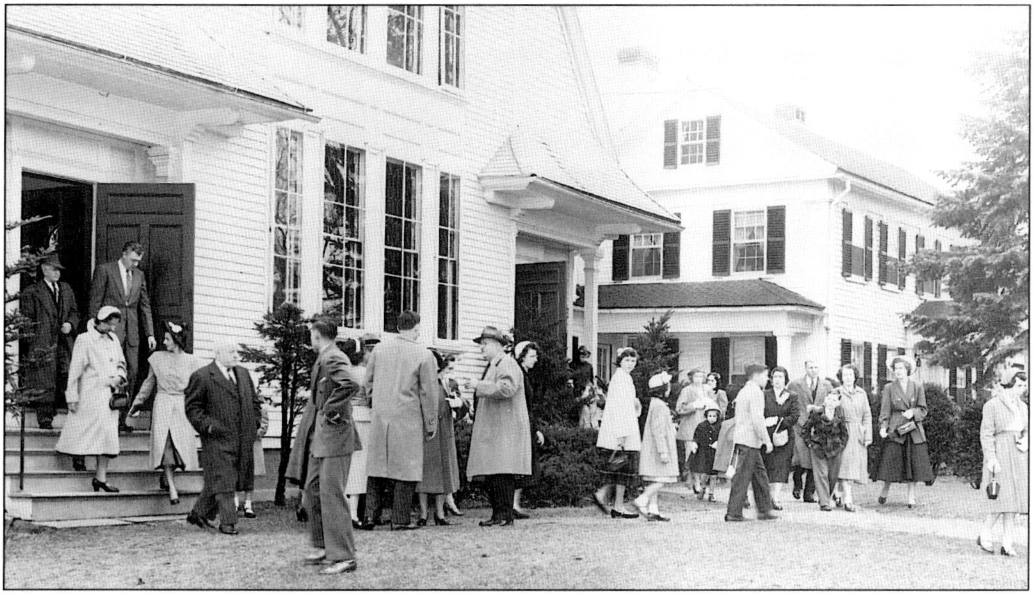

In 1896, after the great fire destroyed their first real church (which had been consecrated in 1858), the people of St. Joseph's immediately built this present church on the same site. It remained sturdy and unchanged until 1987, when a long-desired addition containing classrooms and a large meeting hall was dedicated. This congregation has grown (as has Barre). Now, instead of one Sunday mass, three are celebrated each Sabbath-day weekend. Here parishioners of the 1950s are shown leaving the church on a spring Sunday.

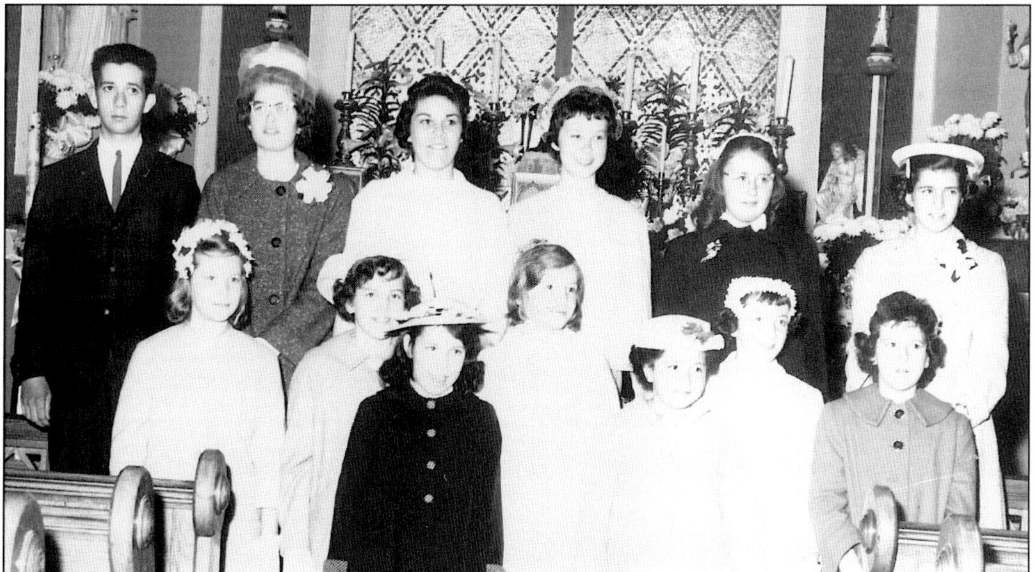

In 1962, the Junior Choir sang at Easter Sunday mass and afterwards was asked to pose in front of the altar. Note the ornate background, which is pre-Vatican II. Also note that every girl wore a hat, as was customary at the time. Seen here, from left to right, are as follows: (front row) Margaret White and Joann Pitisci; (middle row) Joyce Green, Joyce Sykes, Susan Meilus, and Patricia McHugh; (back row) William Whigham (organist), Elizabeth Roberts, Colleen Jannette, Paula Carroll, Kathleen White, and Martha Roberts.

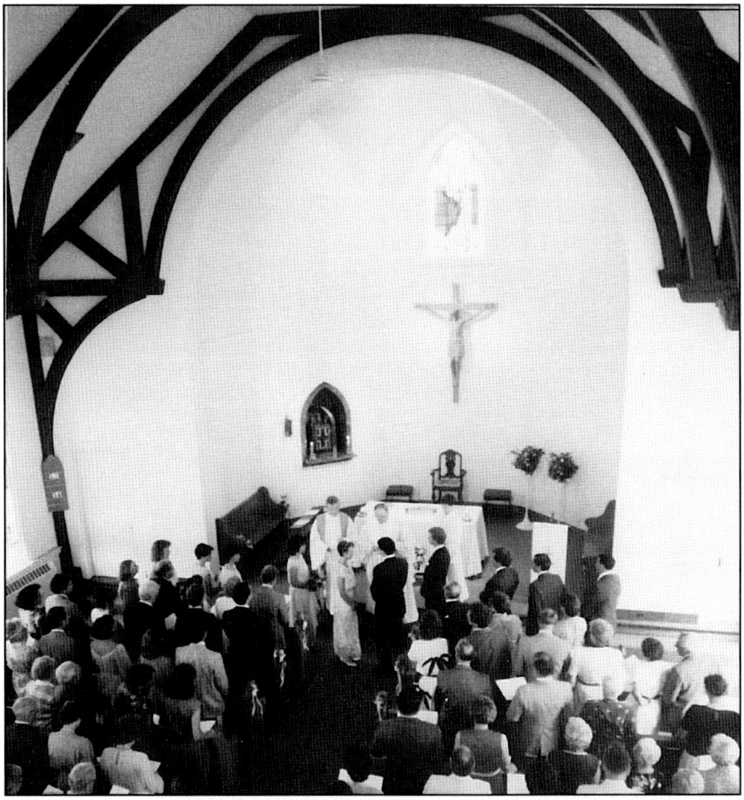

When the addition was made to St. Joseph's in the 1980s, the nave of the church was also redecorated. This 1985 photograph, taken from the organ loft during the wedding of Johanna Carroll and James Delaney, shows the altar rearranged according to the post-Vatican II liturgy.

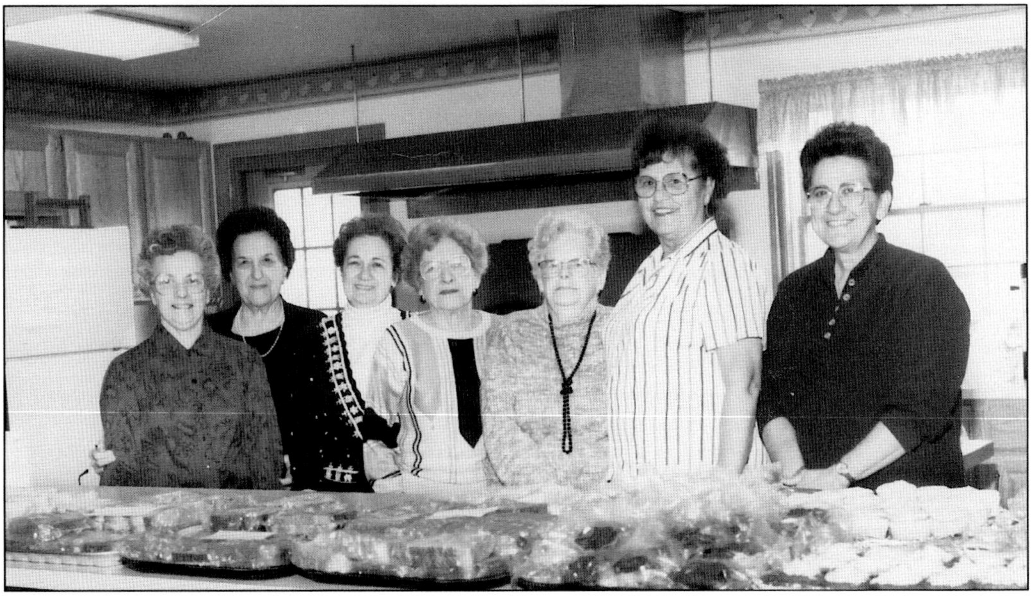

These ladies belong to a loyal group that can always be counted on to serve good things to eat at St. Joseph's Church. In November 1992, they posed in the new church kitchen, cheerfully prepared to serve luncheon to hungry shoppers at the Holiday Fair. From left to right are Pauline Croff, Josephine Mansueti, Rose Stewart, Marie Staiti, Clara Gonsalves, Anita Roy, and Anna Robinson.

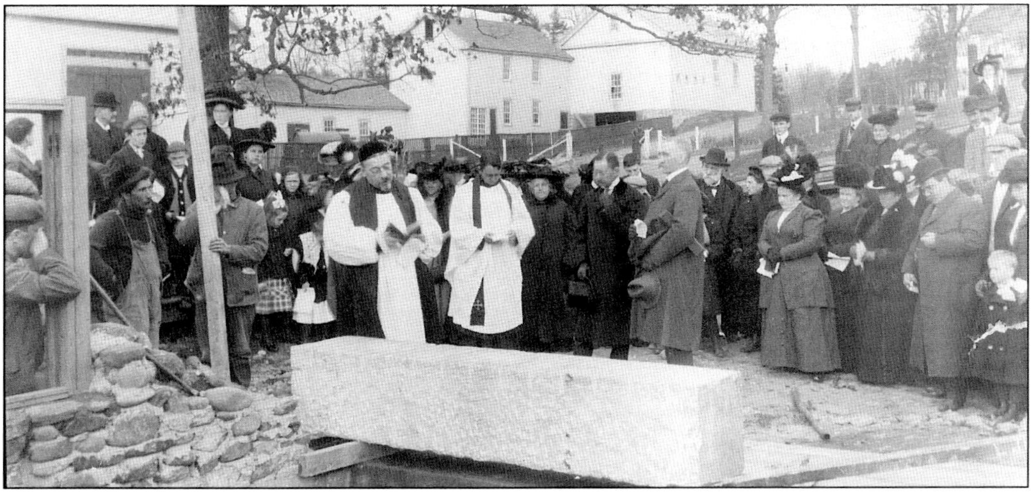

On the chilly afternoon of November 20, 1909, honored guests and parishioners gathered to lay the cornerstone for Christ Episcopal Church in South Barre (the first church to be built in the village). Retired Rev. Alexander Vinton officiated, assisted by Archdeacon Charles Sniffen, who had worked tirelessly to establish the church. Standing to Reverend Sniffen's left is Col. William Gaston of Boston and Barre, an important supporter. Lord Barnby, owner of the Barre Wool Combing Co. Ltd., the church's chief benefactor, is the white-bearded gentleman in the black fedora, to the right of Colonel Gaston.

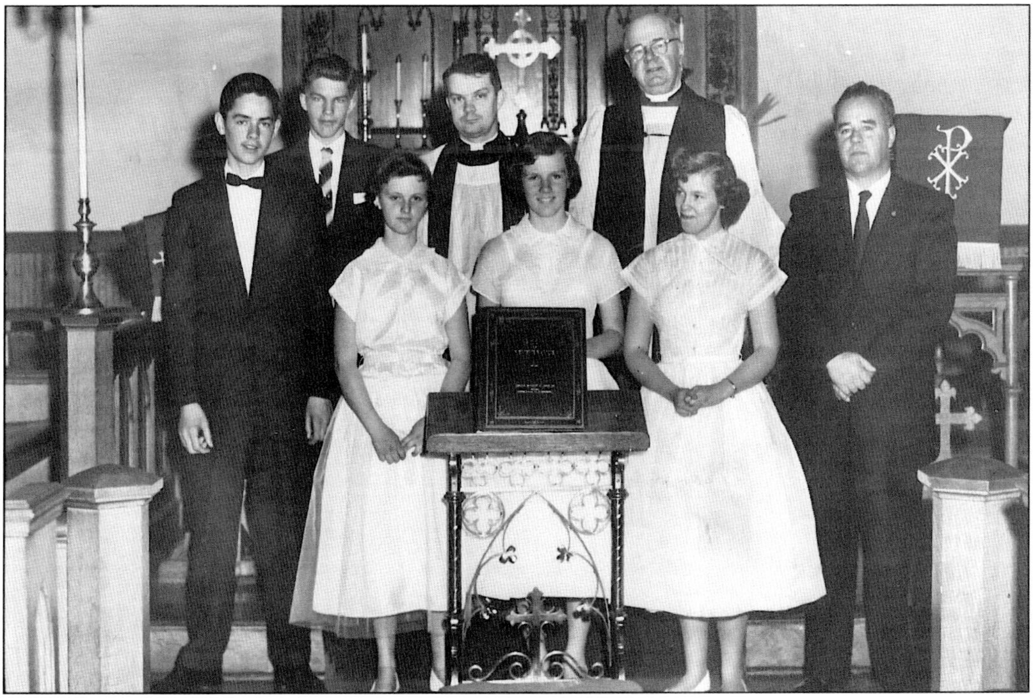

On April 18, 1957, Bishop Appleton Lawrence came to the Christ Episcopal Church to confer the Sacrament of Confirmation on these young people. Seen here, from left to right, are as follows: (front row) Pauline Moyette, Jane Robinson, and Andrea Miknaitis; (back row) Karl Ericson, David Tucker, Vicar James O'Dell, Bishop Lawrence, and Warden of the Church Stanley Ericson.

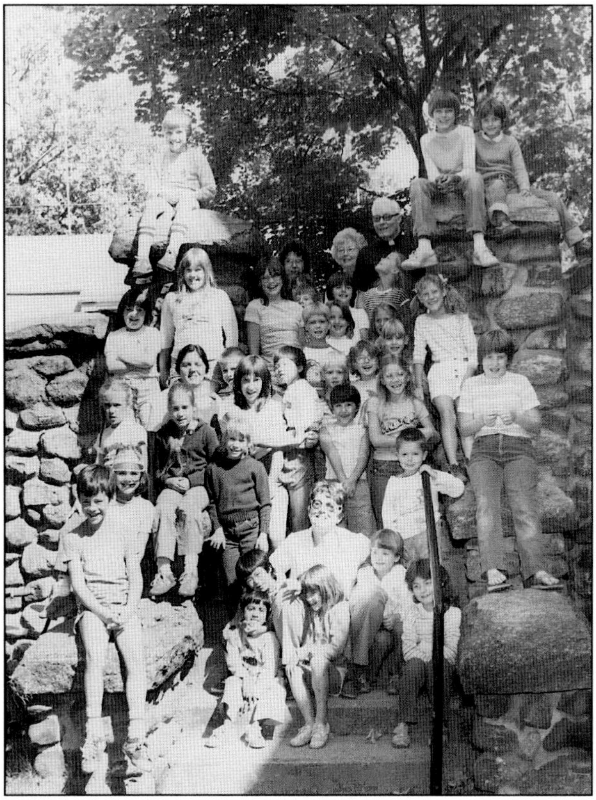

In the summer of 1983, each Barre church takes its turn inviting youngsters of all denominations to a lively week at the Vacation Bible School. This happy group is gathered on the stone steps in front of Christ Church Episcopal in South Barre with Rev. and Mrs. Humbert Thomas and the enthusiastic teaching staff.

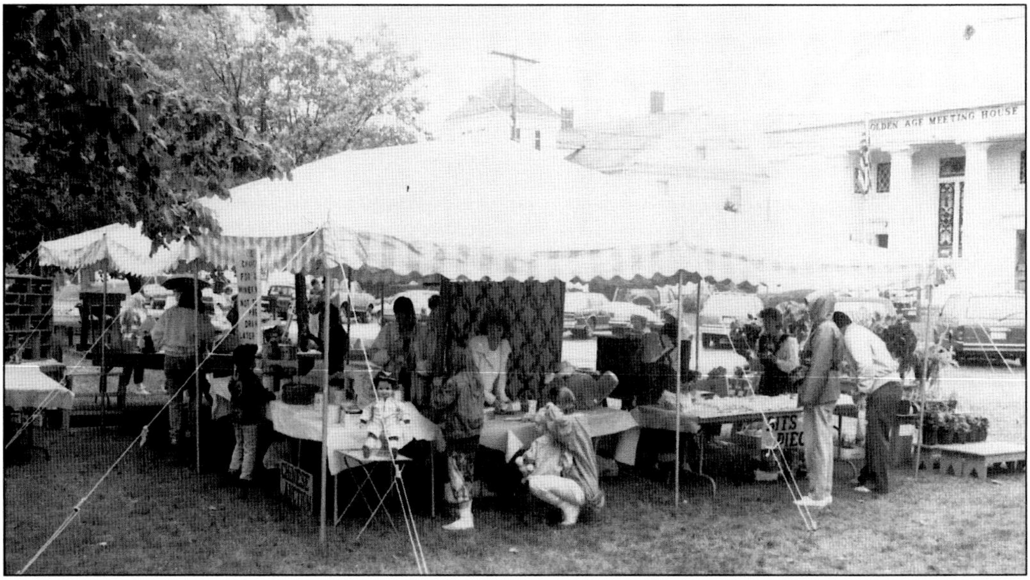

In late September 1991, the parishioners of Christ Episcopal Church decided to hold their Fall Fair under a large tent on the South Common in Barre Center (a change from its usual location on the church grounds). The diligent workers (both women and men) were rewarded with great success, as is shown by many intent shoppers.

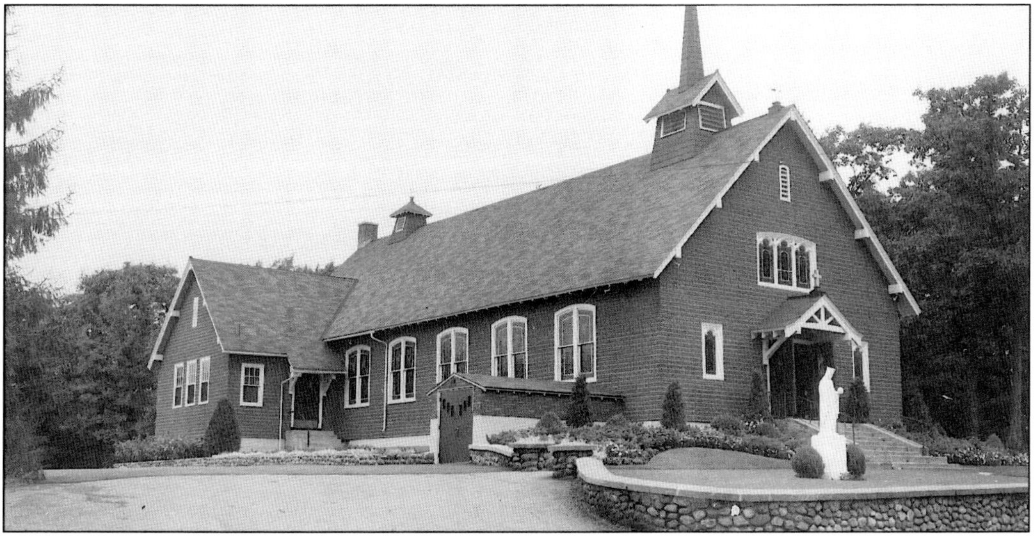

Countless hours of hard physical work by fervent early parishioners combined with gifts of land and labor from the Barre Wool Combing Co. Ltd. culminated in the 1917 dedication of South Barre's Catholic church, named for the English saint Thomas-a-Becket. Three decades later, in 1948, parishioners again volunteered time and skills to excavate beneath the church nave for construction of a fine parish hall. The entrance to the hall is seen on the left side of the building.

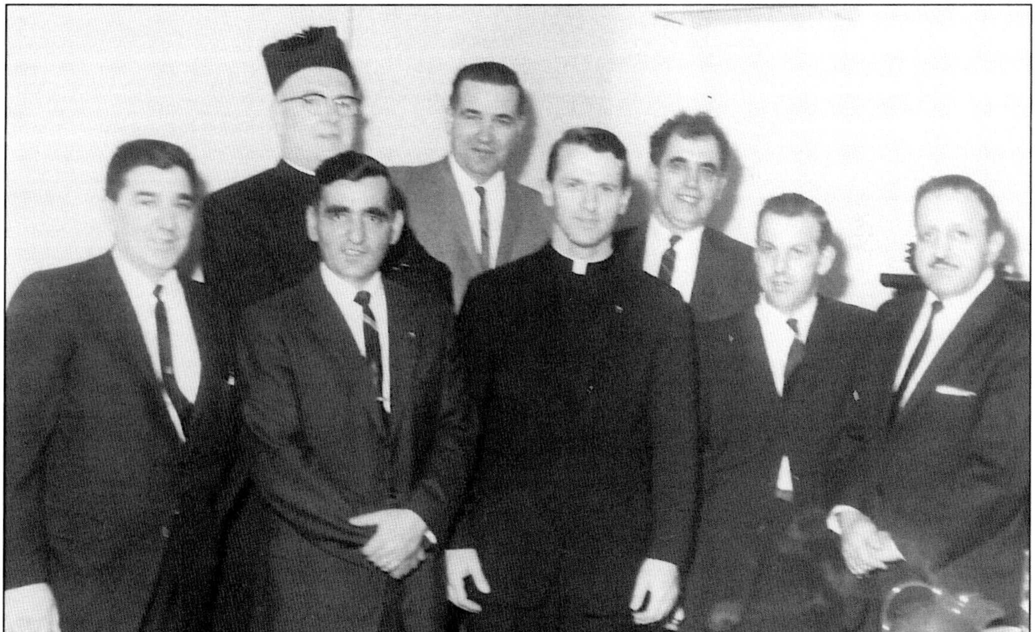

In mid-February 1965, the men's Holy Name Society of St. Thomas sponsored a lecture by Reverend Bourque of the Blessed Sacrament Fathers. Reverend Bourque spoke vividly about his missionary work for the order in Uganda. The committee members, pictured here from left to right, are as follows: (front row) Peter Inzerillo, Michael Caranci, Reverend Bourque, Robert Duval, and Sam Lamacchia; (back row) Rev. Marcus Murtough (pastor), Matthew Towle, and Rudolph Jablonski.

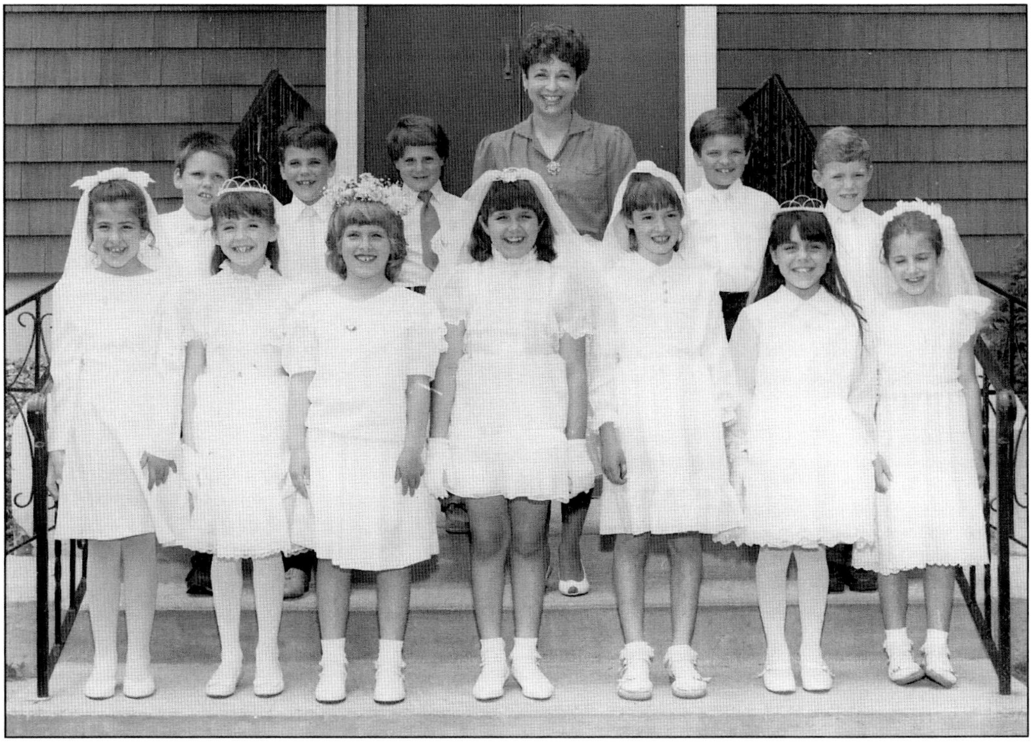

A smiling Victoria King stands on the main steps in front of St. Thomas-a-Becket Church with her First Communion class after mass on May 31, 1987. Seen here, from left to right, are as follows: (front row) Sarah McDaniel, Jillian Johnstone, Kelli Burch, Katie Inzerillo, Ryan Mesch, Heather Petracone, and Sarah Widing; (back row) Harley Bassett, Evan Barringer, Derek Puliafico, Mrs. King, Eric Petersen, and Richard Mansfield.

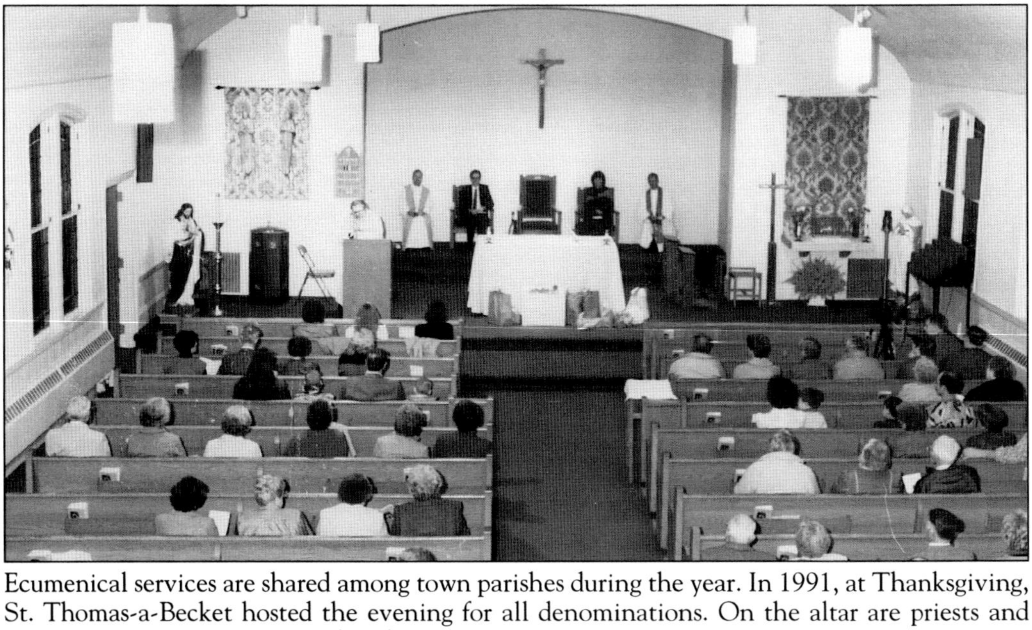

Ecumenical services are shared among town parishes during the year. In 1991, at Thanksgiving, St. Thomas-a-Becket hosted the evening for all denominations. On the altar are priests and ministers representing Barre's churches.

The New Life Assembly of God held its first service in South Barre in mid-August 1979. Since then the parish has purchased, and carefully renovated, the Kaplan store building on Vernon Avenue in South Barre. The throng of youngsters pictured here has just come from services celebrating the church's 10th anniversary in August 1989.

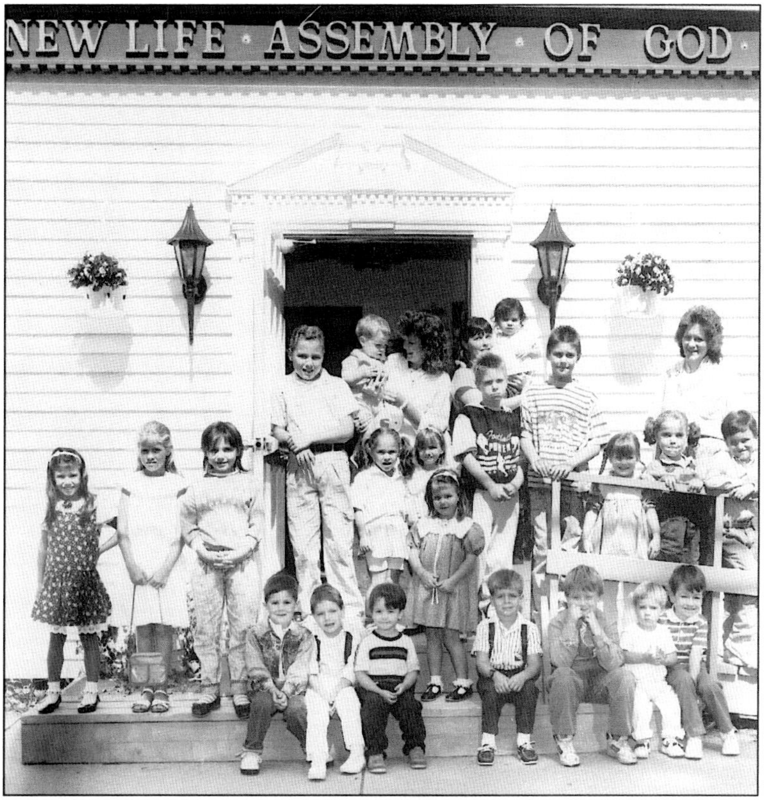

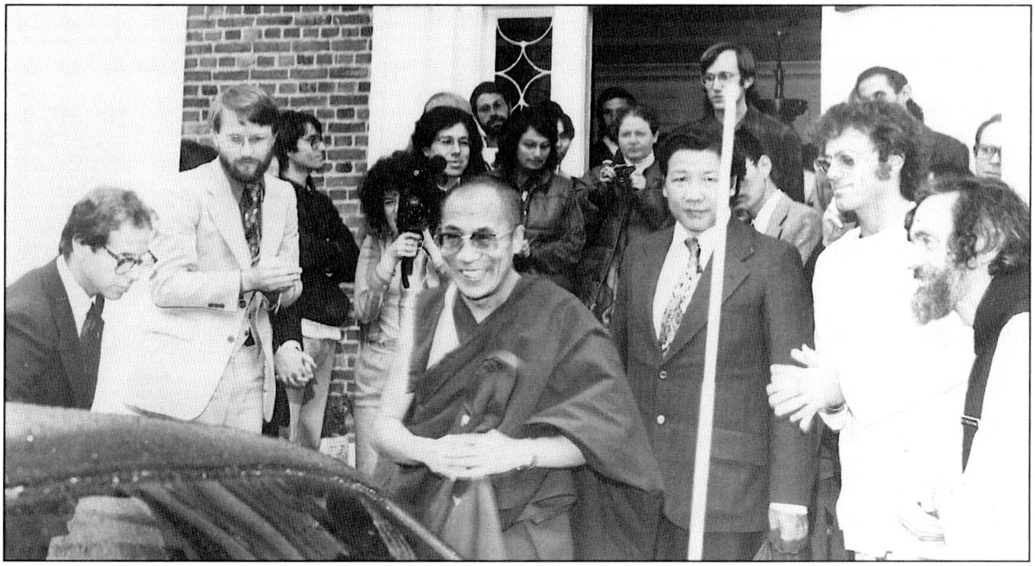

The Insight Meditation Society (IMS) came to Barre in 1975. The great main house was originally built for Col. William Gaston in the early 20th century. For several years after the Gaston family sold it, the mansion served as a novitiate for The Blessed Sacrament Fathers, a Catholic order. IMS offers meditation studies and retreats in the Buddhist tradition. Visitors come from around the world for varying retreat periods. The memorable and joyous visit of the Dalai Lama, the revered Tibetan spiritual leader, took place in October 1979.

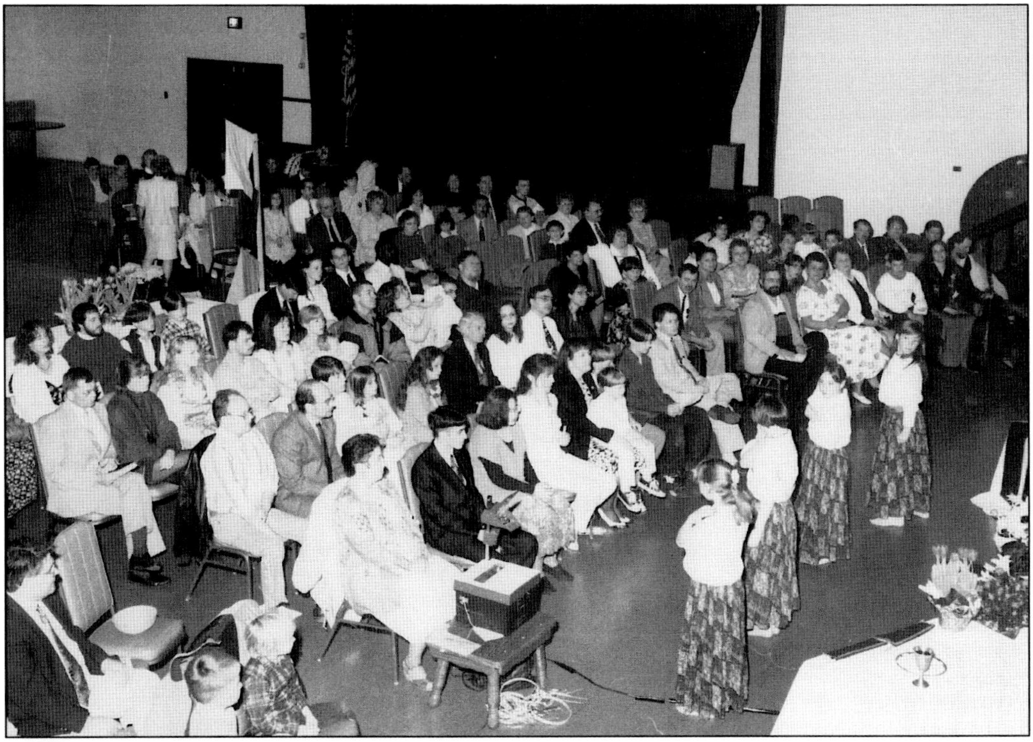

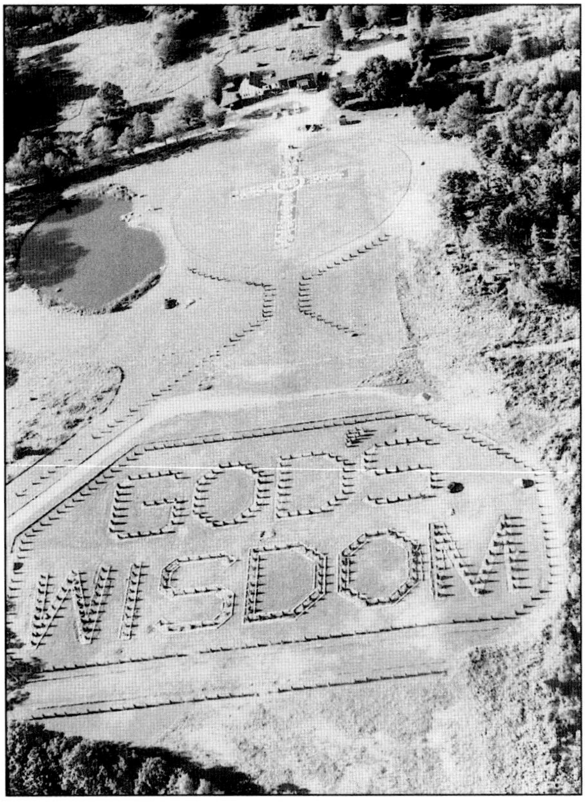

Members of the newly formed Covenant Evangelical Church have been gathering weekly since 1994, in the large hall of the Coldbrook Country Club. This photograph records parishioners attending the Easter Sunday service in 1995.

John Harty, a gentleman of abiding faith, designed and painted this great cross with the help of his daughter Noreen. It is laid out on a paved area near his farmhouse on Harty Road and brings thousands of visitors to view and pray by the cross, on which the Ten Commandments are painted. From a plane flying 1,600 feet or more, the view is splendid and the painted commandments are clearly readable.

Seven

Remarkable Faces and Places

Barre is a place with unusual features both natural and man-made. There are dams, unique buildings and structures, glacial boulders, silvery waterfalls, spectacular views, and an abundance of nature's beauty. Most are enduring. On the other hand, thousands of individuals have passed their fleeting time in our midst. Some enjoyed the simple life in anonymity. Many of these were farmers, mechanics, lumberjacks, artisans, and laborers. Others made an impact on the community by their deeds of leadership and service. It would not be possible to point out and honor all these remarkable people and places. We present just a few here.

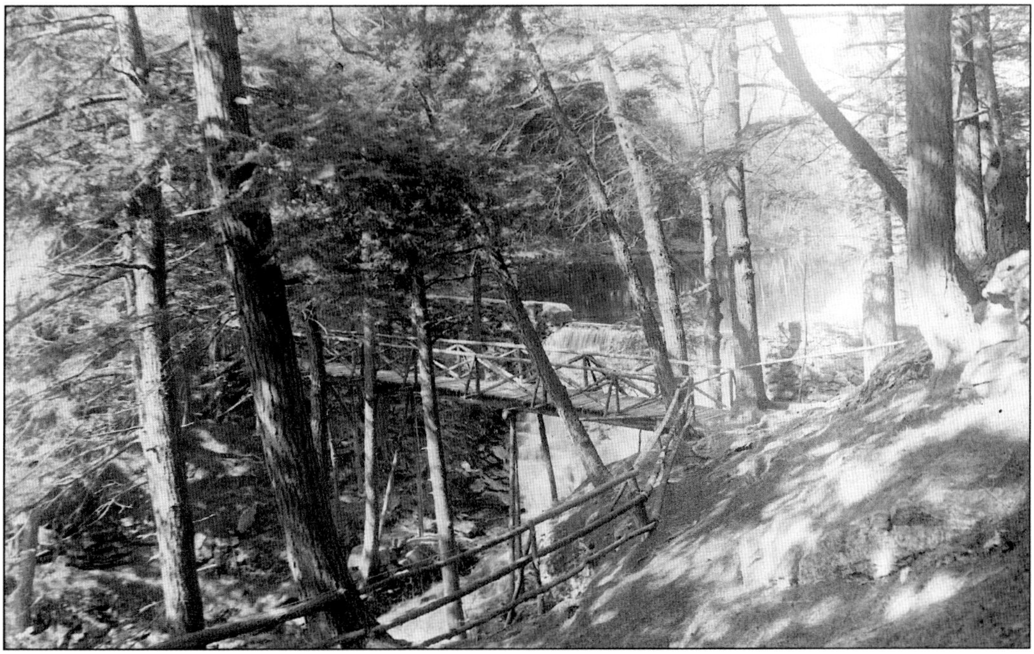

In the first few years, the early settlers discovered and delighted in the series of cataracts formed by Galloway Brook as it splashed downward from South Street to join the Prince River. It was a place of special beauty and they called it Barre Falls.

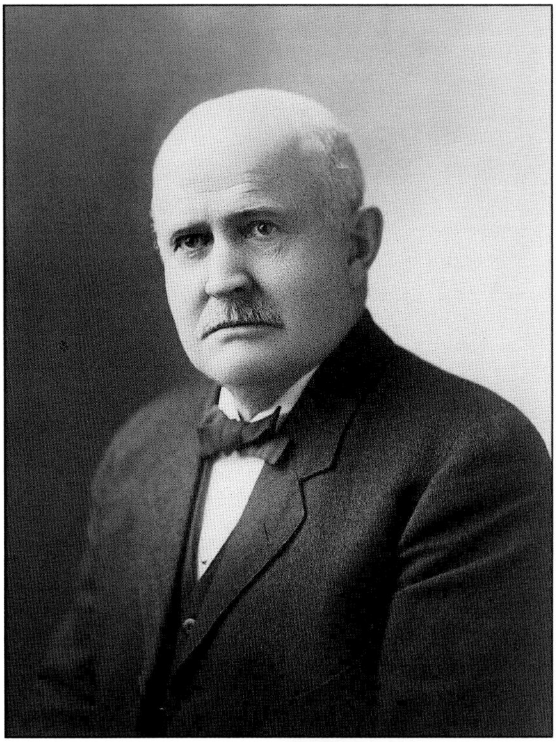

George W. Cook, businessman and county commissioner, acquired his home from his father-in-law, James Davis, and purchased much of the land leading to a canyon through which Galloway Brook flowed. He subsequently restored the whole property to a natural condition. It has ever since been called Cook's Canyon.

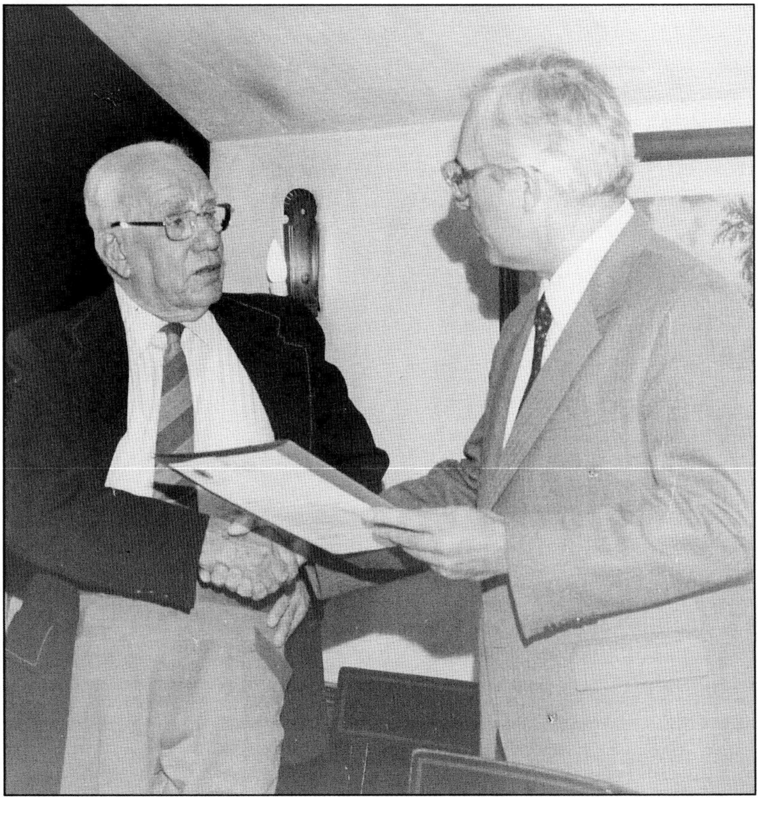

For many years, these two gentlemen worked on behalf of our community, often together. It seemed that Charles Connington (left) was on everyone's board of directors; and Robert Wetmore represented Barre capably in both the Massachusetts House and Senate for many years.

A longtime resident, Ella Elvira Gibson, was our "women's rights" activist. A poet, writer, and public speaker, she espoused many causes, but her claim to fame was her unique service as the only female chaplain of a military unit in the Civil War.

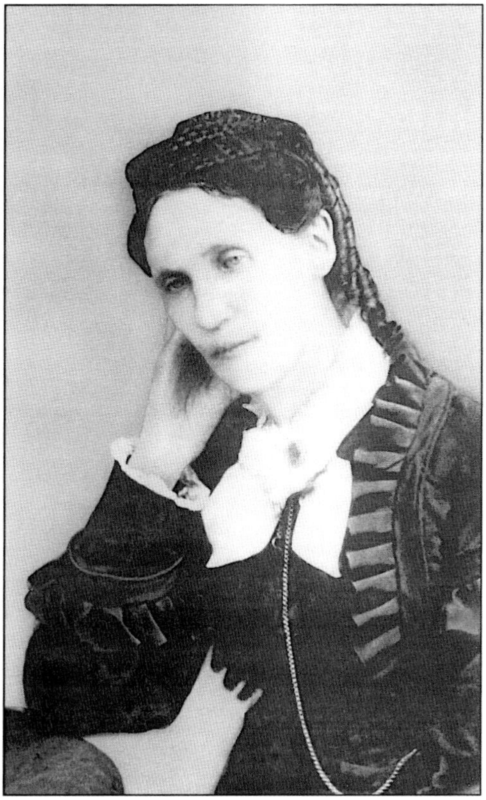

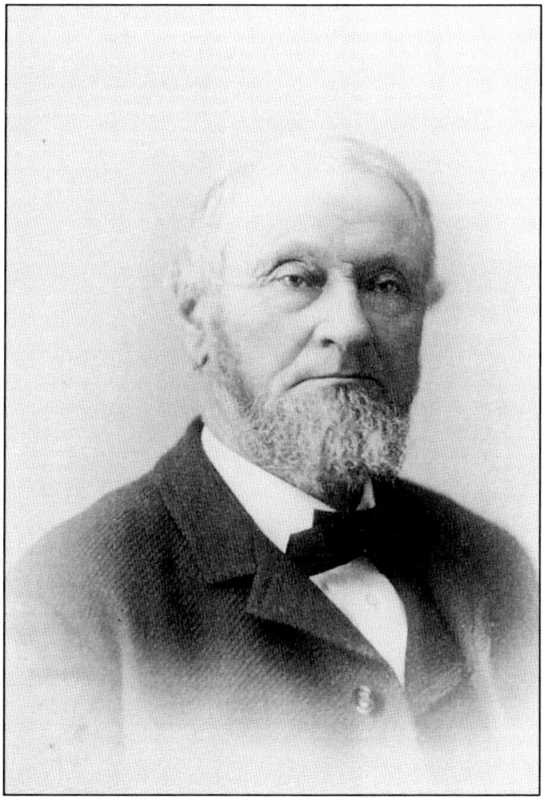

John W. Rice was in the boot and shoe manufacturing business in several locations in the latter half of the 19th century. The concern survived two disastrous fires. With his son Albert, he had an office in the building where his grandson, John S. "Jack" Rice, made and sold his famous popcorn.

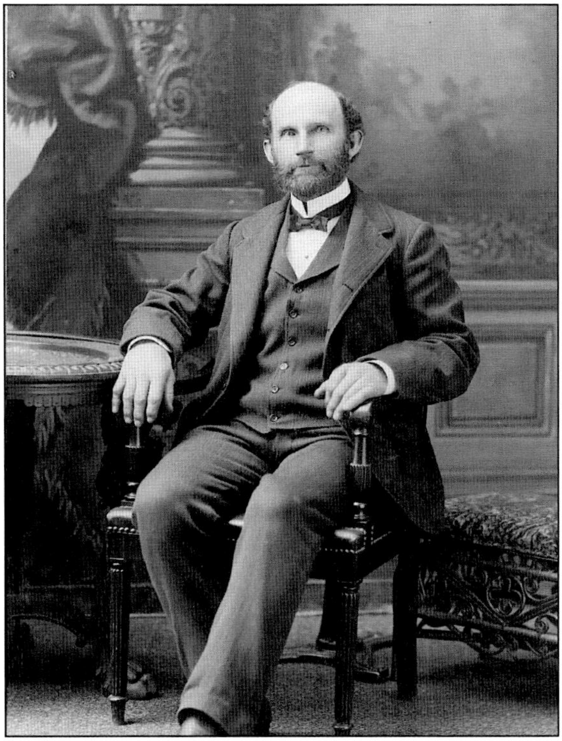

As a devoted public servant, Austin F. Adams served many years in the Massachusetts House and Senate. When he wasn't erecting buildings in Barre Plains, he was often occupied in researching the early history of the town.

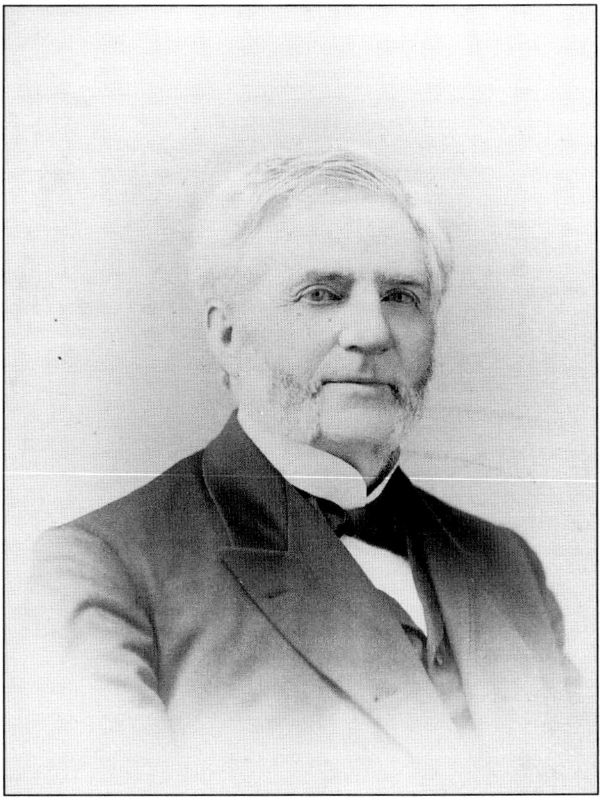

When Hervey B. Wilbur left his school for special youngsters, he turned it over to colleague Dr. George Brown. Dr. Brown (shown here) and his heirs successfully operated the Elm Hill School for nearly 100 years; he became a world-renowned expert in his field.

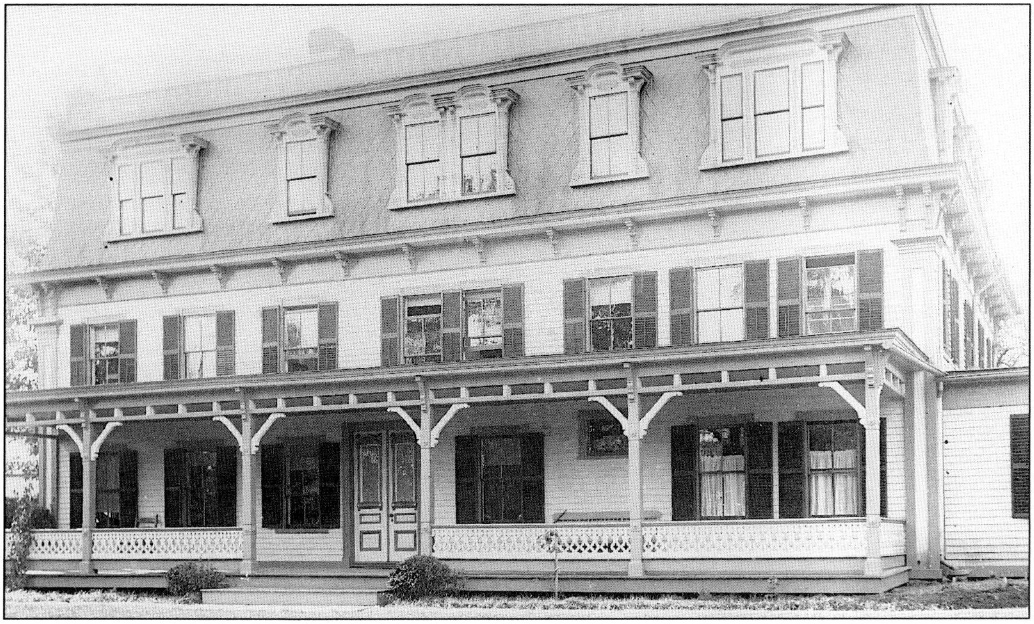

One of the many buildings that constituted the Elm Hill School was called "Der Platz." It was situated on Union Street.

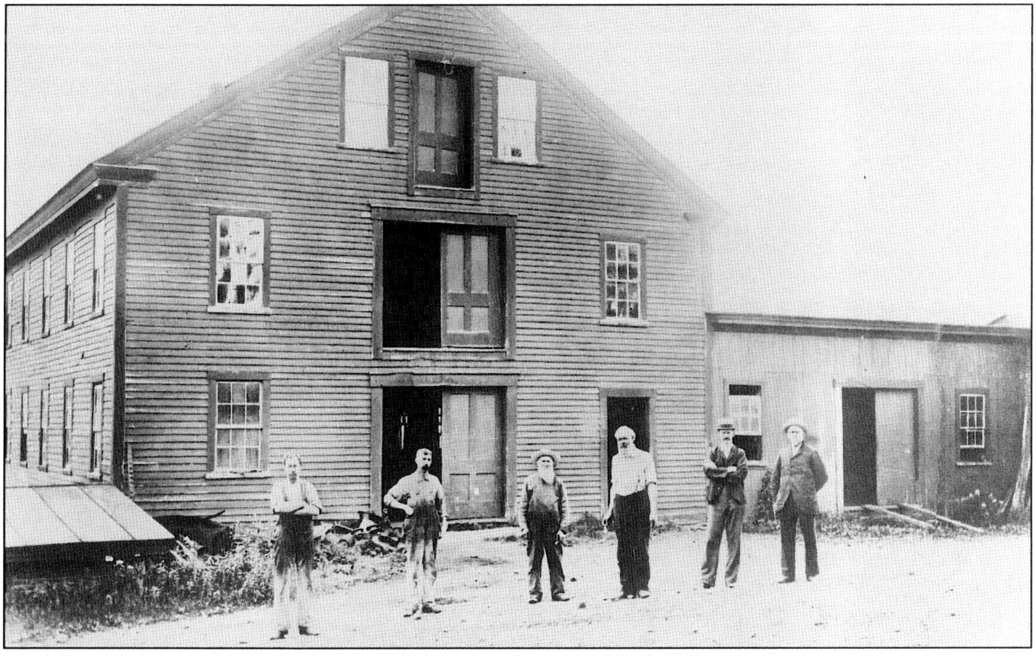

The Heald Co. was an early manufacturing firm on Valley Road. Located near the corner of Mechanic Street, this now-extant building served as a workplace for Barre workers 100 years ago.

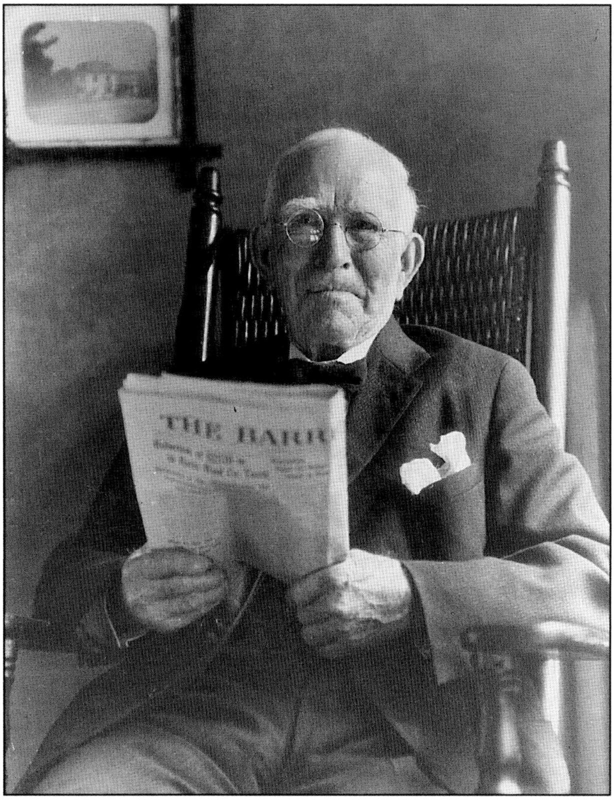

The Heald Foundry, originated by Stephen Heald, flourished for more than 50 years. Boxes, wheels, stoves, components for the Bay State rake, and even kegs were made here. Many workers lived nearby and it became known as Heald Village. Stephen was eventually succeeded by his son Leander S., seen here in his retirement.

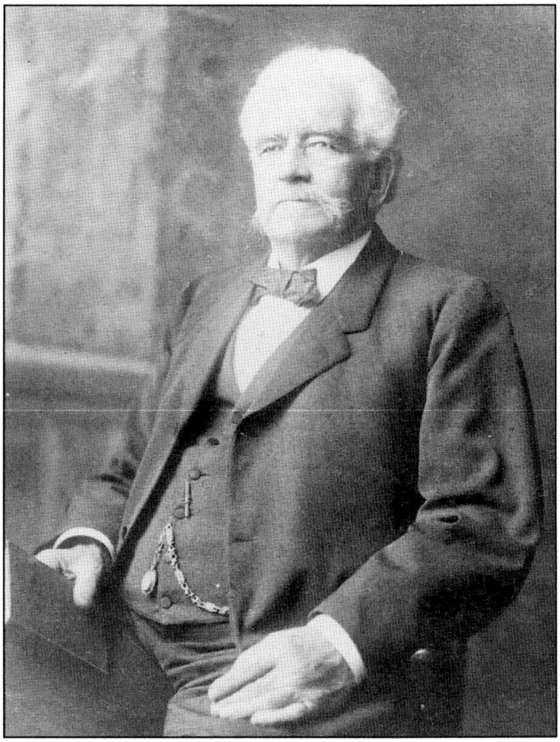

In 1899, Henry Augustus Pevear purchased the large land-holdings of William Ash and his family. Pevear also acquired two other farms with their homes nearby as well as nearly 200 acres. Members of his family spent many summers here.

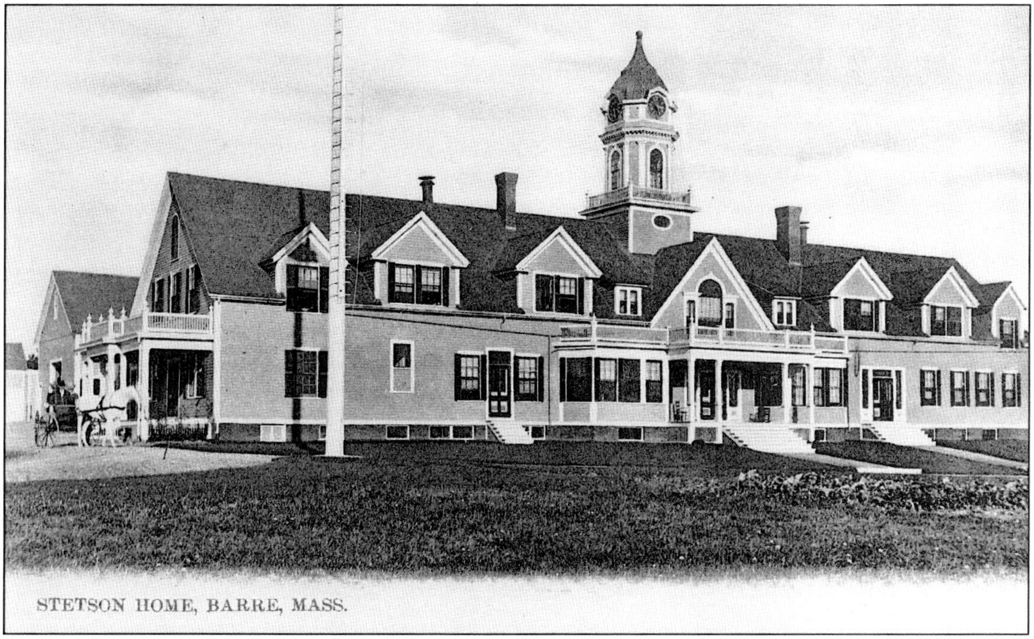

The chief attraction on the Pevear holdings was a large dwelling for boys who did not have a suitable situation at home. Some were orphans, but no matter what their background, they were given the opportunity to live and work on an active farm. Mr. Pevear named it Stetson Home in honor of his mother, the former Mary Stetson.

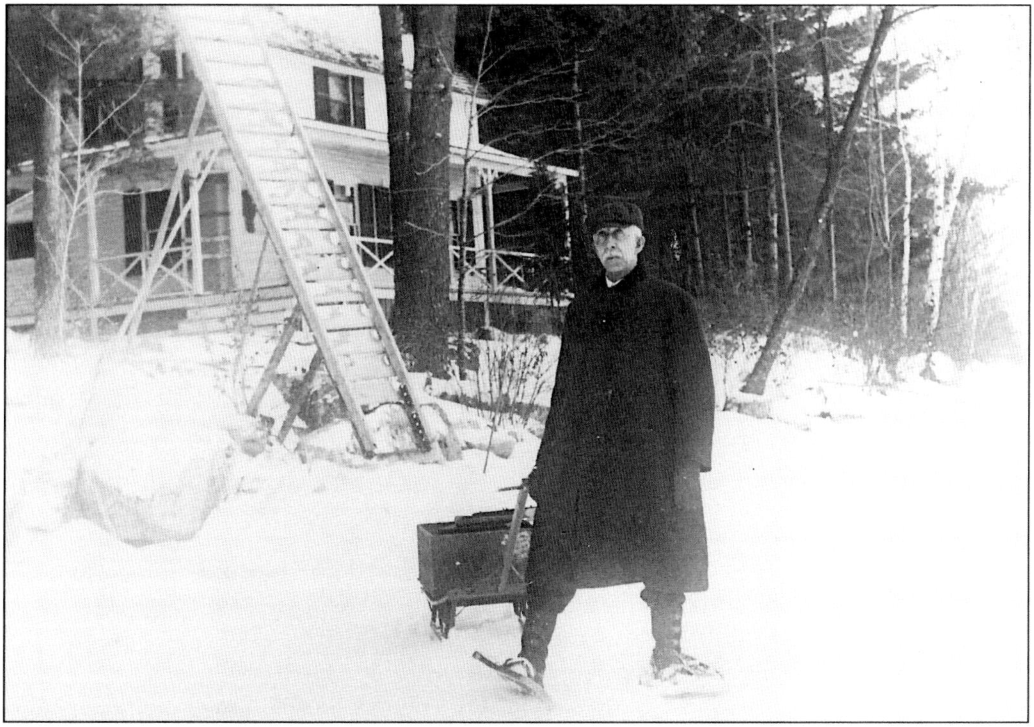

A general practitioner in our town for many years, Dr. Walter Bates used many modes of travel to reach the sick and aged, even snowshoes.

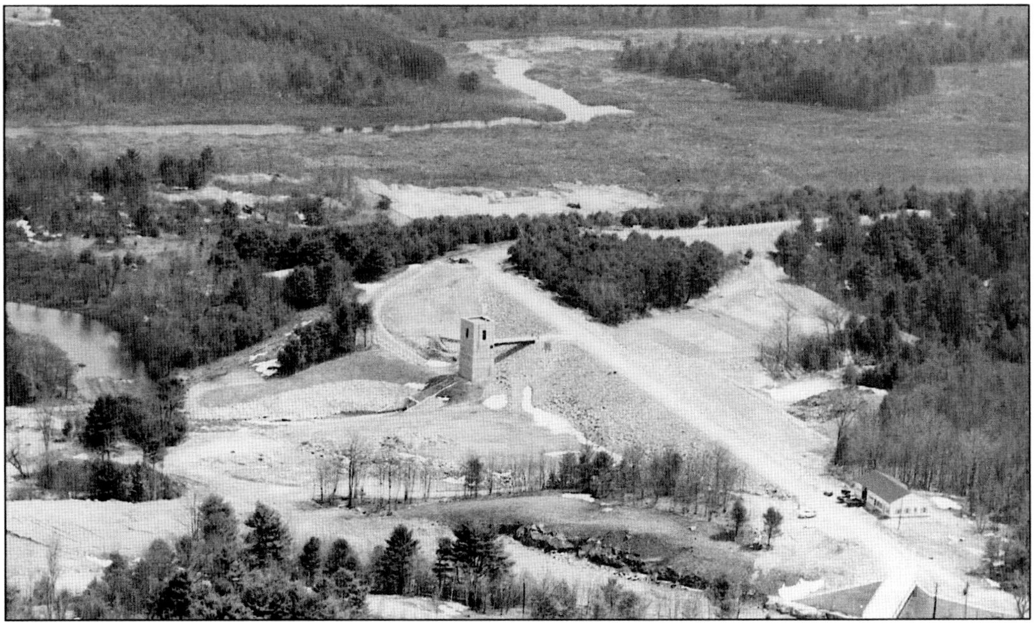

One scenic area of Barre was changed forever when, in the mid-1950s, the U.S. Army Corps of Engineers built a flood control dam obliterating the falls in the eastern part of Barre. This aerial view shows the dam under construction. Now a favorite recreation area once again, its value to residents downstream is immeasurable.

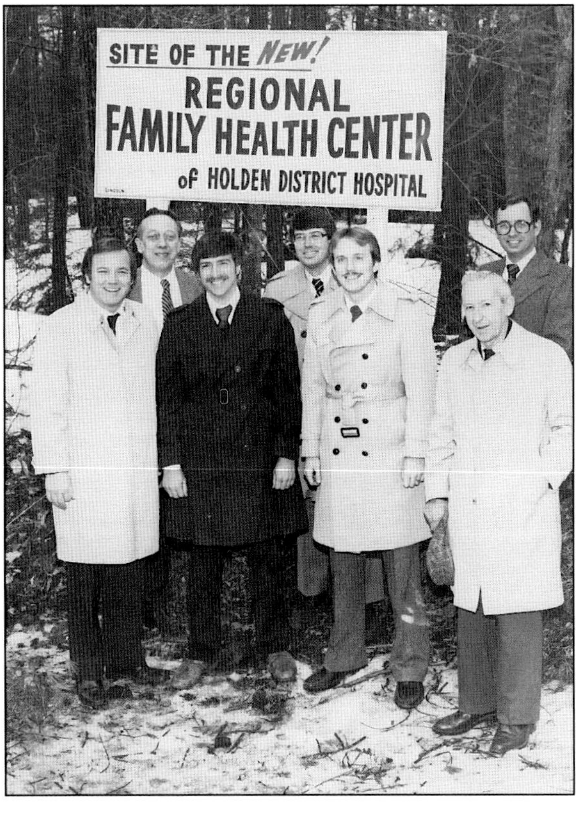

A remarkable achievement, the Barre Family Health Center took a giant step forward when a new facility was built on Route 122. Among the dignitaries present at the ground-breaking ceremony were Dr. Samuel Pickens (second from left) and Dr. Stephen Earls (third from left), who both devoted many years to the successful institution. J. Howard Thompson, the chair of the Barre Board of Selectmen, is pictured at right in the light coat.

After serving in the Civil War, Dr. Charles G. Allen returned to Barre and soon organized a company that manufactured the famous Yankee Hay Rake and the Victor Plow, among many other products.

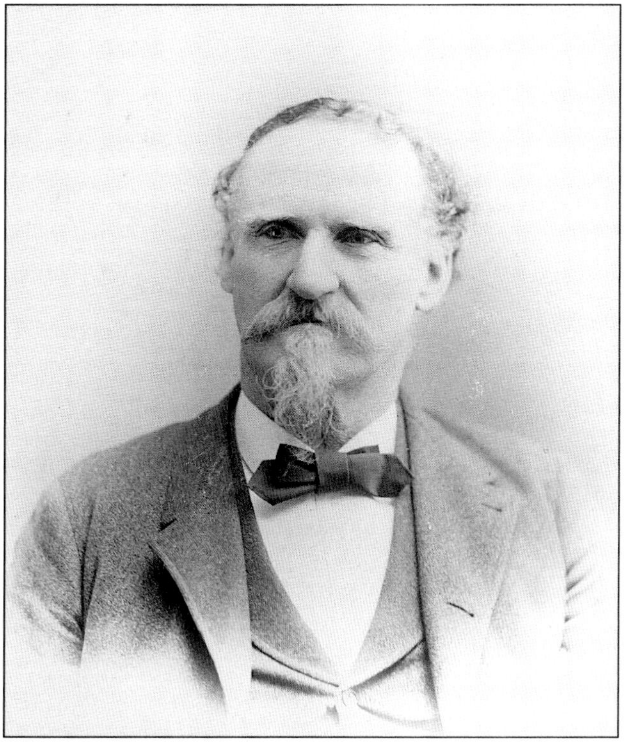

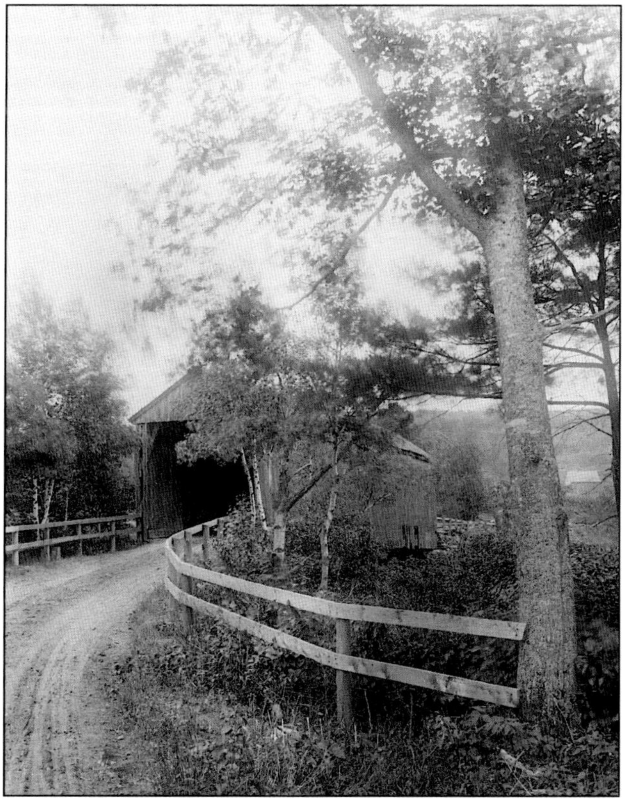

Among the special places was Barre's picturesque covered bridge over the Ware River, located near the old Granger place. It was destroyed by the great hurricane of 1938.

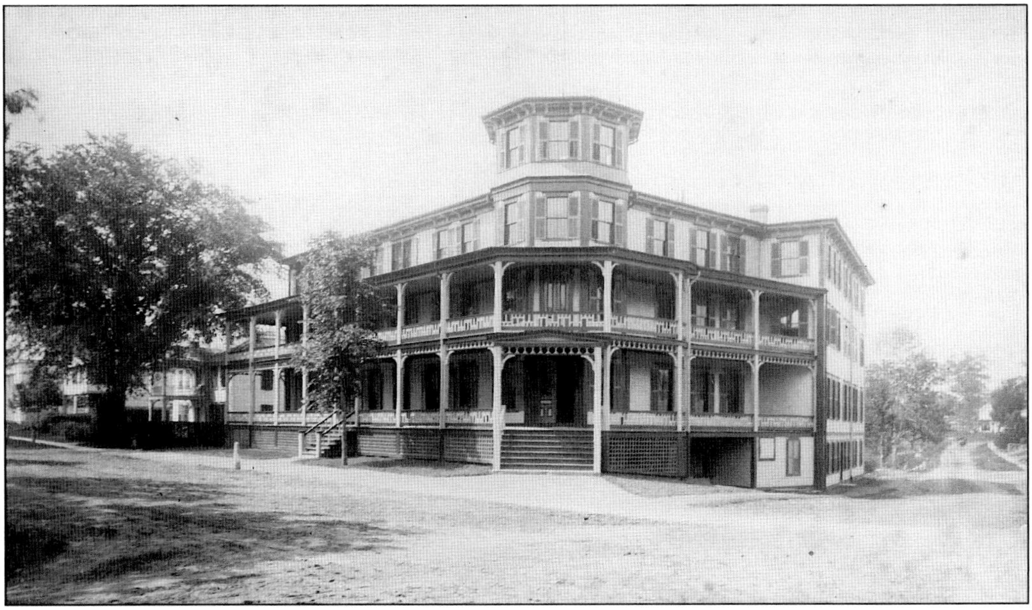

One of the most remarkable places in the area was the Hotel Barre, a vacation destination for many visitors from 1888 until its loss by fire in 1990.

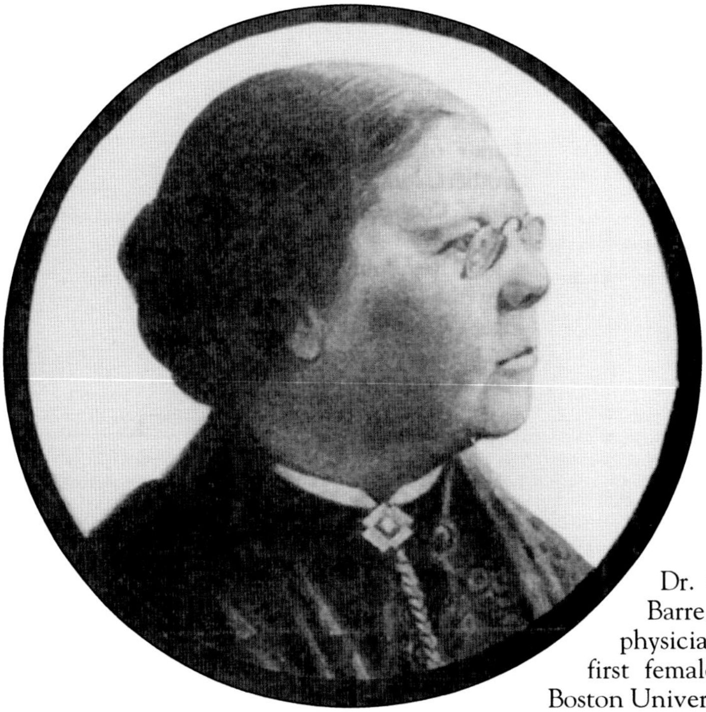

Dr. Caroline Hastings, a native of Barre, was one of the earliest female physicians in the country and was the first female lecturer in anatomy at the Boston University Medical School.

Eight

Memorable Moments

There are some who would argue that any and all moments spent in Barre—surrounded by rolling hills, blue skies, and fresh air—are memorable. The spectacular beauty of the town's landscape is indeed worthy of note, but what truly defines this community are the people who live here. Now and in generations past, Barre's character and strength are symbolized by the individuals who have called this special place "home."

Heroes are created by circumstance, and Barre has had its share of noble human beings. From public servants to veterans of military service, from mothers raising children on their own to fathers earning high school diplomas in their "spare" time while working two jobs to support their families, we are a community of heroes. At work and at play, in the office, home, or on stage, our lives are a reflection of the best we are and hope to be.

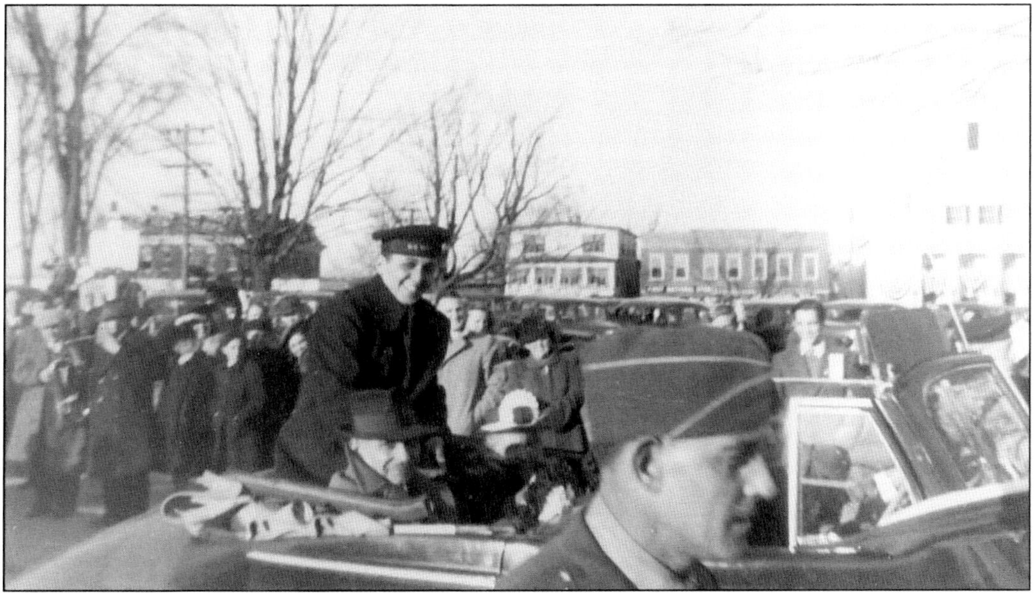

Seamen 2nd Class Basil D. Izzi, one of Barre's true heroes, spent 83 days on a raft in the Atlantic Ocean after the ship on which he was stationed was torpedoed on November 2, 1942. On January 24, 1943, Basil and two comrades were rescued, and on April 11, 1943, the Town of Barre welcomed him home. He was met at Union Station in Worcester by hundreds of "Barre-ites." Every business in town closed for the day to honor our young hero!

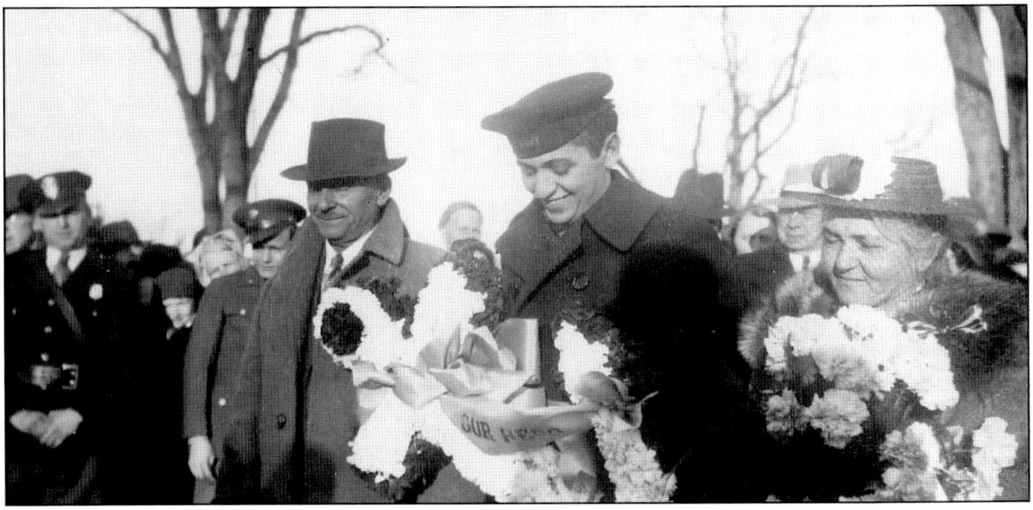

After many months of waiting and praying, Basil Izzi came home to a gala celebration and a very happy mom and dad. Pictured here, from left to right, are Dominic Izzi, Seaman 2nd Class Basil Izzi, and Rosa Izzi. Mrs. Izzi never gave up hope and always believed her son would return home.

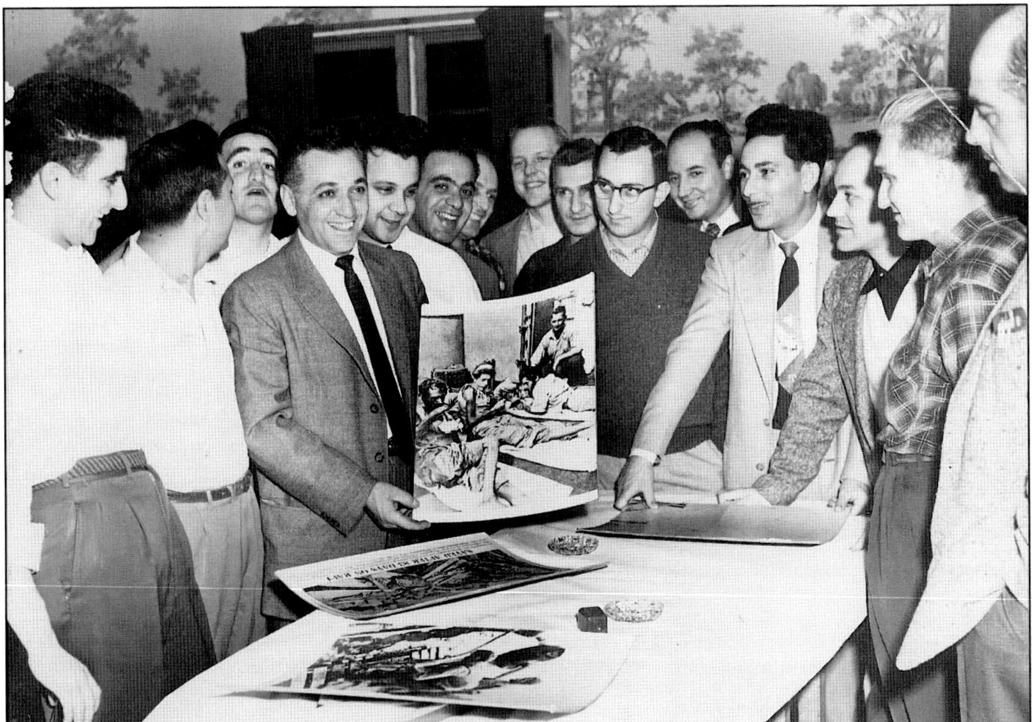

In 1958, 15 years after Basil Izzi was rescued, a group of Basil's friends gathered to celebrate and listen to his detailed story of the 83 days he spent on a raft. This get-together was at the Post 404 Legion Hall in South Barre. Seen here, from left to right, are Cleveland Trifilo, Joseph Lamacchia, Eugene Caranci, Basil Izzi, Amerigo Simeone, Gildo Simeone, Frank Valente, George Thorng, Peter Rosselli, Dominic Spasaro, Fido Neri, Joseph Chilleri, Reginald Franciose, John Rosselli, and John Fargnoli.

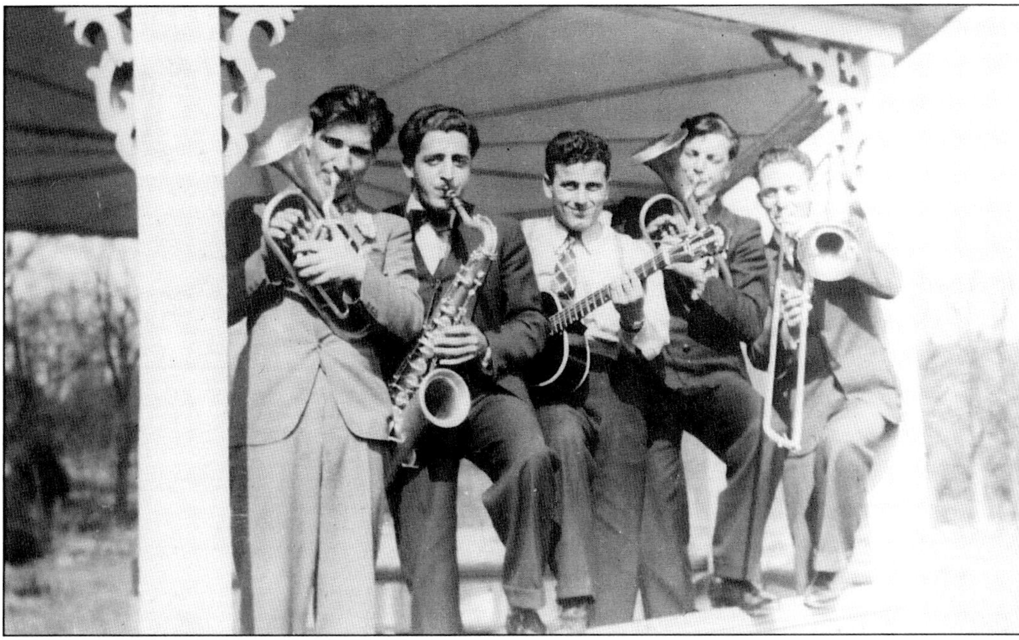

These young gentlemen of South Barre formed a band called The Five Wacks and played at functions. Practicing at the Rocking Stone Park Bandstand (which is no longer there), from left to right, are John Aliquo, Salvatore Lamacchia, Frank Borelli, Louis Franciose, and Frank (Mimo) Valente, who still leads "Mimo's Band." As you can see, the dress code of the day, in 1937, was suits, white shirts, and ties—a far cry from the fashions of today!

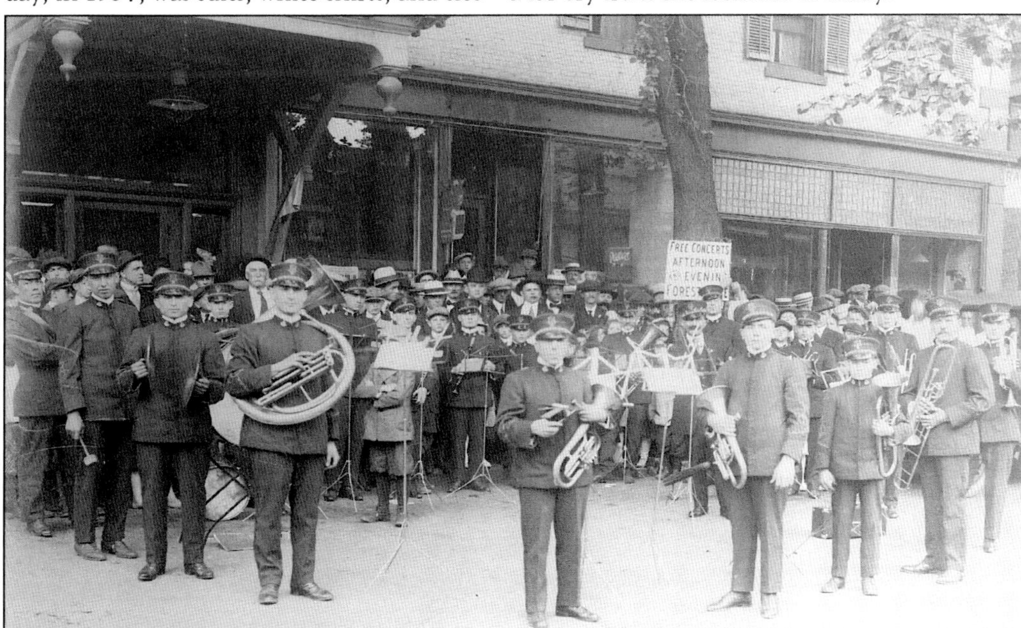

In 1914, the Barre Wool Combing Co. Ltd. donated a building so Italian men could gather and spend a few leisure hours together. The building was also used for band practices. It was around this time that the South Barre Brass Band was formed. Some of the bandleaders through the years include Edward Spinelli, Charles Colletti, John Franciose, and Severino D'Annolfo.

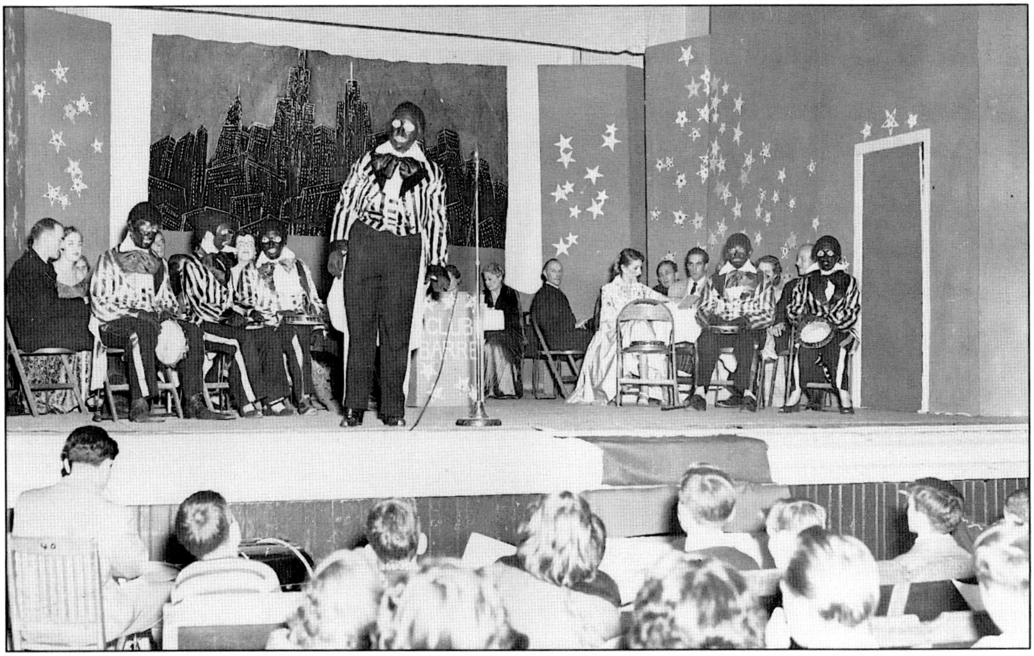

The Barre Teachers Club presented an old-fashioned minstrel show in 1952. This was one of the many productions presented by the club. The proceeds, which totalled $2,500 one year, were used for scholarships.

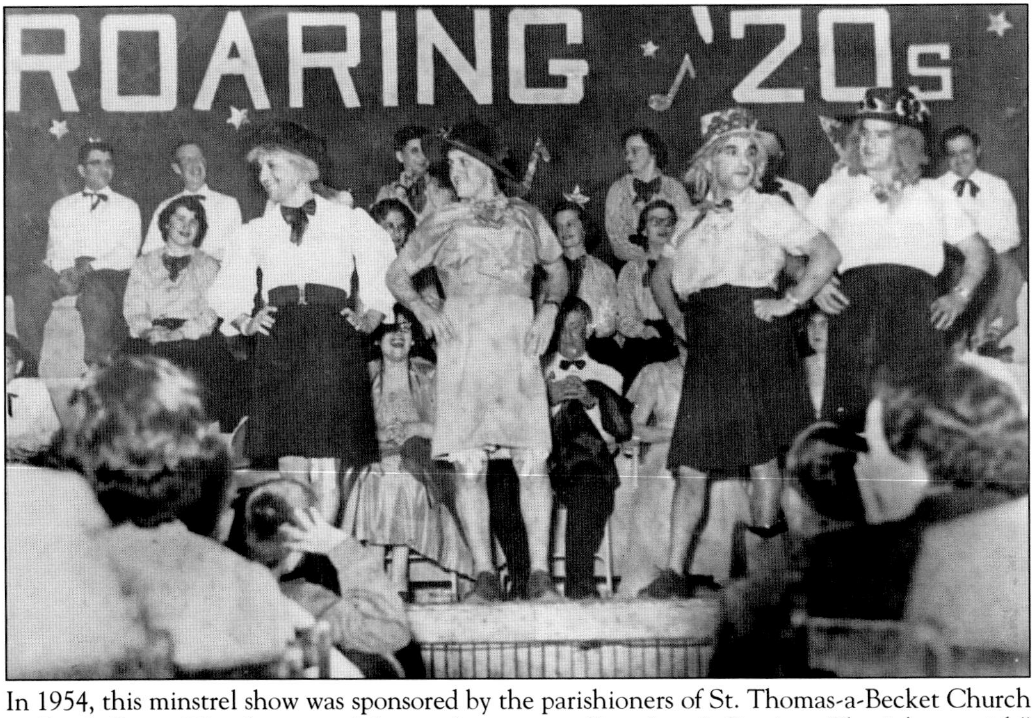

In 1954, this minstrel show was sponsored by the parishioners of St. Thomas-a-Becket Church in South Barre. The director of the production was Rev. Leo J. Battista. The "chorus girls" pictured here, from left to right, are Joseph Lamacchia, Joseph Petracone, Joseph Giarusso, and John Corso.

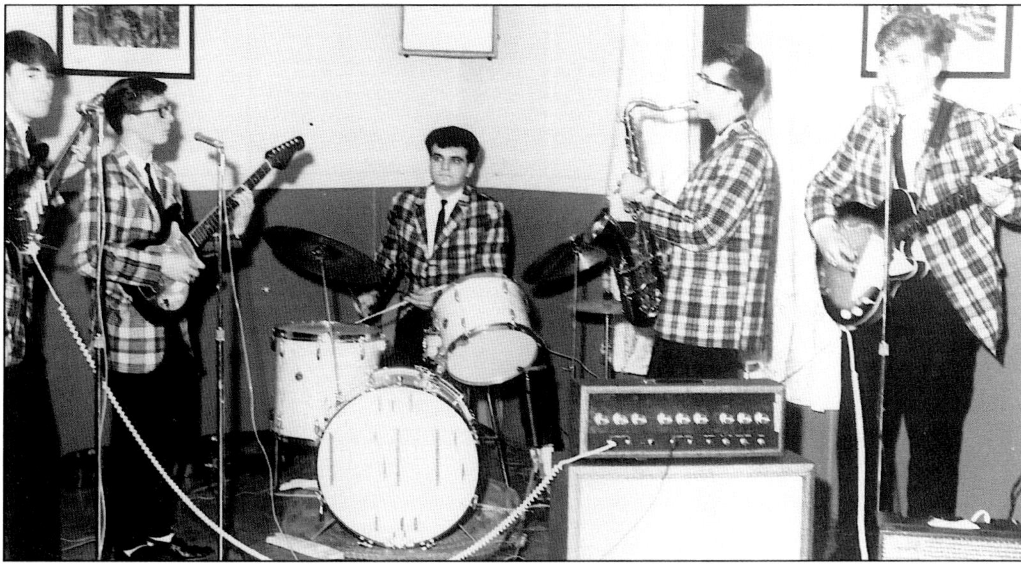

In the mid-1960s, the above combination was very popular in this area. The band was arranged by Nick Mallozzi, who operated Nick's Barbershop at that time. Seen here, from left to right, are Bill Powers, Richie Zbikowski, Nicky Mallozzi, Don Whigham, and George Benouski. The jackets certainly were an eye-catcher.

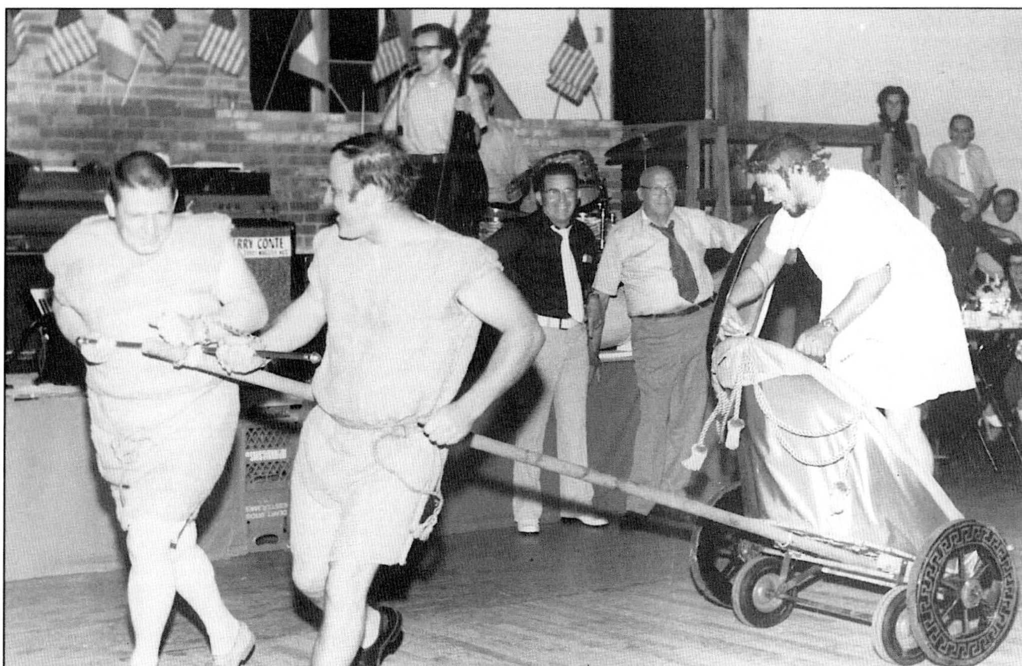

As part of Barre's bicentennial celebration, a Roman Festival was held on August 3, 1974, at the Coldbrook Country Club. A scrumptious seven-course meal was served. Pictured in this photograph, from left to right, are Earl Sample and Fred Smith (slaves), Ralph Giarusso and Joseph DiFonzo (onlookers), and Anthony Pitisci (driver).

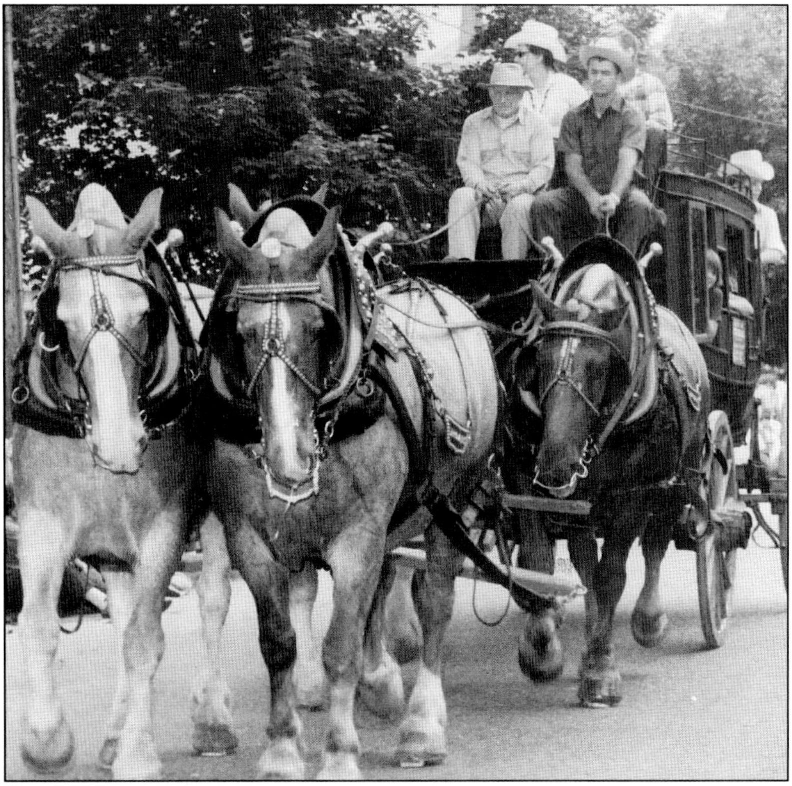

Barre's Concord stagecoach was one of the many attractions in the Barre Bicentennial Parade in August 1974. The people in the photograph are unknown.

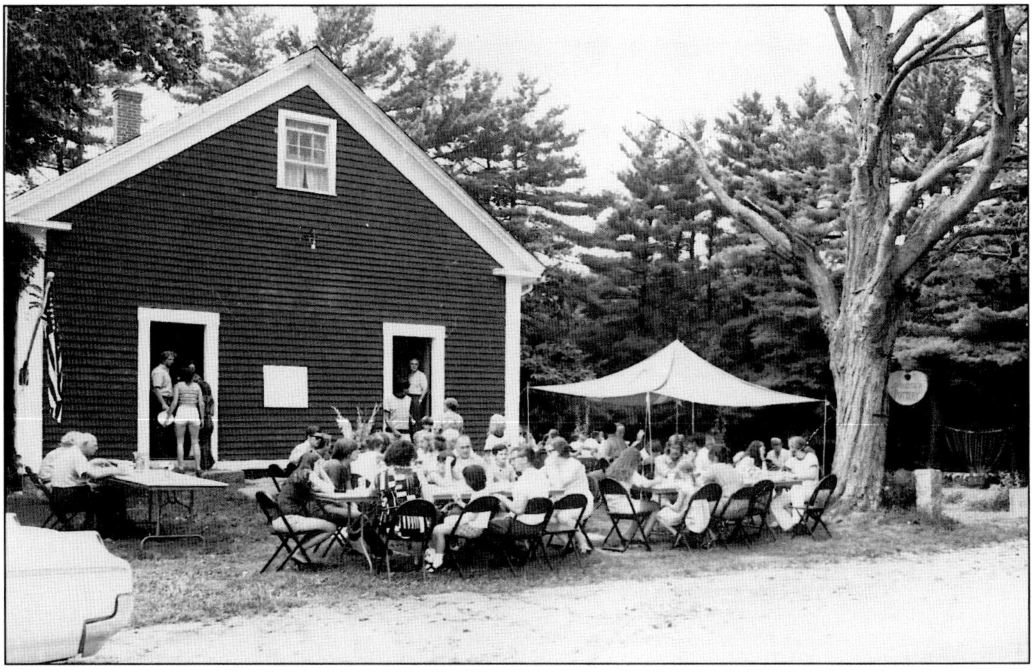

The home of Howard and Jinx Hastings was the former Rice Village School. Each year the alumni held an annual get-together here. After the Hastings purchased the school, they carried on the tradition of the picnic. In the mid-1970s, they sold the house to John and Catherine Brandon.

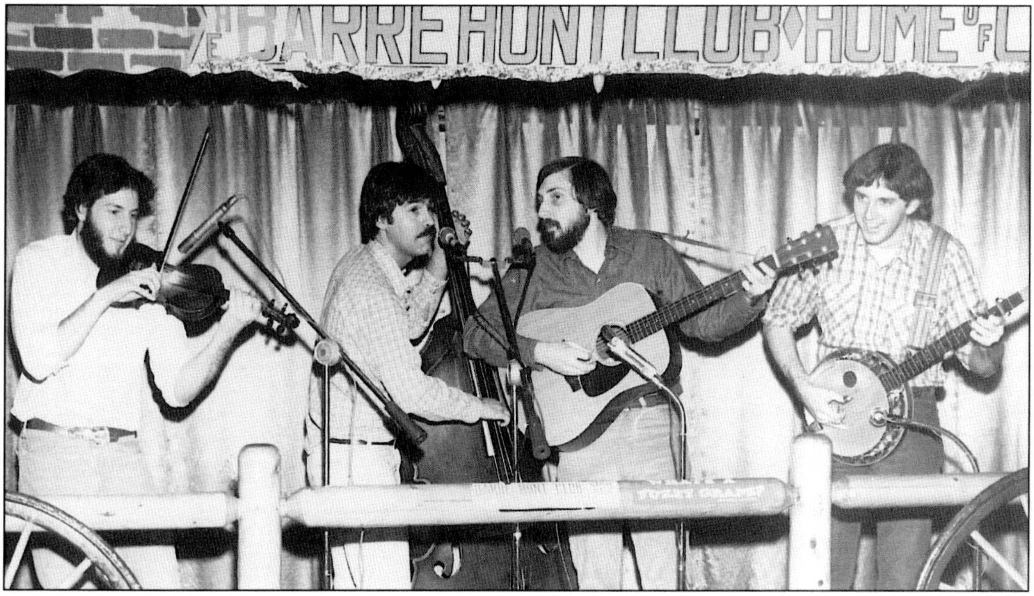

The Panaccione brothers, with the help of another member, played bluegrass music in the area. They performed at the Barre Hunt Club and at many bluegrass festivals and fairs. Seen here, from left to right, are Mark Panaccione, Pete Travisono, Paul Panaccione, and Danny Panaccione. The band was formed in 1979 and disbanded in 1982.

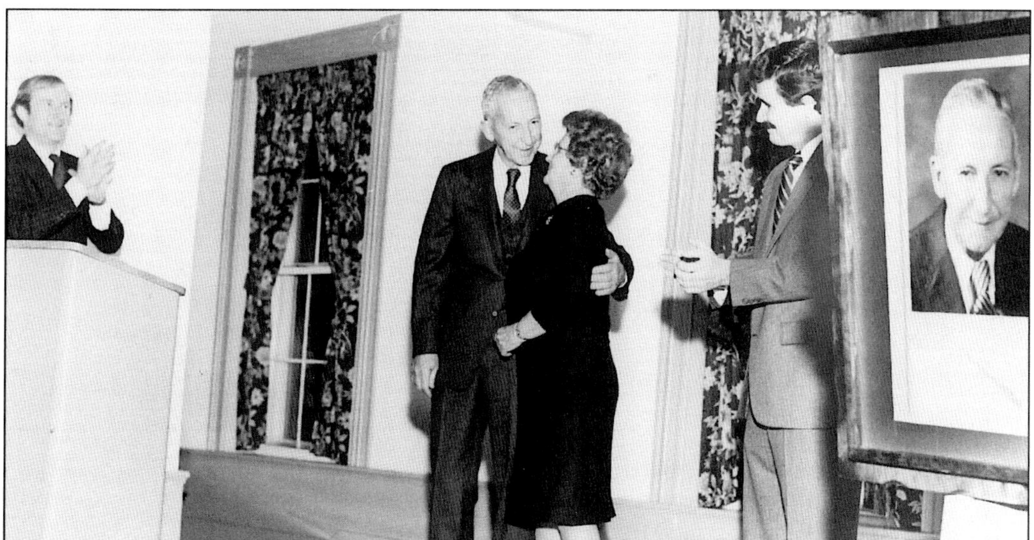

The original structure of the Barre Town Hall was completed in 1839. The second floor of the building was used as a normal school and later as a high school. Many organizations have used this building throughout the years. The Barre Players produced many wonderful plays here. In 1981, fire destroyed a large portion of this building. The Barre Town Hall was restored to its original beauty and was rededicated on October 23, 1982. Seen here, from left to right, are Stephen Brewer, J. Howard Thompson, Mary Thompson, and their son, John D. Thompson. The rededication ceremony was dedicated to Howard Thompson.

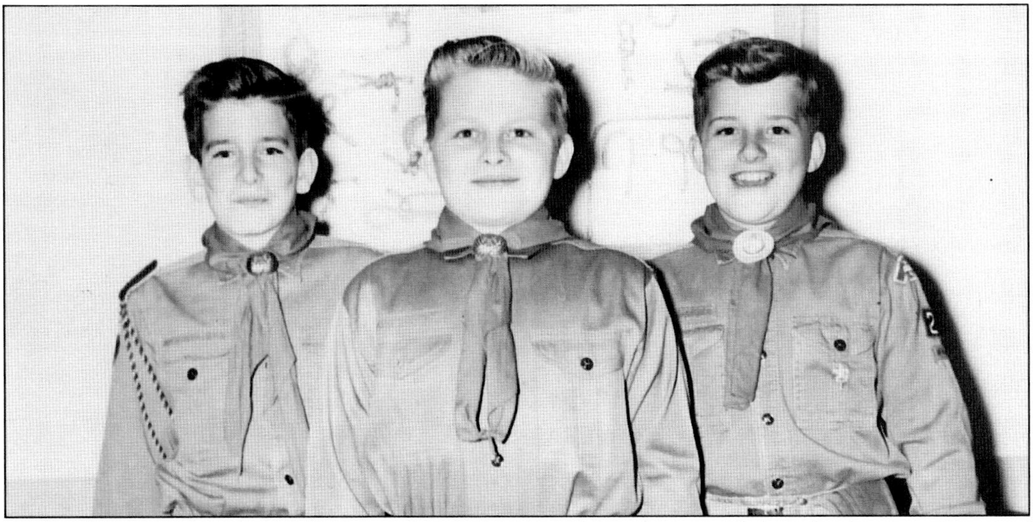

Boy Scouts have been an integral part of life for Barre boys for several decades. Barre's Troop 26 has fostered the goals of scouting by imparting values that help build character and encourage citizenship. The spirit of scouting is captured in these young men at the February 1960 God and Country observance. Seen here, from left to right, are Glenn Allen, Walter Madsen, and J. Lawrence Higgins.

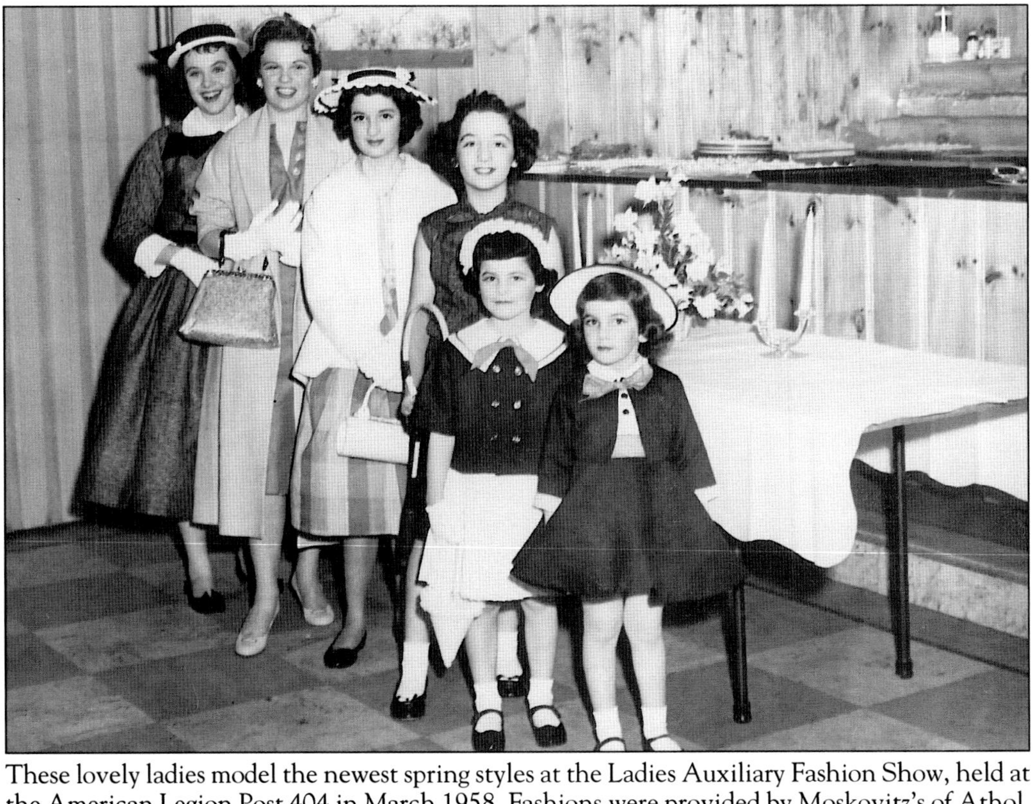

These lovely ladies model the newest spring styles at the Ladies Auxiliary Fashion Show, held at the American Legion Post 404 in March 1958. Fashions were provided by Moskovitz's of Athol, Massachusetts. Seen here, from left to right, are Ginger Klein, Mary Messier, Sharon Brown, Madeline Duval, Kathy Mallozzi, and Debbie Trifilo.

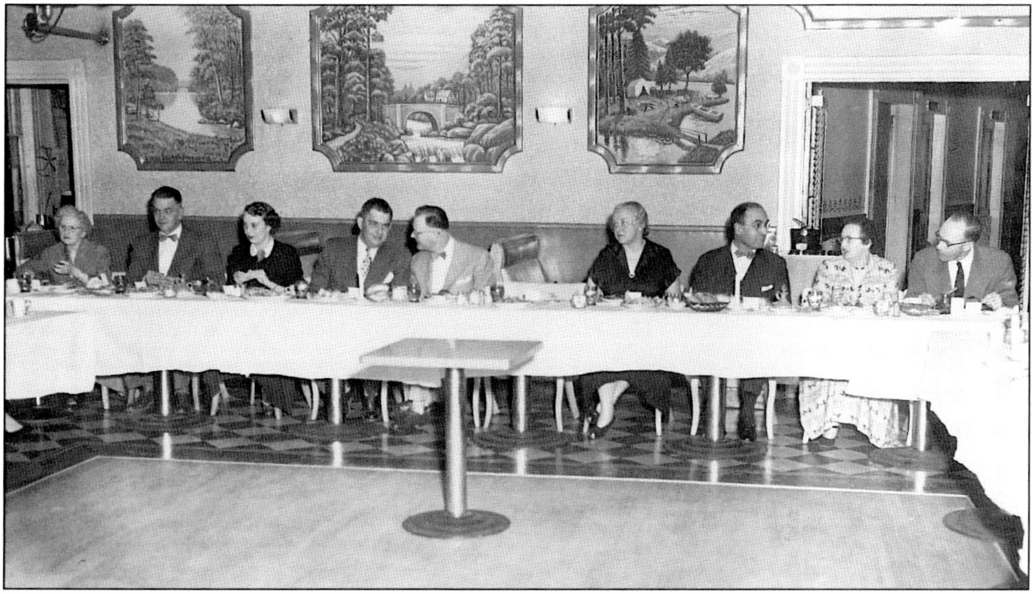

The Barre Wool Combing Co. Ltd. held a banquet at the Hotel Barre for those who completed a human relations and public speaking program in April 1953. Pictured in front of the hand-painted murals that graced the walls are, from left to right, Mr. and Mrs. George Hellman, Mr. and Mrs. John Wytrwal, Frank Wand (instructor), Mr. and Mrs. Levon Yacubian, and Mr. and Mrs. Clarence Damon.

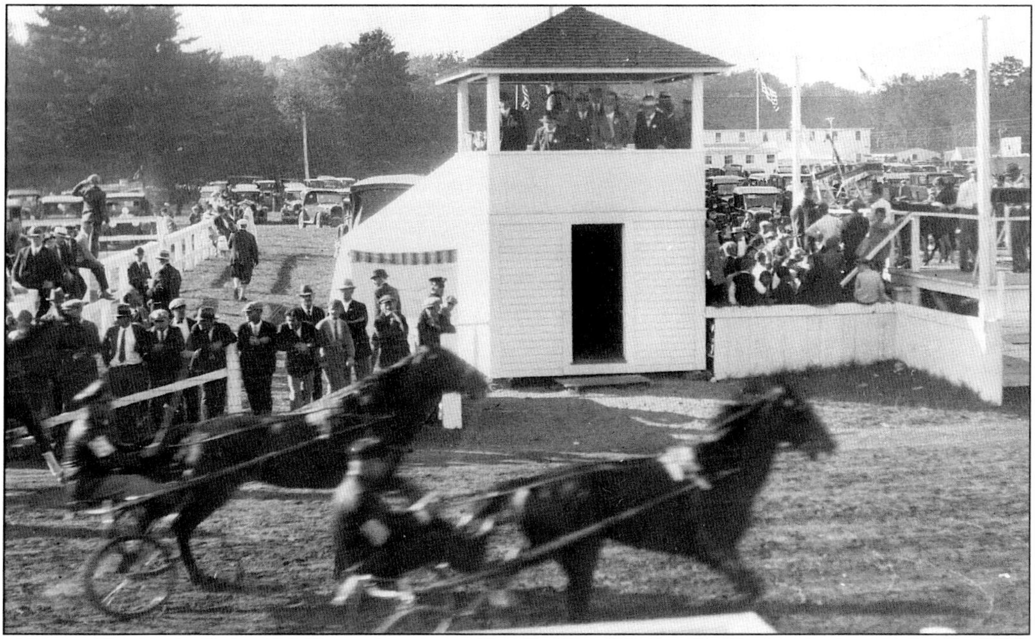

Spectators cheer as sulkies race around the track at the Barre Fairgrounds. Flags fly full in the breezes overhead as the judges intently watch for the winner. Since 1865, this parcel of land, known as Felton Field, has been used as a fairground for agricultural fairs and later for recreational and athletic events. The early fairs were sponsored by the Worcester West Agricultural Society and for many years were the biggest annual event in the area.

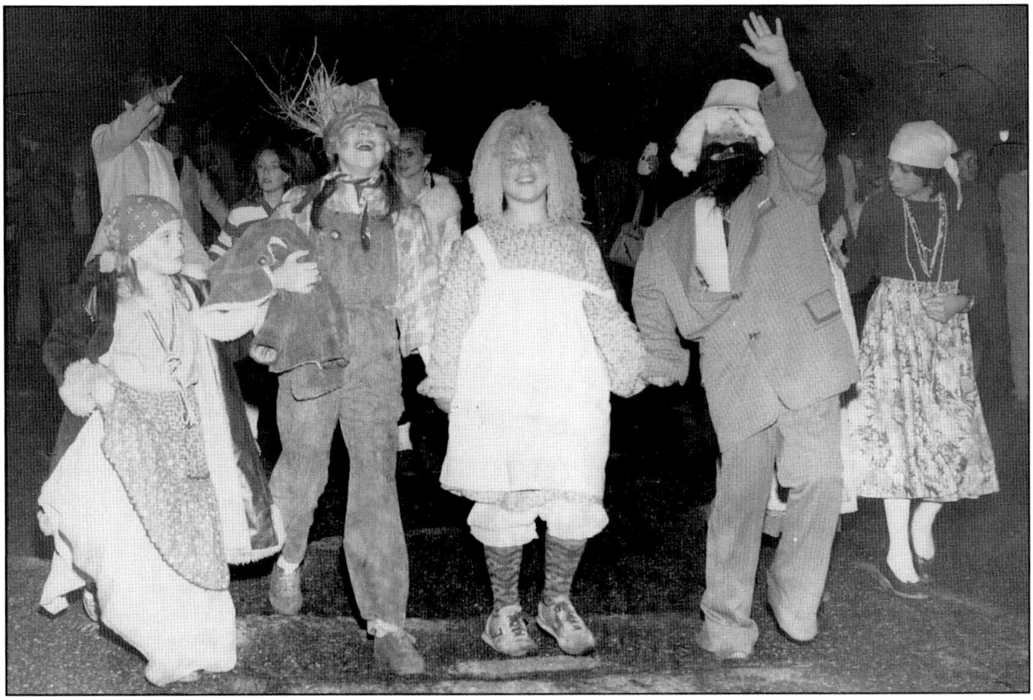

These unidentified youngsters are caught up in the excitement that fills the air on the spookiest night of the year! They are among many children who joined in the Halloween parade on Vernon Avenue in South Barre, 1992. The parades are a long-standing tradition within the community.

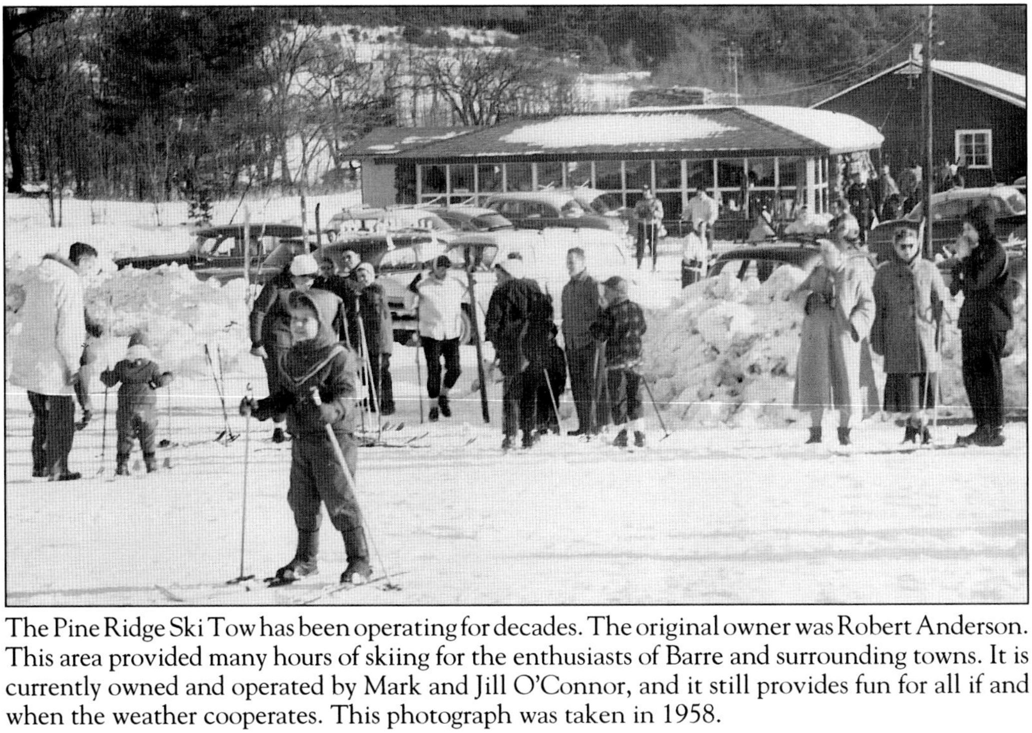

The Pine Ridge Ski Tow has been operating for decades. The original owner was Robert Anderson. This area provided many hours of skiing for the enthusiasts of Barre and surrounding towns. It is currently owned and operated by Mark and Jill O'Connor, and it still provides fun for all if and when the weather cooperates. This photograph was taken in 1958.

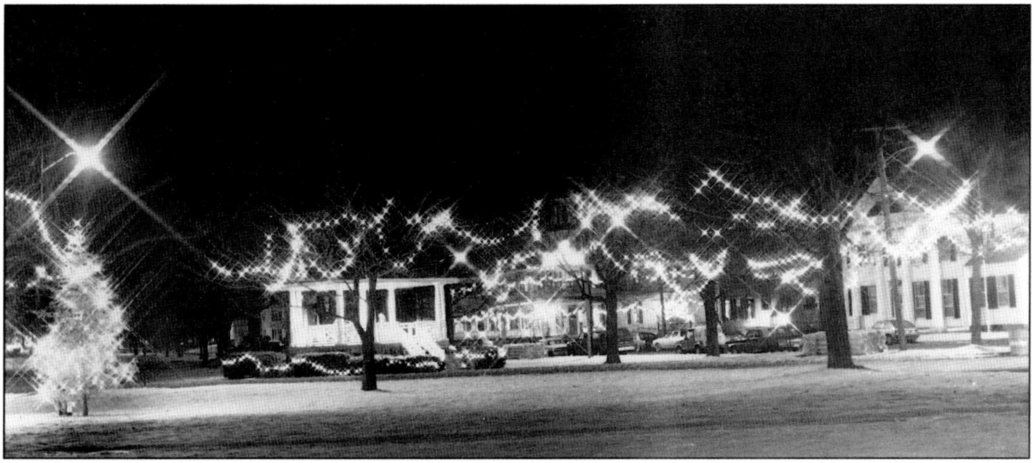

For many years Barre Common has been aglow with hundreds of tiny lights at Christmas time. Since this photograph was taken in December 1987, there have been many new decorative additions. Little Christmas trees in wooden tubs, which are lit, a decorated tree on the bandstand, a nativity scene, and wire-framed deer with lights all enhance the beauty of Christmas in Barre.

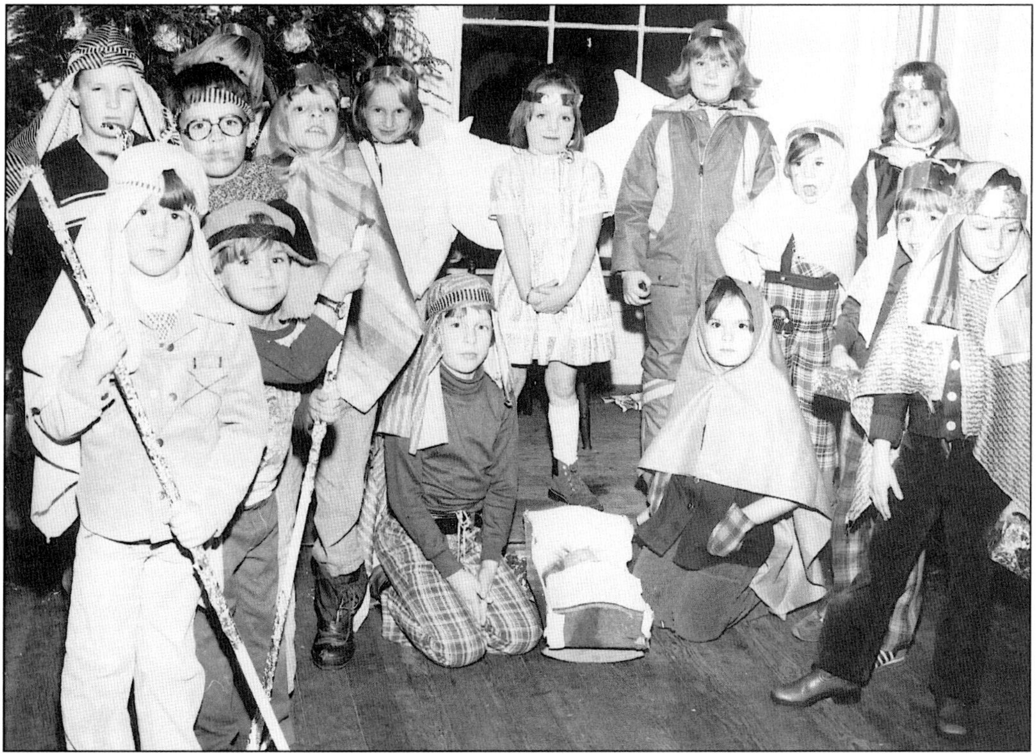

A living nativity was part of the Christmas celebration in 1977 at the one-room No. 4 Community School located on Farrington Road. Seen here, from left to right, are as follows: (front row) Jeremy Kelley, Chad Cummings, David Rogers, Allison Dea, Christopher Barnicle, and Christopher Harty; (back row) Arthur LeBlanc, John LeBlanc, Christina Dea,Joseph Rogers, Diana Rogers, Johanna Jenneson, Doreen LeBlanc, Brandi Pimental, and Darlene LeBlanc.

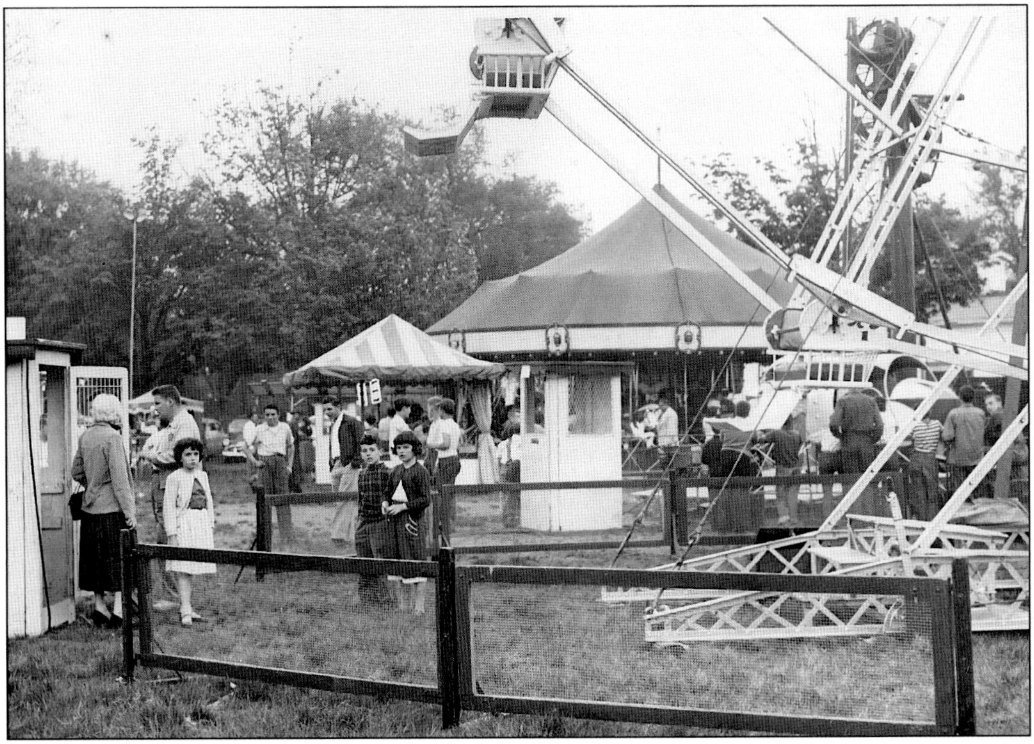

The Kiwanis Club sponsored an annual carnival that was held in the field adjacent to the Barre Plains Fire Station. This organization, made up of local businessmen, held fund-raisers to support their civic projects, such as summer swimming programs. This 1955 view captures youngsters ready to board the Ferris wheel.

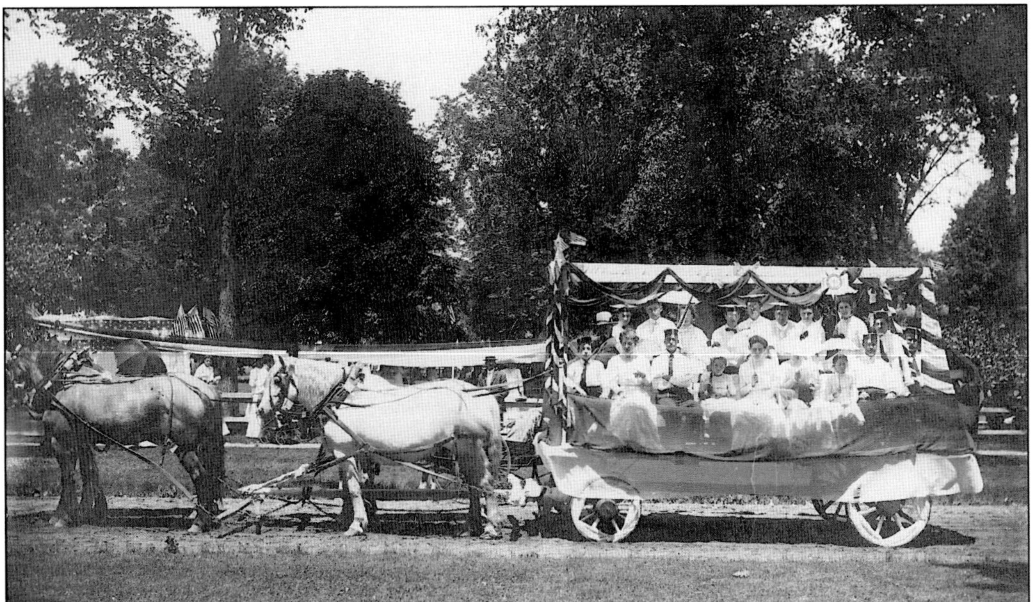

This is the Epworth League Float in the July 4, 1910 celebration on Barre Common. The Epworth League was a women's group of the Methodist Church.

Nine

TRANSPORTATION

Transportation in Barre started as, and has returned to, a "do-it-yourself" operation. During the first half of the 19th century, Barre was the hub of several bustling stagecoach routes. The Barre Stage, originally owned by entrepreneur Ginery Twitchell, ran from Worcester through Barre to Athol, and is presently on display during shop hours at Village Green Antiques on West Street. While the stage is drab and in need of professional restoration, experts say it is one of fewer than five such elegant Concord coaches still in original condition. The layers of darkened varnish probably cover high-quality oil painting with gilt backgrounds on the door and wall panels.

Twitchell went on to become president of several key railroads and a member of Congress. The long-haul stage lines were replaced by 1880 with railroad service to Barre Plains, South Barre, and Coldbrook on two competing railroads. Stagecoaches continued to bring passengers from there as well as from Hubbardston Station up to Barre Center. In this century, the Prescott and Roberts bus lines each provided service to Worcester up until the 1970s. Since then, Barre citizens have once again been "on their own."

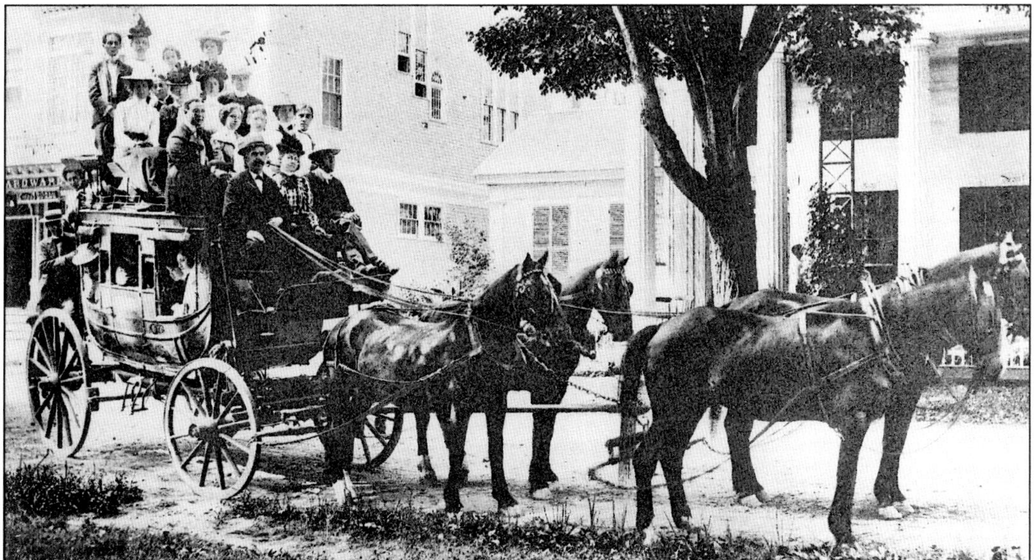

In this 1900s postcard scene, the Barre stagecoach sits on Common Street in front of the Williams Block and the Barre Historical Society building (at right).

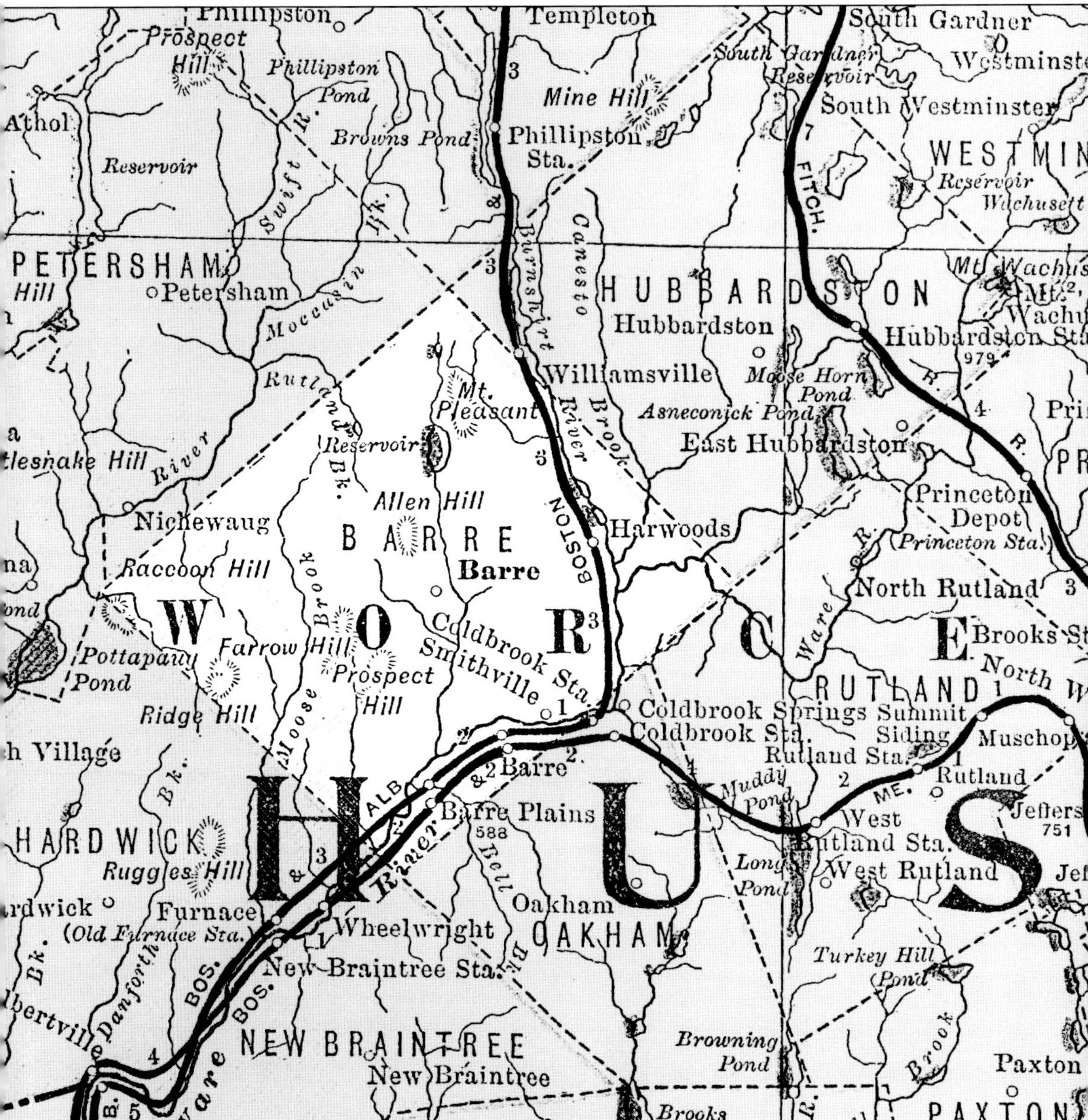

This section of the National Publishing Company's Boston Railroad Map, *c.* 1902, shows the three railroads that served Barre: the former Massachusetts Central Railroad, now the Central Massachusetts Branch of the Boston & Maine (B&M); the Boston & Albany (B&A); and the Fitchburg Railroad. The B&M came north from Ware, crossed over the B&A at Hardwick, ran through Barre parallel to the B&A up to Coldbrook, then climbed to Rutland. The B&A tracks (which were taken over in 1980 by the new Massachusetts Central Railroad Corp.) followed a parallel route to Coldbrook, then turned north toward Templeton and Winchendon. The Fitchburg Railroad (originally the Boston, Barre & Gardner RR, and presently the Providence & Worcester) ran from Gardner through Hubbardston Station and on to Jefferson, where there was a junction with the B&M. Despite promises to the contrary, no railroad was ever built uphill to Barre Center.

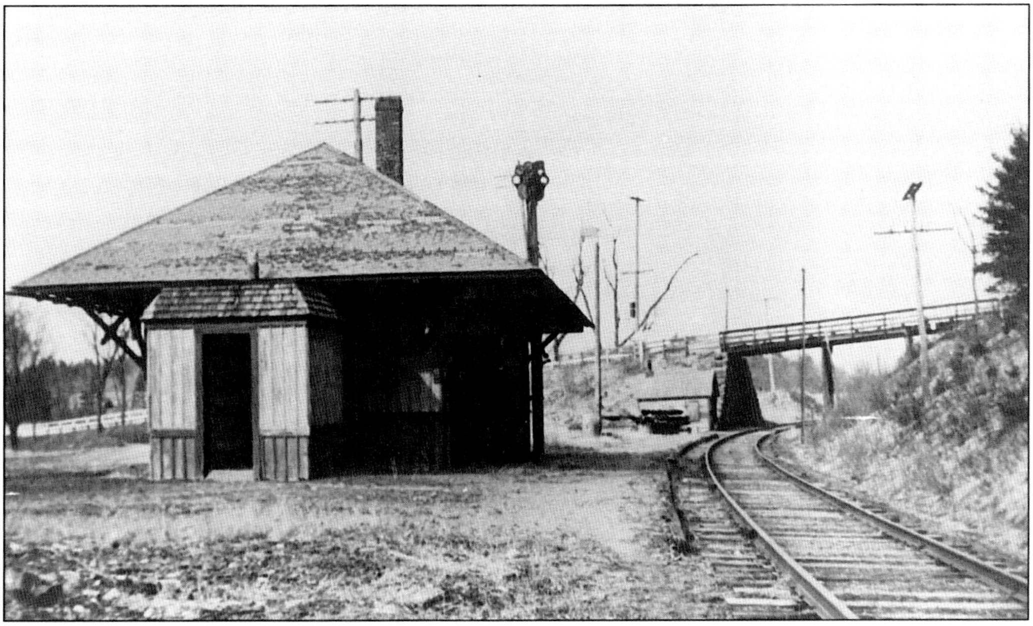

The Barre Plains station on the Massachusetts Central looks east under the present Route 67. The left-hand stone abutment is still visible on the east side of Route 67, north of Oakham Road.

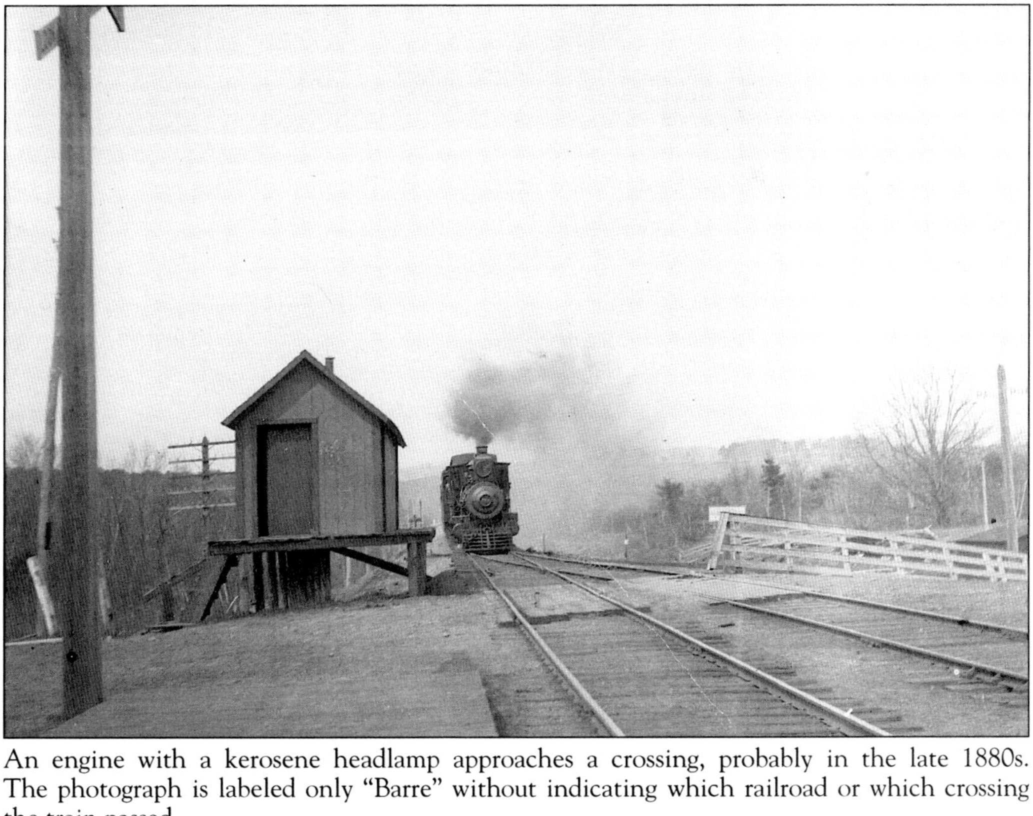

An engine with a kerosene headlamp approaches a crossing, probably in the late 1880s. The photograph is labeled only "Barre" without indicating which railroad or which crossing the train passed.

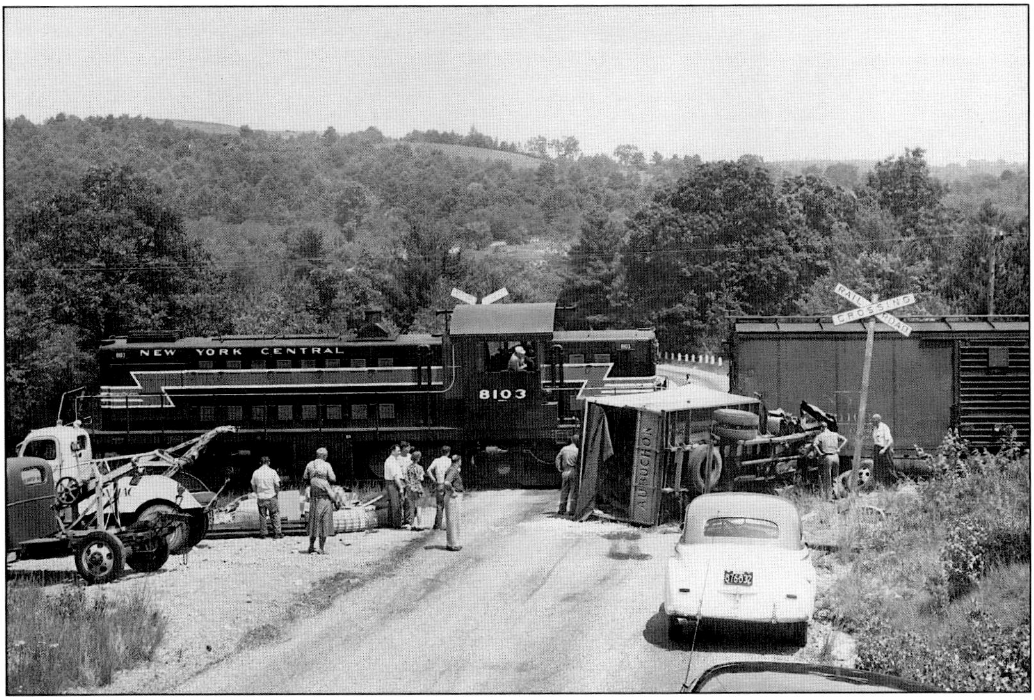

This accident was at Harwood's Crossing (Hubbardston Road—Route 62—at Granger Road) in the 1950s. Note the still-open fields at the top center at the former Jacob Riis farm.

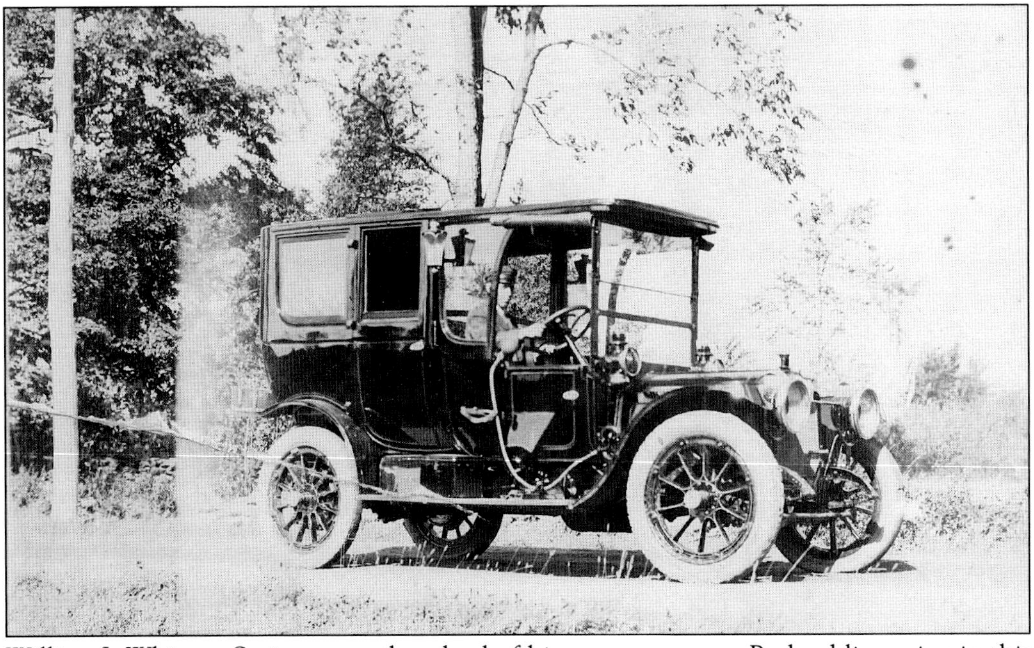

William J. Whippee Sr. is seen at the wheel of his seven-passenger Packard limousine in this c. 1915 photograph. The car allowed Whippee to conduct a jitney service between hotels in Barre and the railroad station in Williamsville, the first time such service was undertaken by an automobile. Whippee, a native of Lincoln, Massachusetts, moved to Barre and married Grace Lovering Sheldon in 1914.

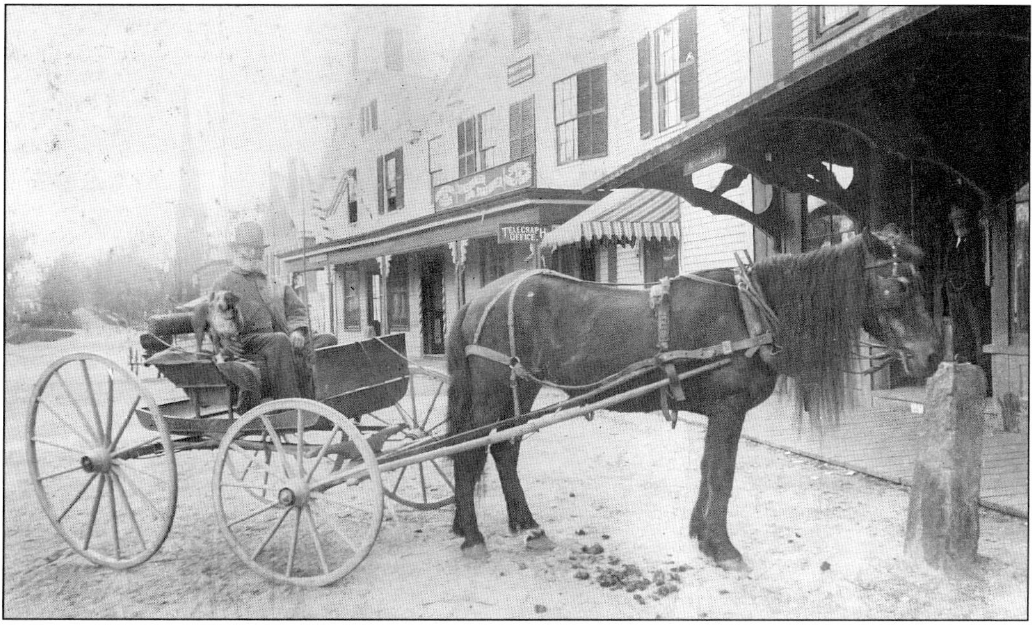

A horse, driver, and dog wait patiently on Exchange Street. Note the Light House Block in the background with two connected peaked roofs and the angled addition to their right.

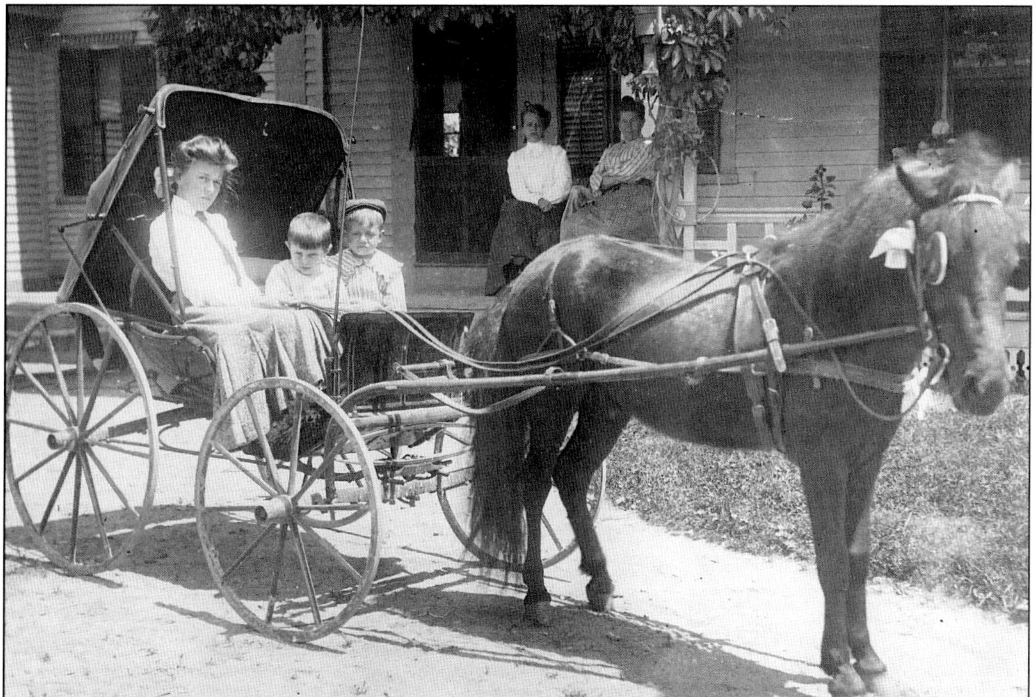

This young lady, ready to take two youngsters for a buggy ride, was likely receiving maternal advice from the porch.

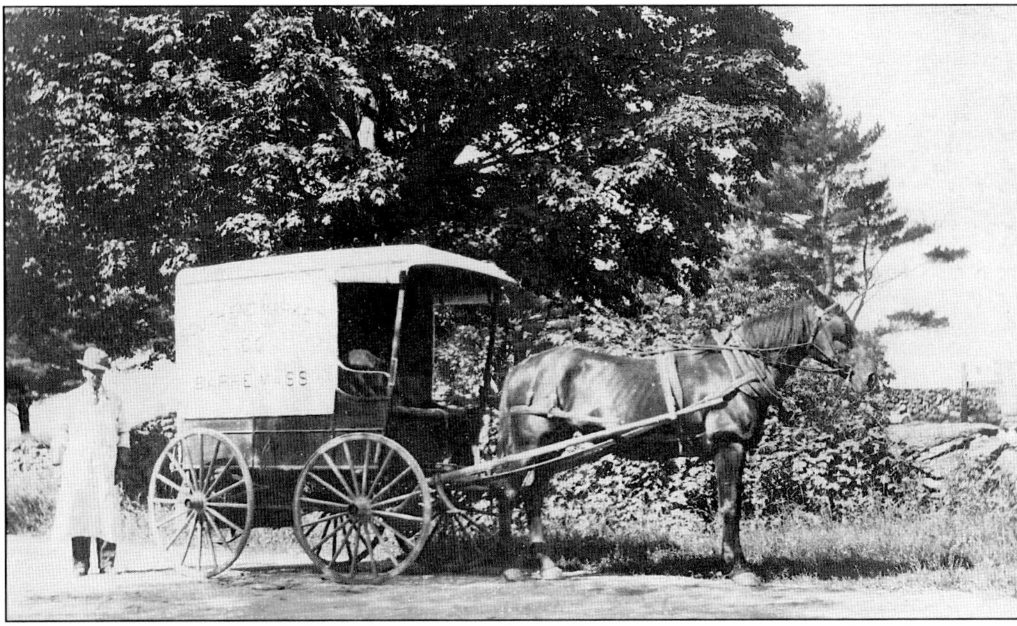

The South End Market delivery wagon is shown here in Barre.

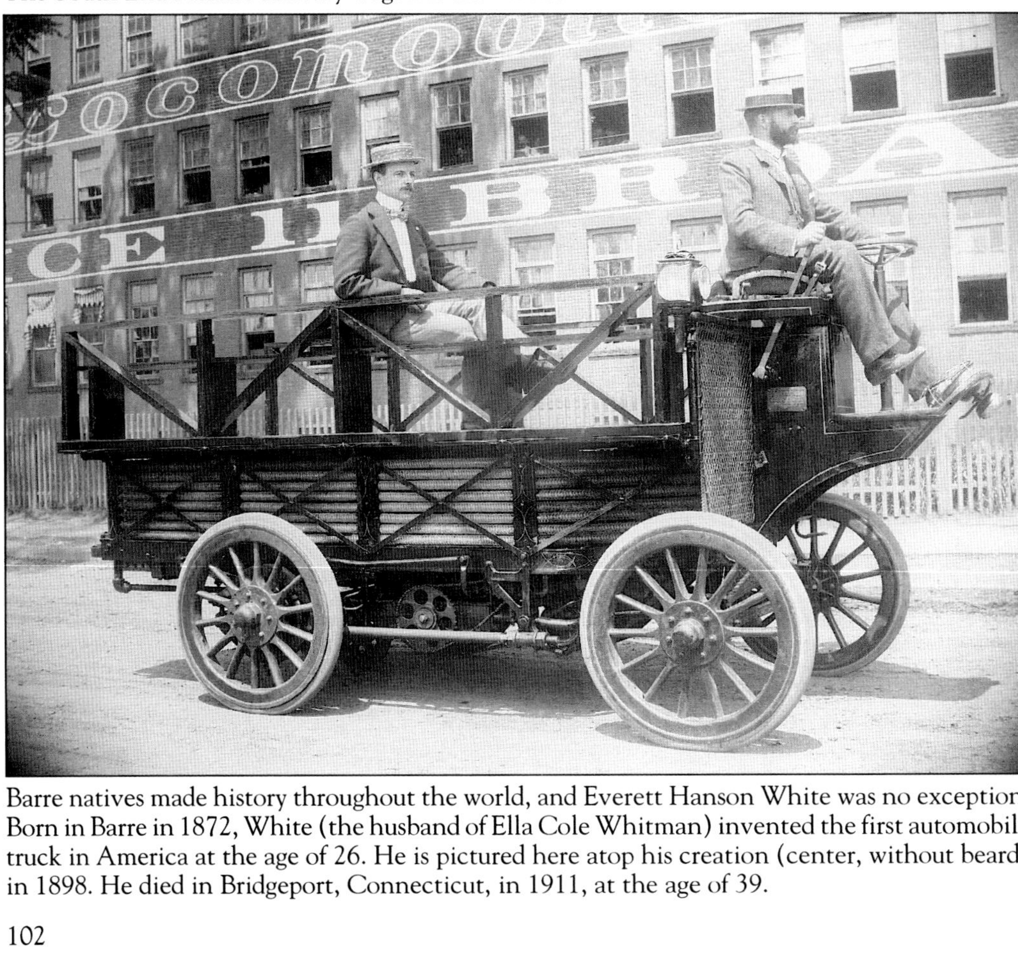

Barre natives made history throughout the world, and Everett Hanson White was no exception. Born in Barre in 1872, White (the husband of Ella Cole Whitman) invented the first automobile truck in America at the age of 26. He is pictured here atop his creation (center, without beard) in 1898. He died in Bridgeport, Connecticut, in 1911, at the age of 39.

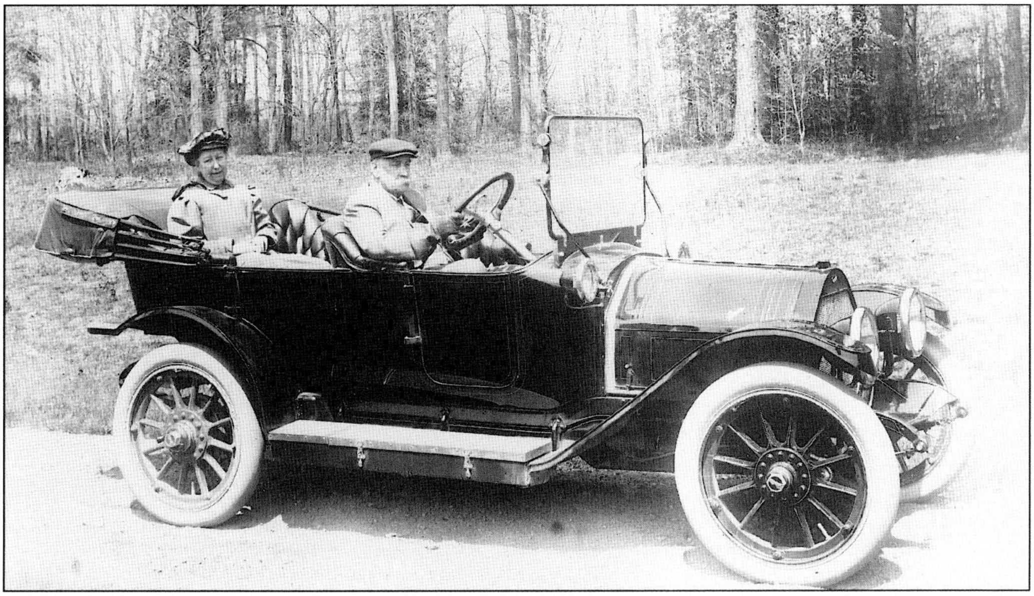

Out for a Sunday drive in their new Chandler touring car, Barre Postmaster Ben Brooks and his wife are suitably attired for motoring in the country. The fact that this automobile has right-hand drive indicates the picture was taken prior to 1914, when steering wheels in America began to be positioned on the left.

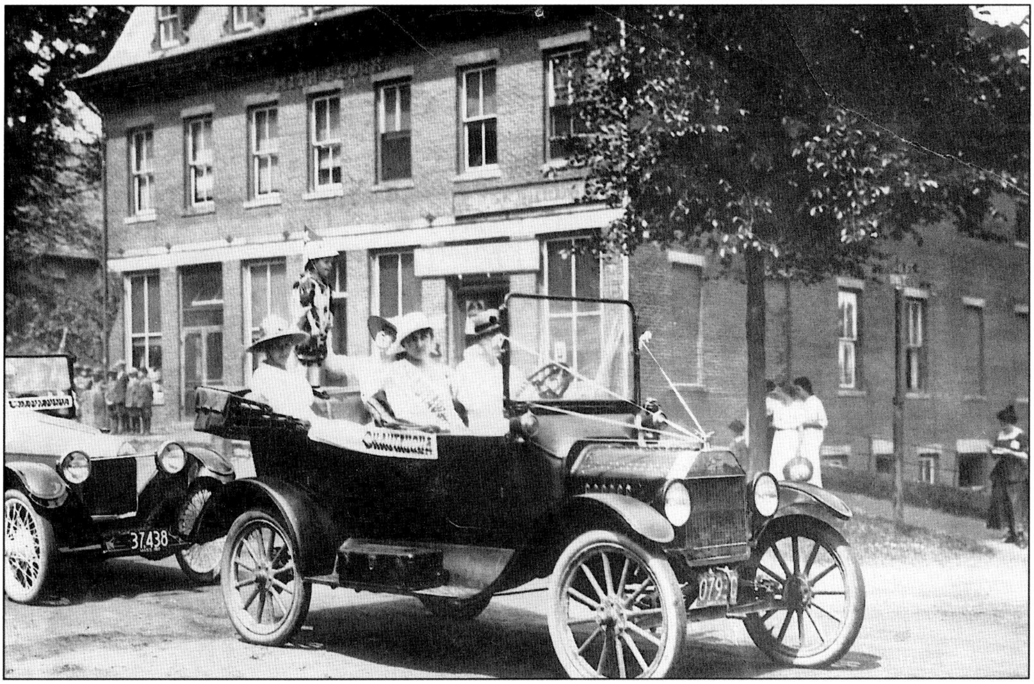

In Chautauqua, New York, a school was established in 1874 to promote the sciences and humanities. Wildly popular, this led to the creation of adult education in America. As its fame spread, "chautauquas" became a summer staple, traveling from town to town presenting concerts and lectures, often in circus tents. Shown above is a "chautauqua parade" at the intersection of Broad and School Streets in 1917.

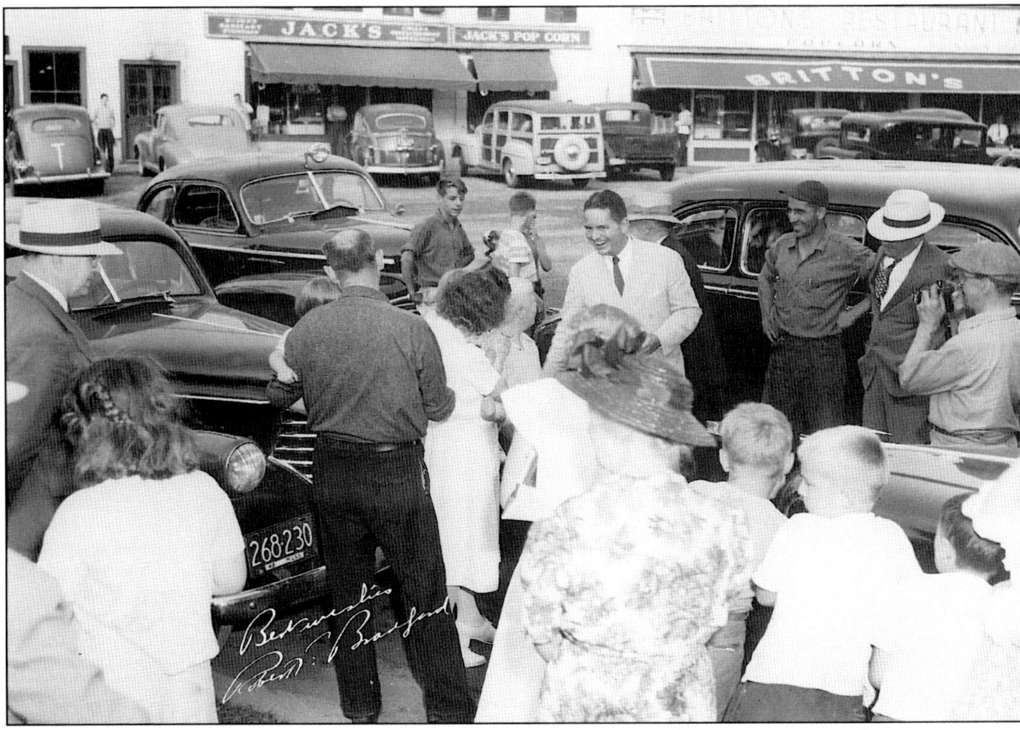

Massachusetts Governor Robert Bradford (in light suit) stopped in Barre to greet his constituents in 1948. Those in this crowd on Barre Common included Merton Baker (far left), Tillman Taylor (dark shirt, back to camera), Blanche Paull (in hat), Edgar Dahart (in cap, hands on hips), and Bill Tuttle (in T-shirt). Note the cars—how many can you identify?

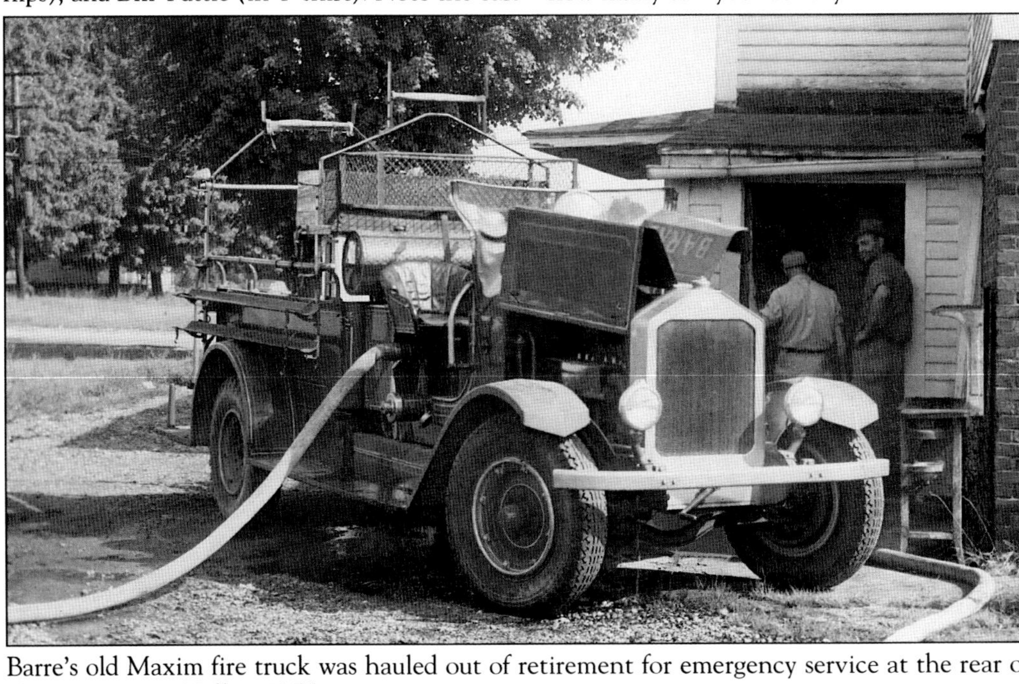

Barre's old Maxim fire truck was hauled out of retirement for emergency service at the rear of the Barre Town Hall in 1955.

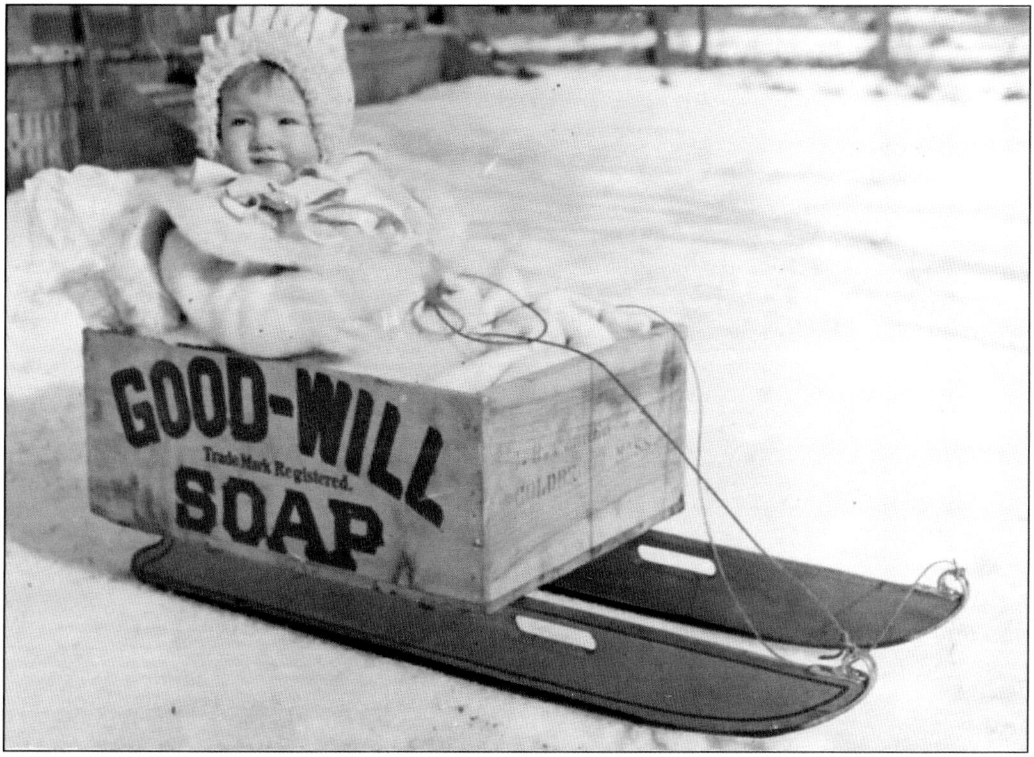

This *c*. 1898 soapbox sled is addressed to Coldbrook, Massachusetts. Not all transportation was store-bought!

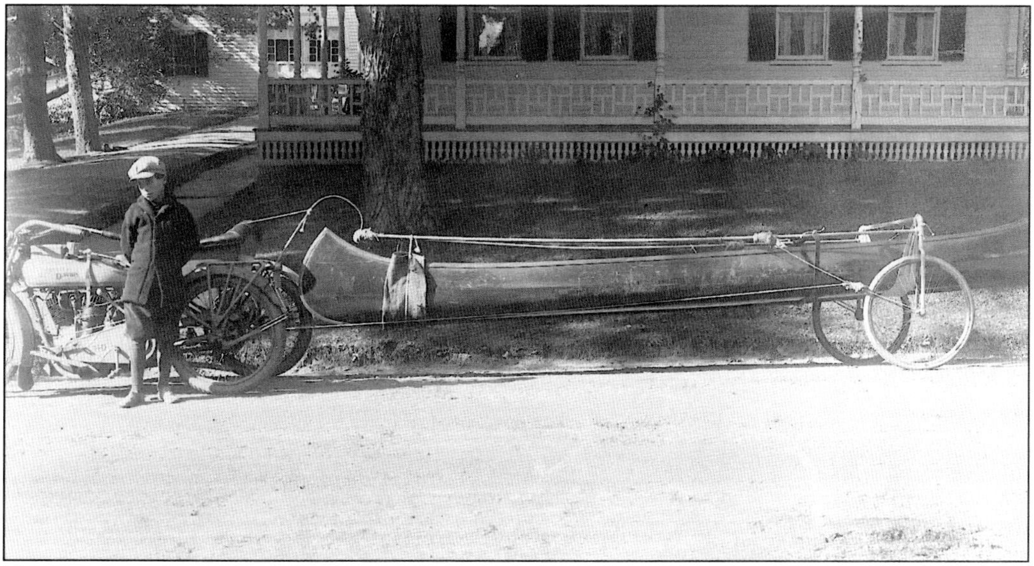
This is a Harley-Davidson motorcycle with multi-use trailer, shown pre-1916.

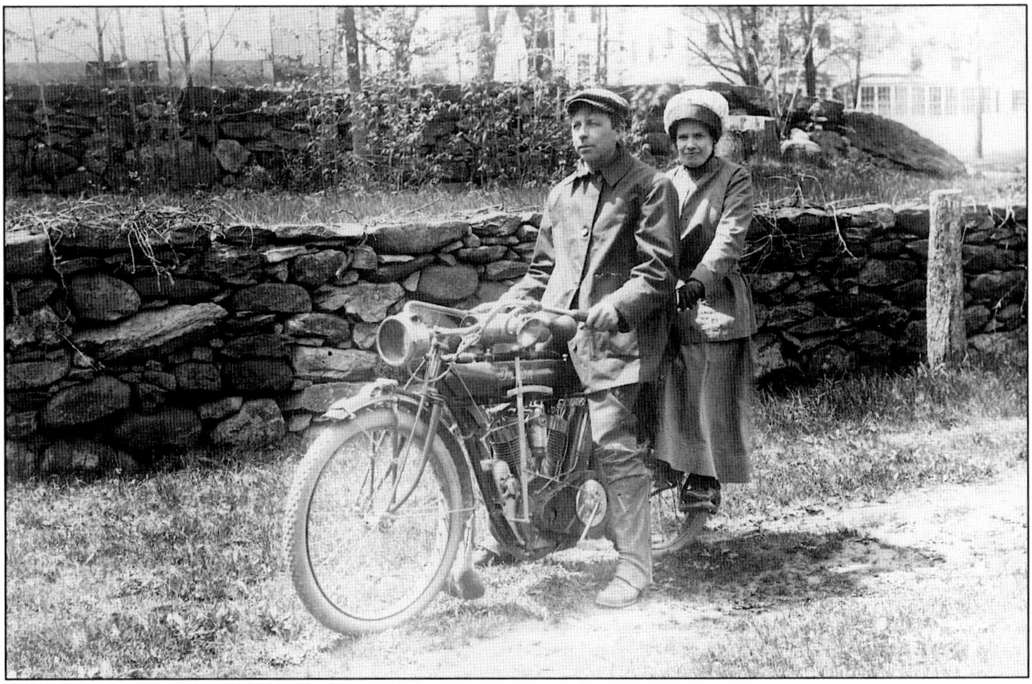

Here is Edgar Glidden and an unknown passenger. The motorcycle appears to be a 1910–1914 Indian, made in Springfield, Massachusetts. The photograph dates from that time.

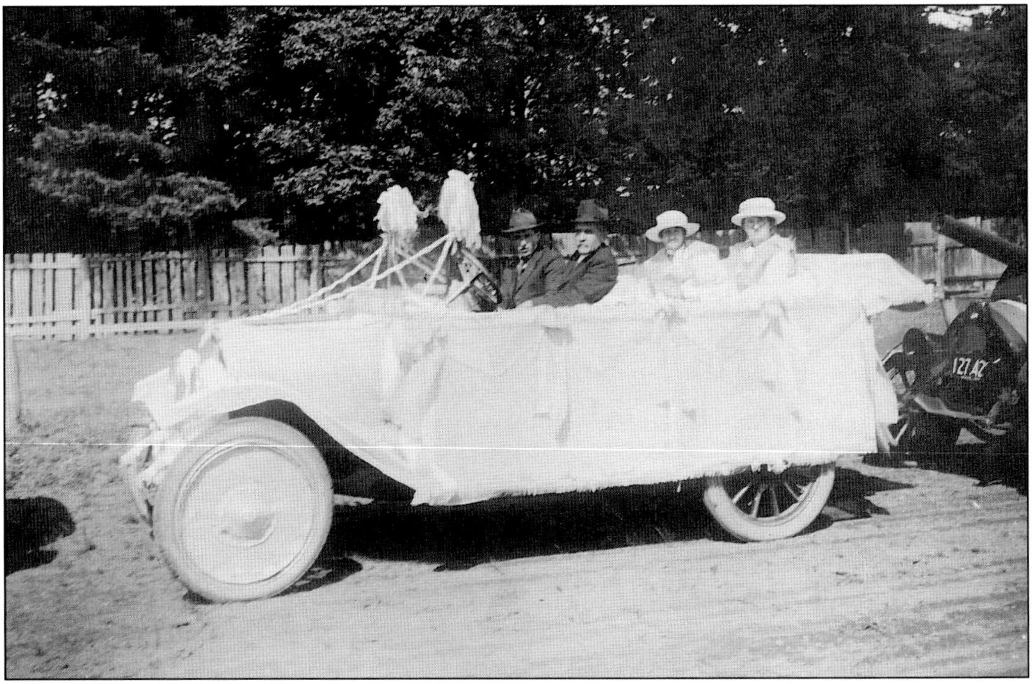

When World War I was over, Barre celebrated. This bedecked car is from the Welcome Home Day parade in 1919. Shown here, from left to right, are Lewis E. Paquin Sr., George W. Paquin, Lila (Paquin) Smith, Ruth (Smith) Clark (infant), and Lillian E. (Stowell) Paquin.

Ten

SCRAPBOOK

The configuration of Barre Center has always been an evolving process and that is true even to this day. It seems that each generation has its own idea about how shops and streets can harmoniously coexist in the middle of town, while simultaneously preserving Barre's unique character.

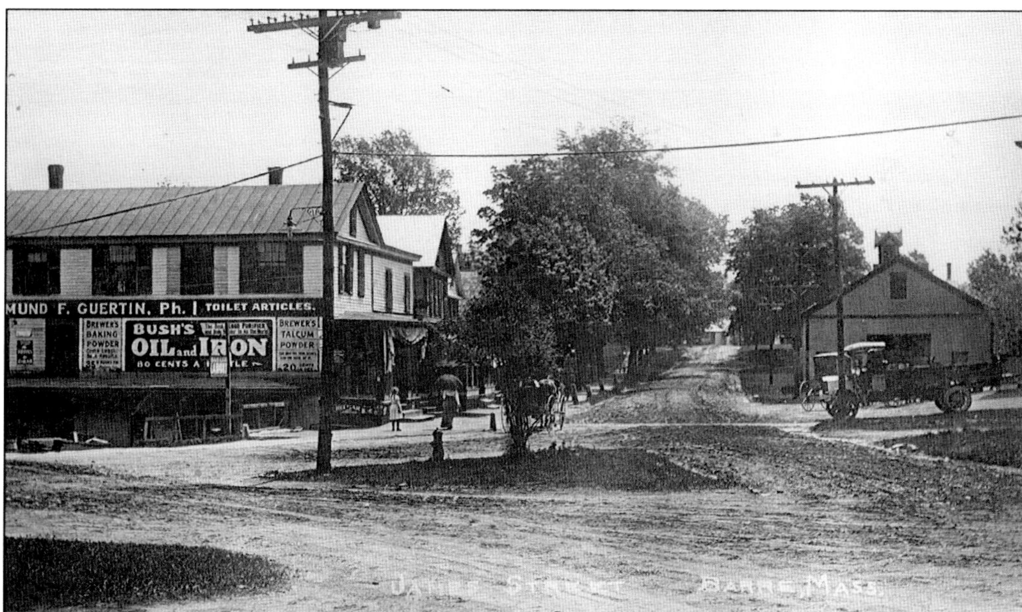

This photograph was taken c. 1912, and shows the intersection of Summer (left) and James Streets. Guertin's drugstore stands on the left, on the site of what is now the Honey Farms store. The barn, pictured on the right and owned by Mary Brimblecom Martin, stood where the parish hall for St. Joseph's Church is today. Note the presence of electric light poles and the "new" delivery truck, which had to share the muddy roadways with carriages and pedestrians.

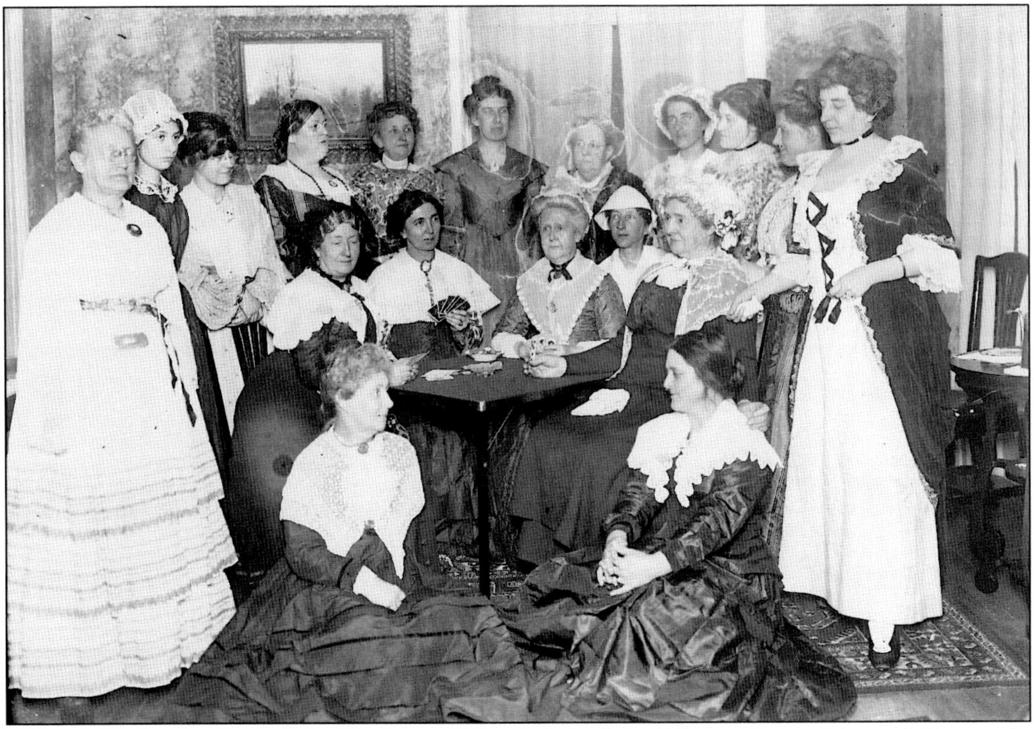

This ladies' costume party took place in 1912. Standing, from left to right, are Marian Whitcomb, Iris Williams, unidentified, Avis Williams, Mrs. Ed. Haven, Blanche Allen Garfield, unidentified, unidentified, Bertha Cox Allen, Bessie Allen, and Carrie Allen. Among those sitting are Etta Smith, Mrs. Bartholomew, and Mrs. Atwood.

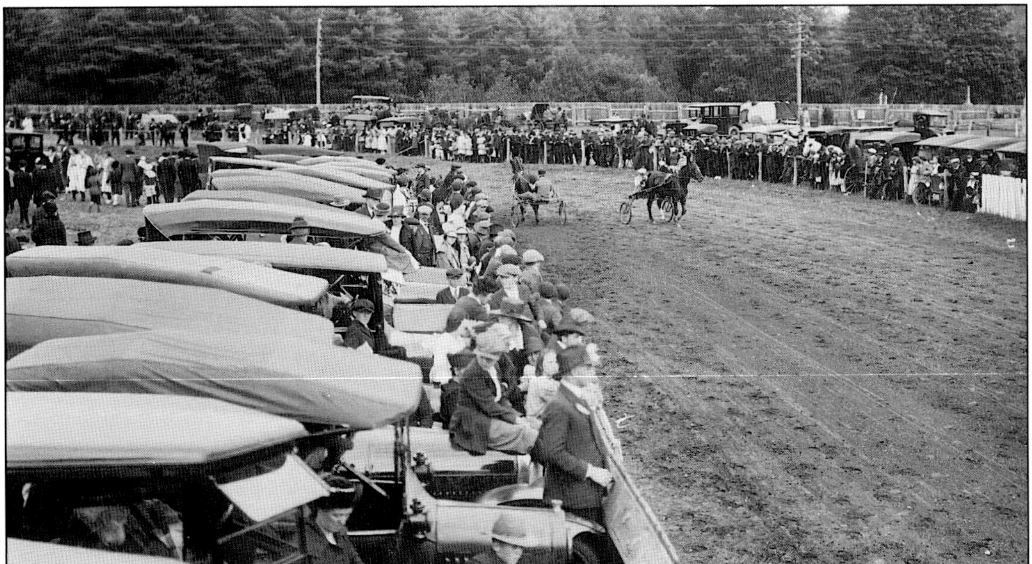

Spectators gather at the fence in front of their canvas-topped automobiles to watch harness racing at the Barre Fair at Felton Field, c. 1912. This event occurred about the time Boston Mayor John F. "Honey Fitz" Fitzgerald came to town and made an appearance at the fair. Fitzgerald was the maternal grandfather of President John Fitzgerald Kennedy.

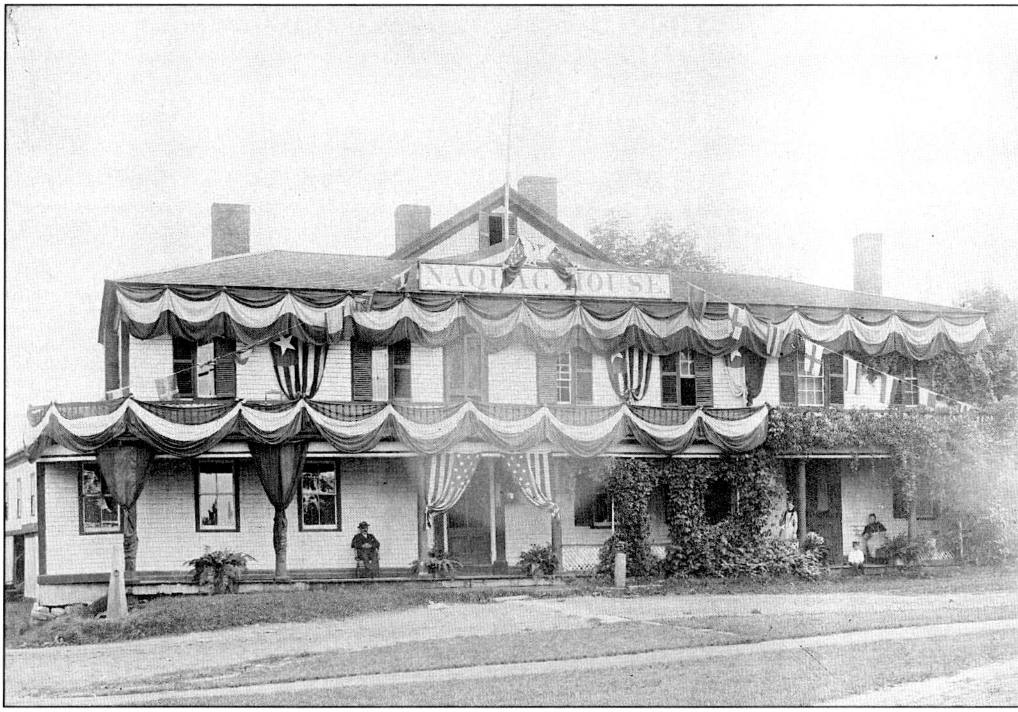

The Naquag House was one of Barre's many hostelries; it was located on the site of the present-day Barre Pizza/Cumberland Farms building. The hotel is shown here as it appeared *c.* 1890, festooned with flags and bunting for the Fourth of July. The building was destroyed by fire shortly thereafter and replaced by the Wheeler Block.

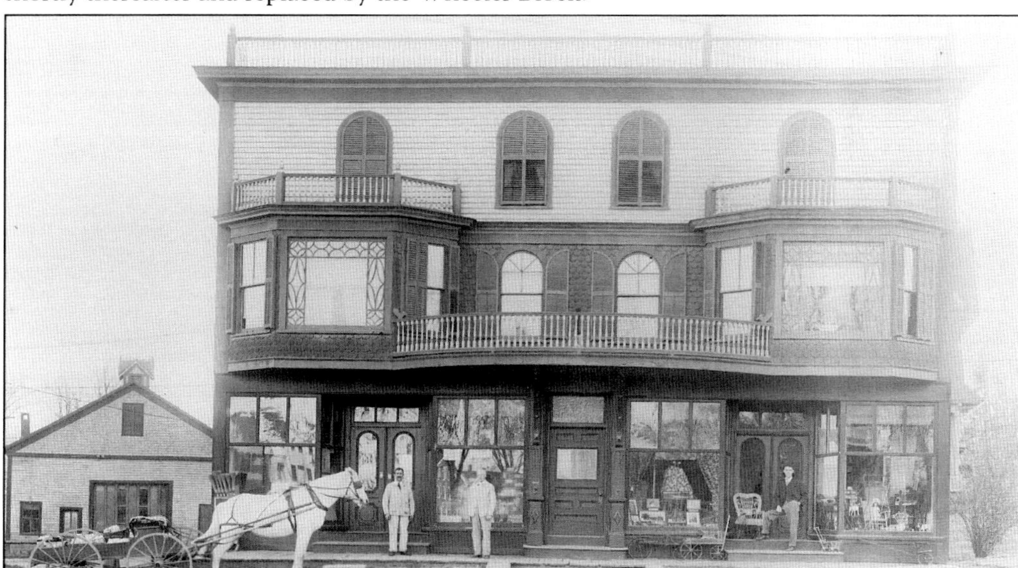

The newly constructed Wheeler Block, *c.* 1900, still stands today on land between James and South Streets on Barre Common. The two men in front of the horse are Michael Higgins (left) and James B. Taylor. The third man, standing in the doorway of the emporium on the right-hand side of the building, is unidentified.

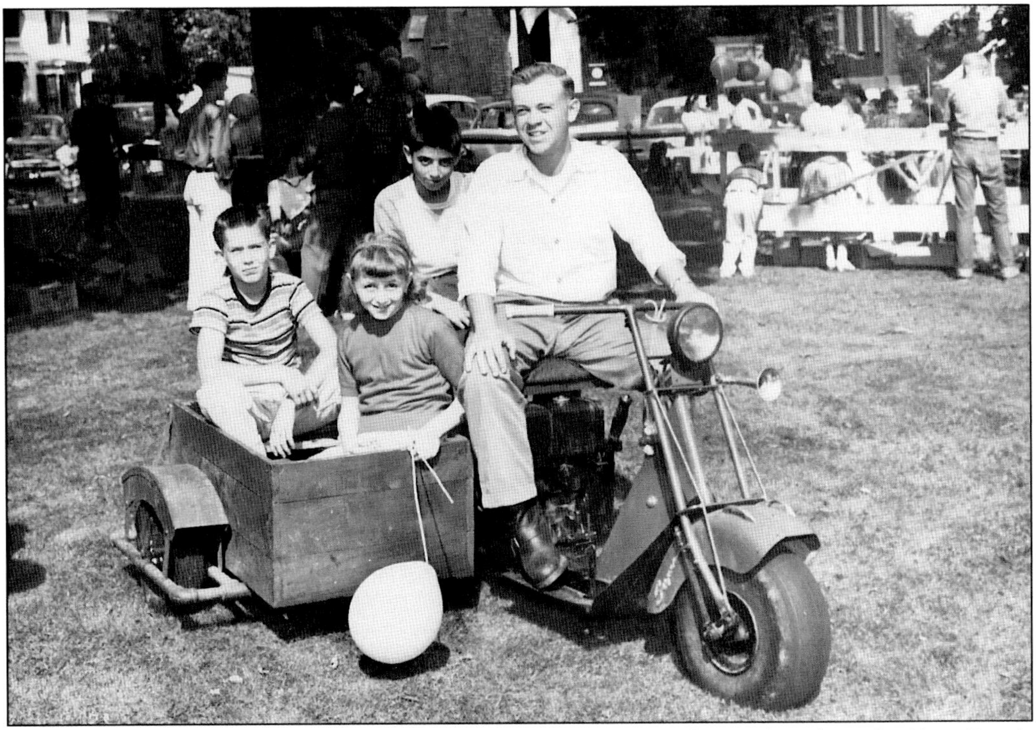

Fun in the late-summer sun was the order of the day in September 1958, when the First Parish Church (Unitarian) held its fair on the northeast corner of Barre Common. Shown riding with motor-scooter driver Richard Stevens are, from left to right, Wayne Smith, Elizabeth Rankovic, and Bobby Puliafico. The "Brown Church," as it was commonly known, stood where the parking lot next to the Mortell home is today.

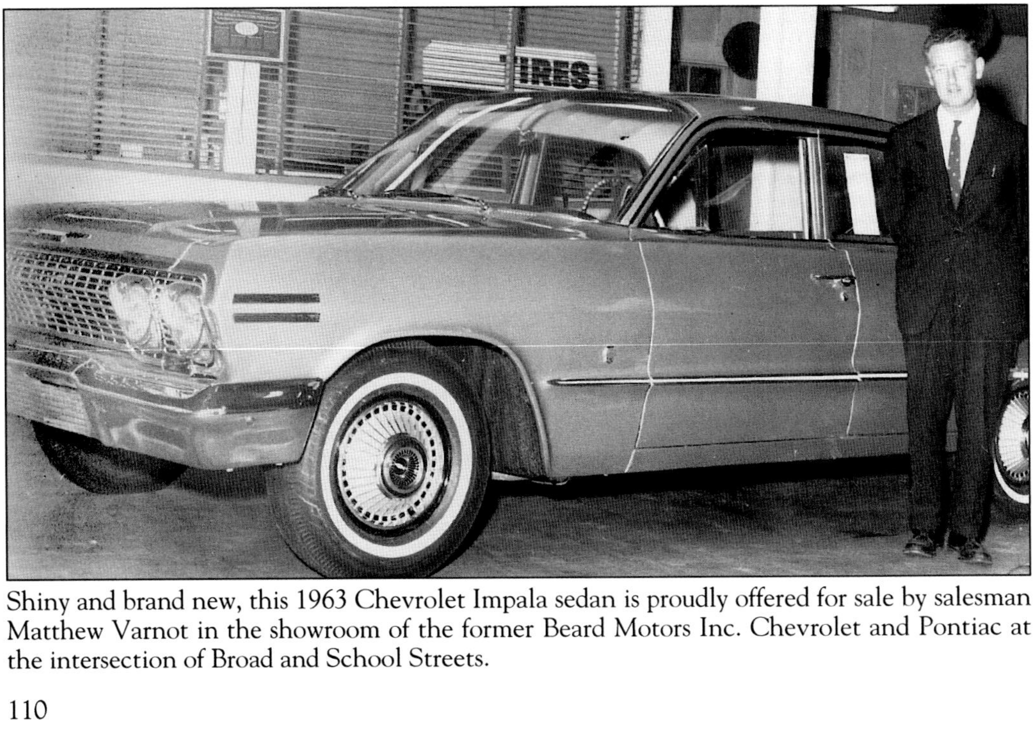

Shiny and brand new, this 1963 Chevrolet Impala sedan is proudly offered for sale by salesman Matthew Varnot in the showroom of the former Beard Motors Inc. Chevrolet and Pontiac at the intersection of Broad and School Streets.

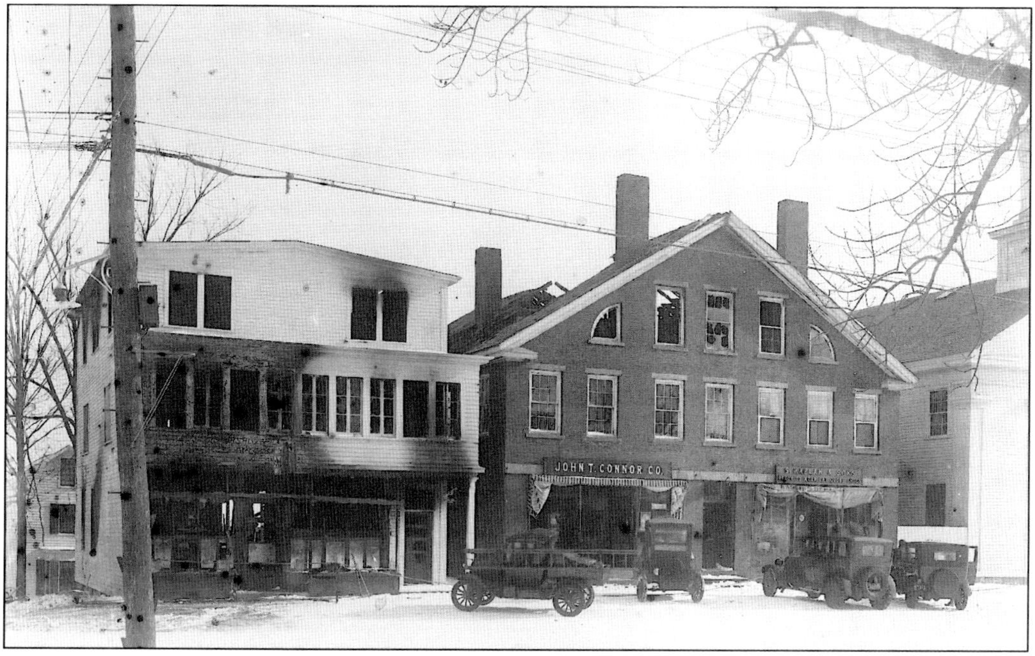

This is the aftermath of the Barre drug store fire in 1927. The building on the left (presently the site of Neylon Real Estate) was owned by Edmund F. Guertin, the town's pharmacist for more than 30 years until his death in 1946. The fire occurred at 4 a.m. on January 14, and was set by a burglar to cover up a break-in. Barre's Town Hall appears at extreme right.

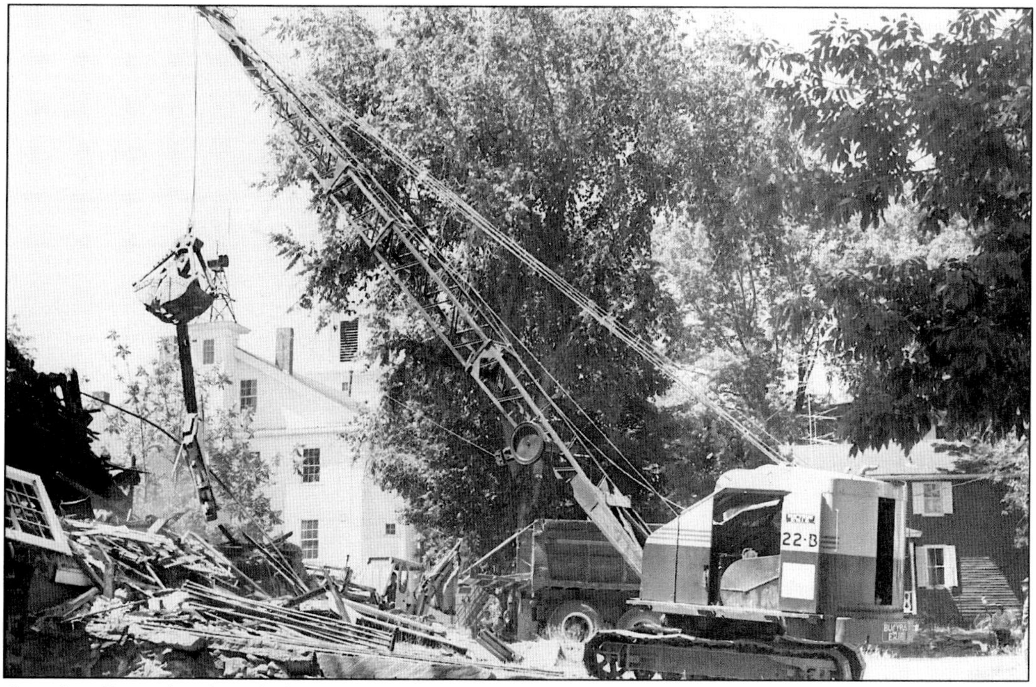

Another Barre landmark disappears forever. This photograph was taken in July 1966 at the site of the Barre Center School, which had been destroyed by fire the previous spring. The school was located on School Street, on the site of what is now Barre's municipal parking lot.

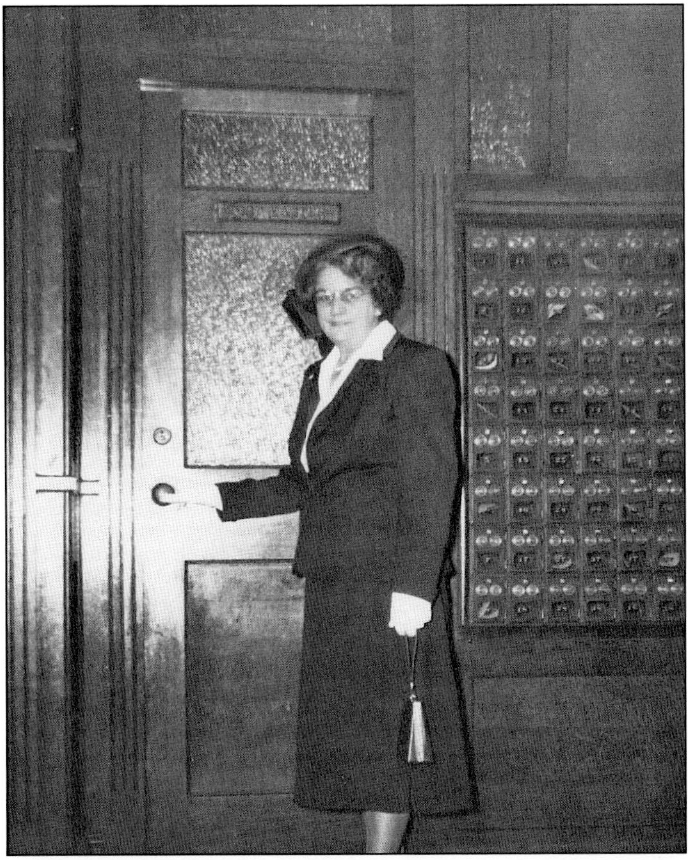

Barre Postmaster Grace S. Whippee stands at the door of the "old" Barre Post Office, located where the *Barre Gazette* currently has its operations in the Light House Block on Barre Common. The picture dates from 1948, when Whippee was appointed by President Harry S. Truman as the town's first female postmaster.

Note the "combination" mailboxes. Can you remember them?

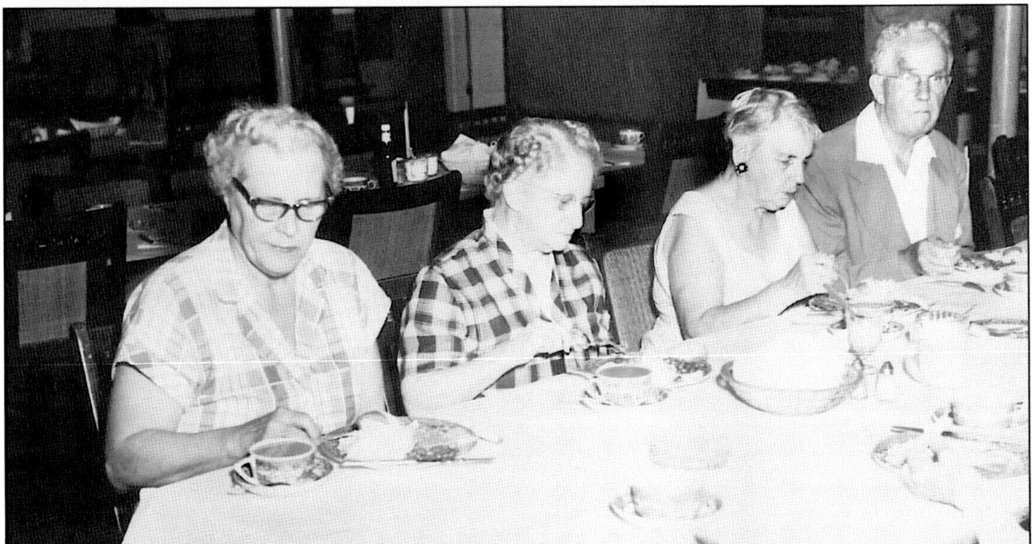

Eating out for a good cause, these dinner guests enjoy the fare during the Lend-a-Hand Plate Supper at the First Parish Church (Unitarian) in Barre on July 31, 1958. Shown here, from left to right, are Marian Johnson, Helen Gilmore, Nellie Clark Murphy, and her husband, James "Big Jim" Murphy.

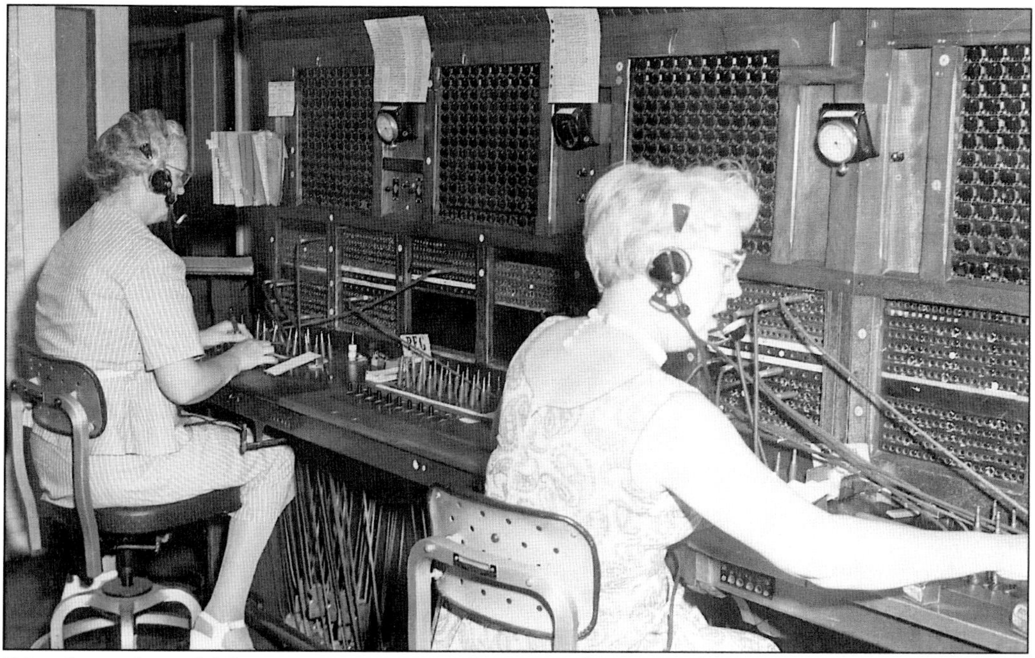

"Number, please." This scene may seem foreign today, now that cellular telephones are in popular use. Not so long ago—in August, 1955, to be exact—this is how telephoning was done in Barre. The switchboard, located in the Merton Baker home on South Street, handled all the calls. The two operators shown here on duty are Bertha Carpenter (left) and Mary Awtry.

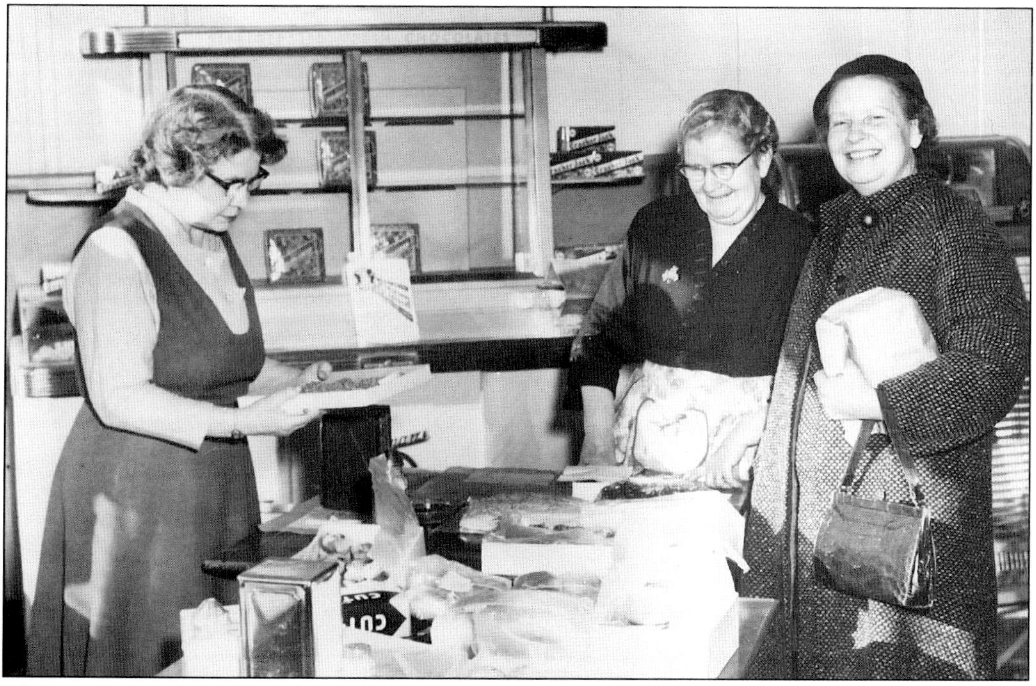

There's nothing quite like homemade baked goods. This Barre Grange food sale was held on February 12, 1959. Delighting in the selection, from left to right, are Clara Jacobson, Mabel Ozenbaugh Smith, and Gladys Armstrong. Note the abundant use of waxed paper!

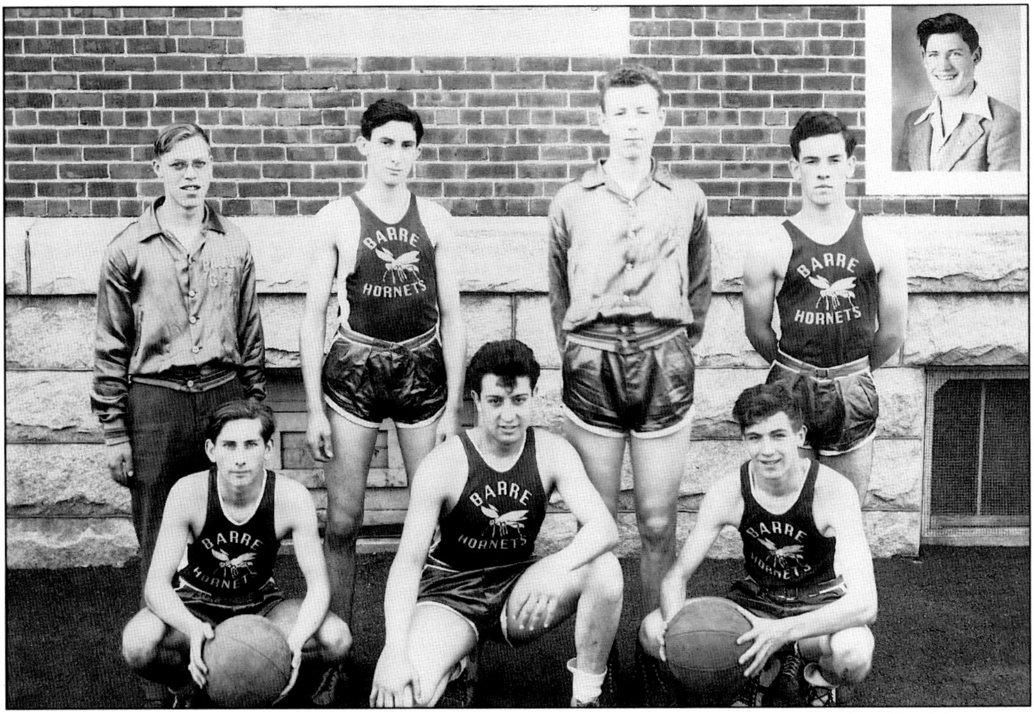

Sports have always been a major part of life in Barre. In particular, our high school athletes are a source of considerable pride. This is a photograph of the Barre High School basketball team, taken on June 18, 1943, at the height of World War II. Shown standing, from left to right, are Alan Ohlson, Joseph Panaccione, Thomas Finan, and Paul Salvadore. The gentlemen in front are unidentified.

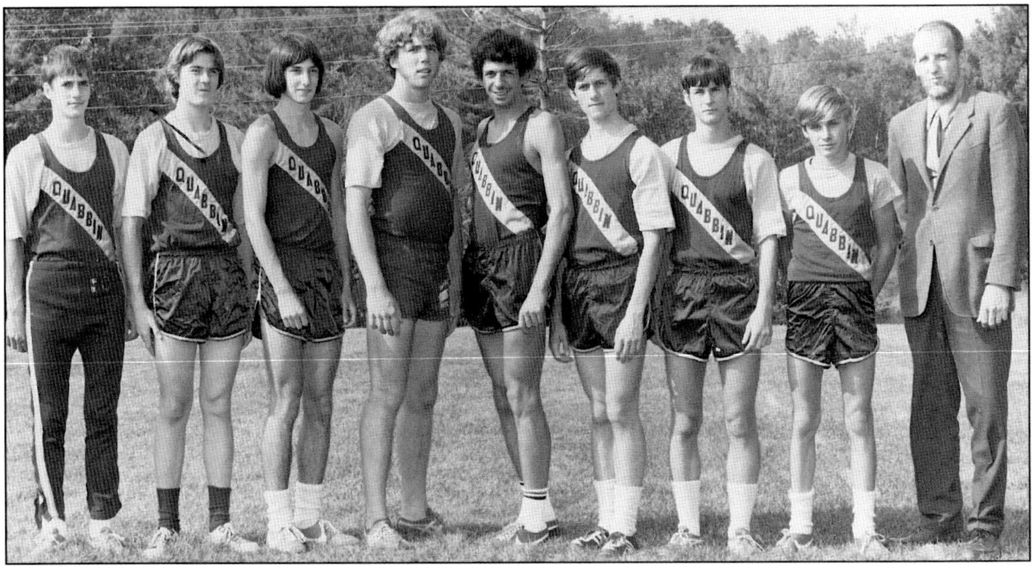

Quabbin Regional High School's cross-country team for 1973 included, from left to right, Peter Halfrey, Albert Plimpton, Louis Panaccione (nephew of Joseph Panaccione in the previous photograph), Bert Allen, Dino Lamacchia, Bruce Newcomb, Gary Halfrey, Lyman Clark, and Coach Richard Lyon Jr.

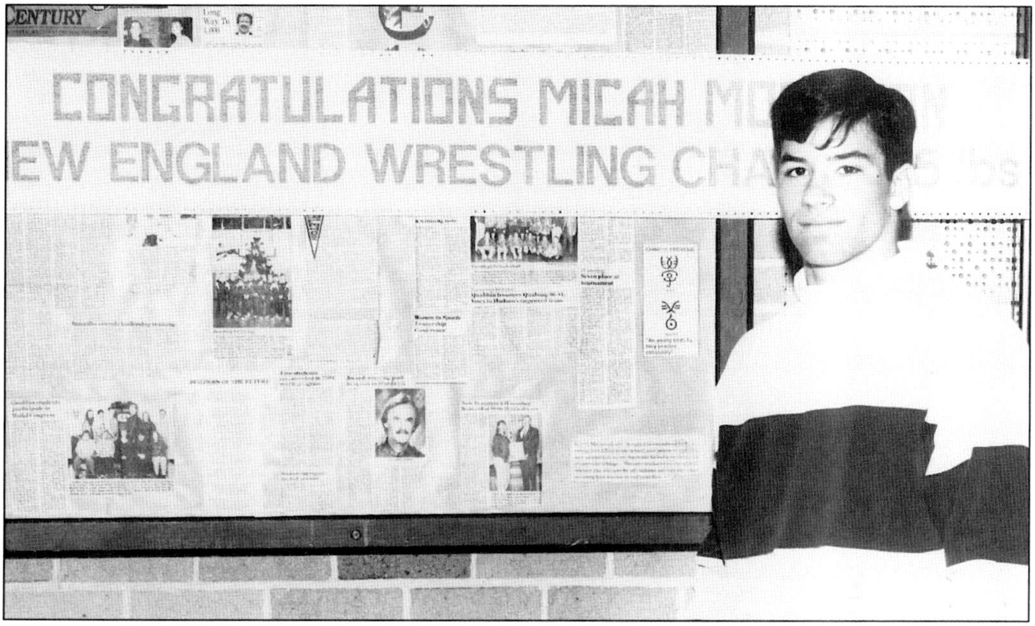

The sport of wrestling has been a vital part of Quabbin Regional High School's long list of athletic achievements. The team has garnered numerous, well-deserved honors over the years, but perhaps the greatest was when Micah Morrison became Quabbin's first New England wrestling champion in March 1994.

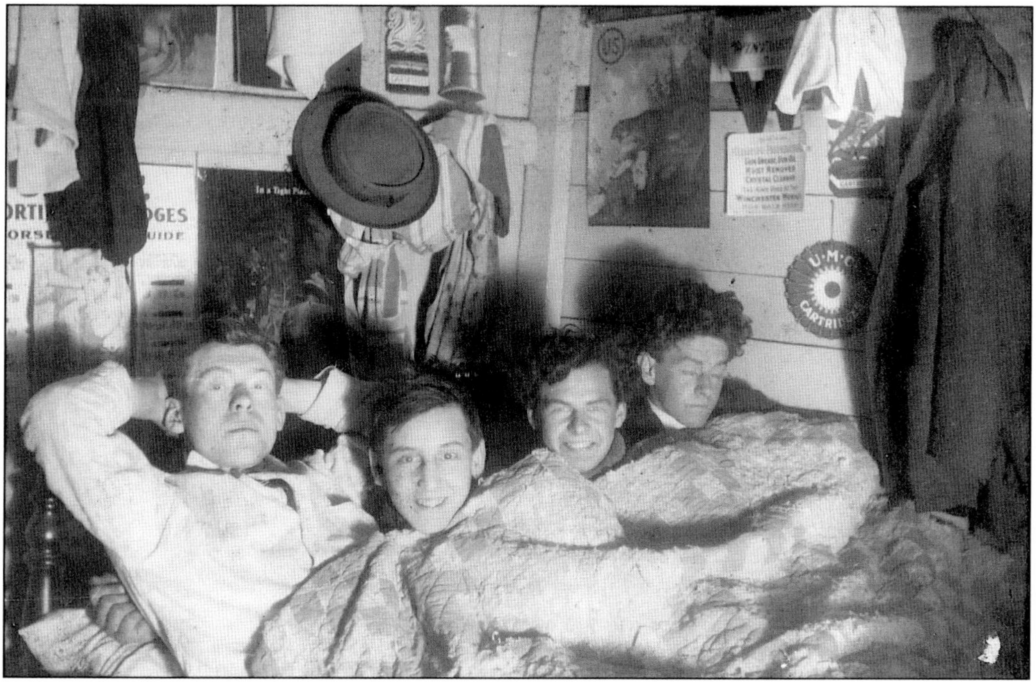

Surprise! These sleepy campers were awakened by a photographer's flashbulb at 5:30 a.m. on February 28, 1909, as they slept at the Prince River Camp in Loring Park, overlooking what is now the Chas. G. Allen Co. on School Street. Sharing a bed to ward off the chill are, from left to right, Allen J. Colby, Leigh Tower, Roscoe Johnson, and a still-slumbering Laurence Rice.

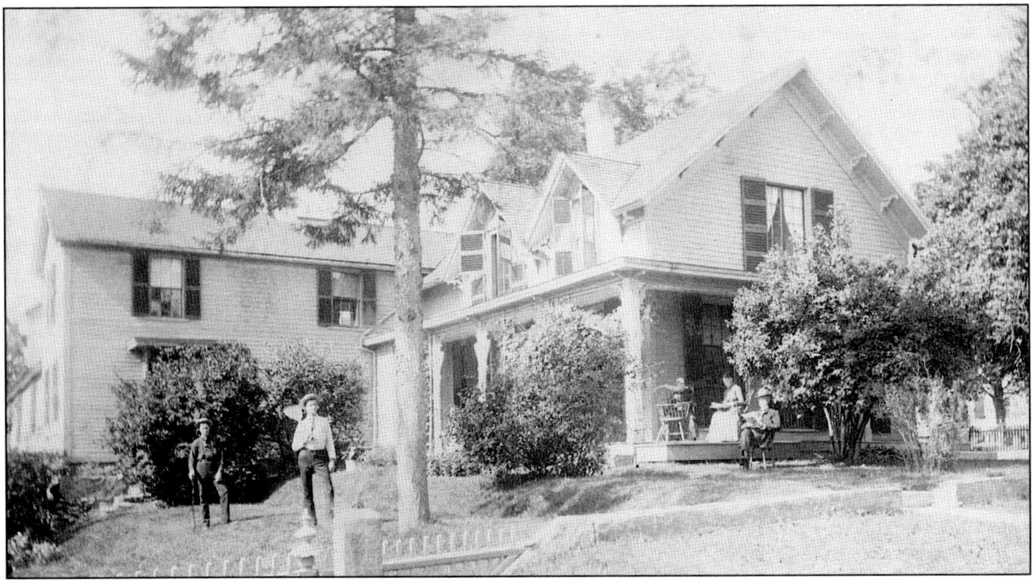

Now a Barre bed-and-breakfast inn of considerable reputation, the Jenkins House, at the corner of Pleasant and West Streets, has always been a gracious home. This picture, taken *c.* 1890, shows the Jenkins family enjoying a summer's day. Note the ornate fence, which conforms to the gentle slope of the lawn, and the south facing, second-story shutters opened to receive the sunlight.

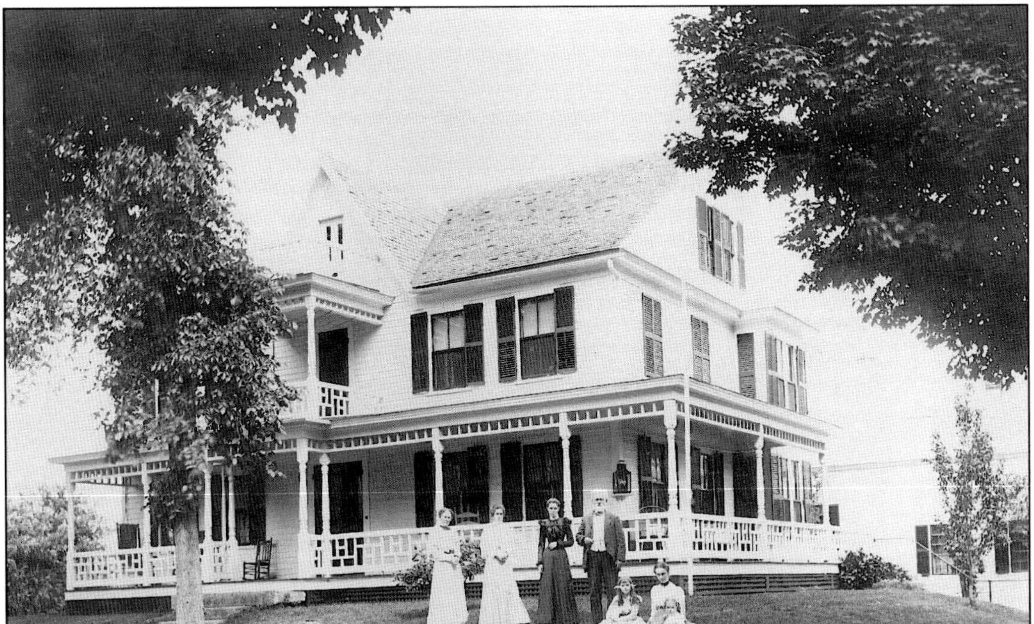

Barre has another Jenkins House, this one located on School Street, across from the current fire station. The home of Harding Jenkins, shown here *c.* 1900, was spacious and tall. The standing gentleman is Pliny Babbitt, father of Mrs. Harding Jenkins, who stands to his right in the dark dress. The woman seated on the ground is Ruth Jenkins, who later became Mrs. Frederick Stedman. The others remain unidentified.

Eleven

PRODUCTIONS AND ORGANIZATIONS

One of the things that makes Barre so special is the dedication and commitment of its citizens. Not only do they care for their families and pridefully tend their homes and gardens, there is a spirit of community service that runs deep here. For many, there's always time for one more committee, one more club, one more just cause. We salute them all.

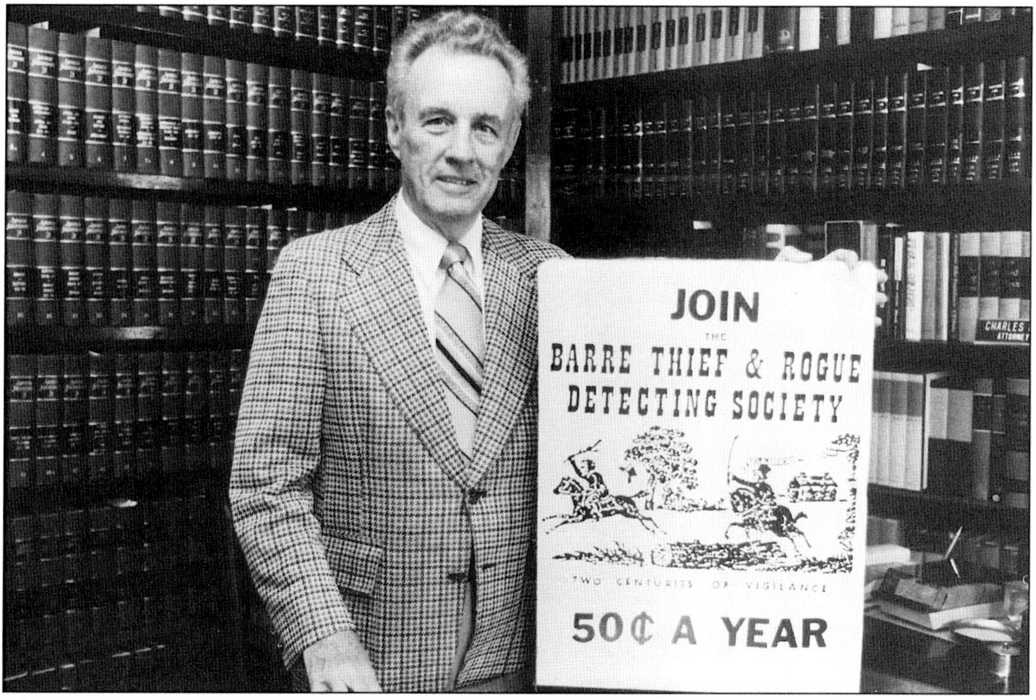

The Barre Thief and Rogue Detecting Society, founded in 1780, is the oldest crime protection organization in the country. Its original purpose was to capture horse thieves. The group posts bonds and rewards to encourage the apprehension of vandals of public property. Due to the late Charles Wyman's personal interest in the society, membership has increased to 50 members and has become more active in the community. Any person or business may join the society for a fee of 50¢ per year, which has remained unchanged for two centuries.

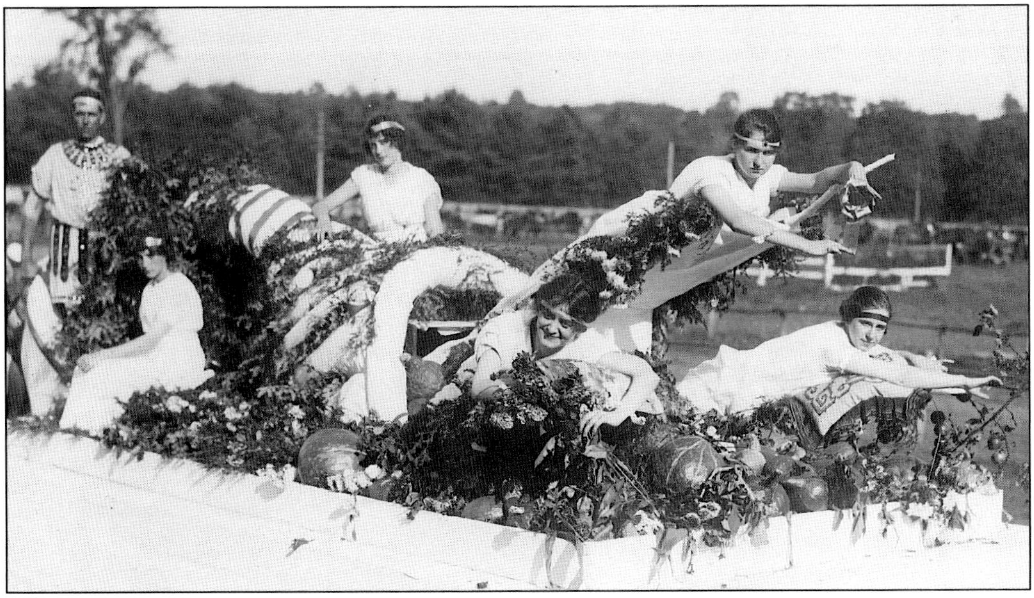

Pictured here are the ladies of the Grange participating in the Welcome Home Celebration float called the "Horn of Plenty" for the servicemen of World War II.

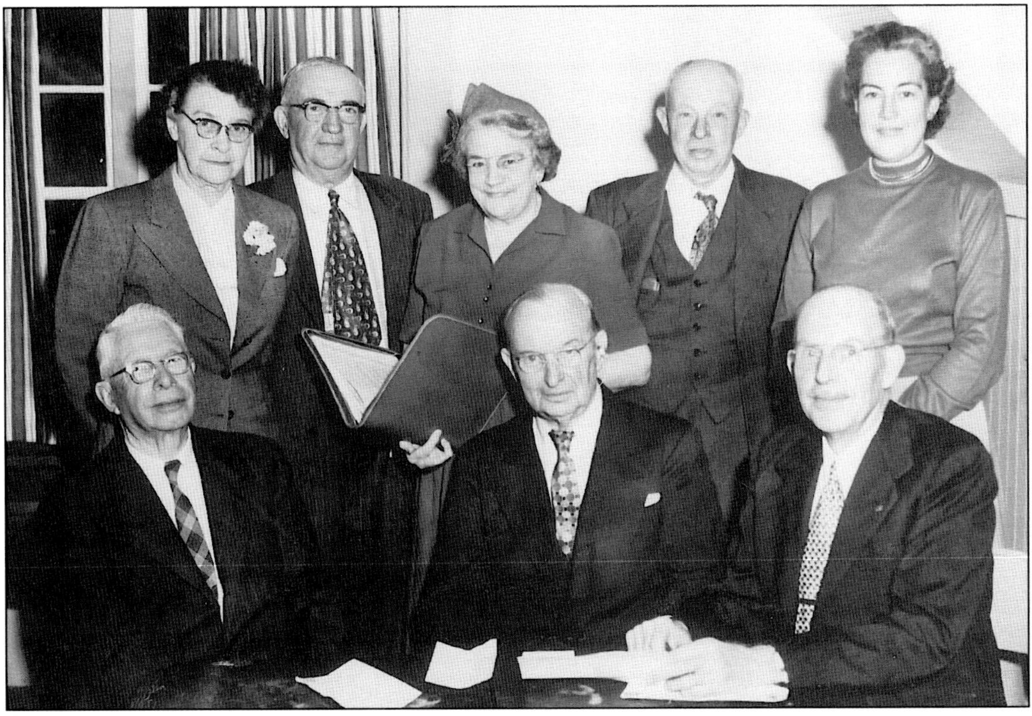

Members of the Barre Historical Society are shown in 1958, before the acquisition of their building on the Common. The society was formed in 1954 for the purpose of maintaining a museum for the preservation of local history and the protection of historical sites and buildings. Seen here, from left to right, are as follows: (front row) Charles Harwood, Joseph Rogers, and Herbert Rice; (back row) Elsie Smith, Joseph Higgins, Grace Whippee, Ernest Pratt, and Helen Connington.

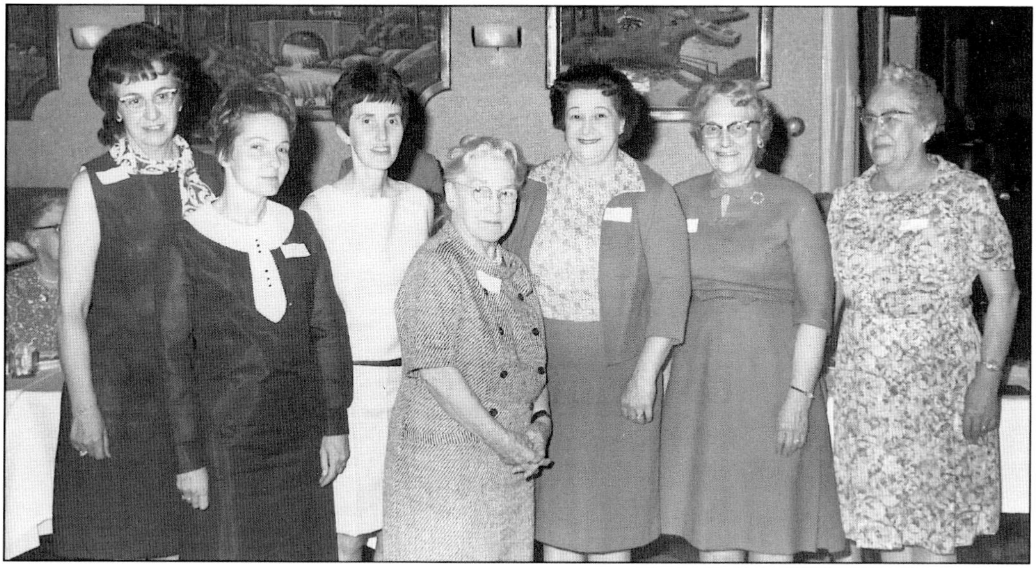

The Barre Woman's Club was formed in 1916 with Miss Lucy Rice as president. Open to all women in the community, the club is dedicated to community service. It joined the Massachusetts State Federation of Women's Clubs in 1952. Shown in 1968, from left to right, are Margaret Bentley, Andrea Goodwin, Gloria Castriotta, Alice Roper, Gladys Mara, Betty Gariepy, and Ettie Glidden.

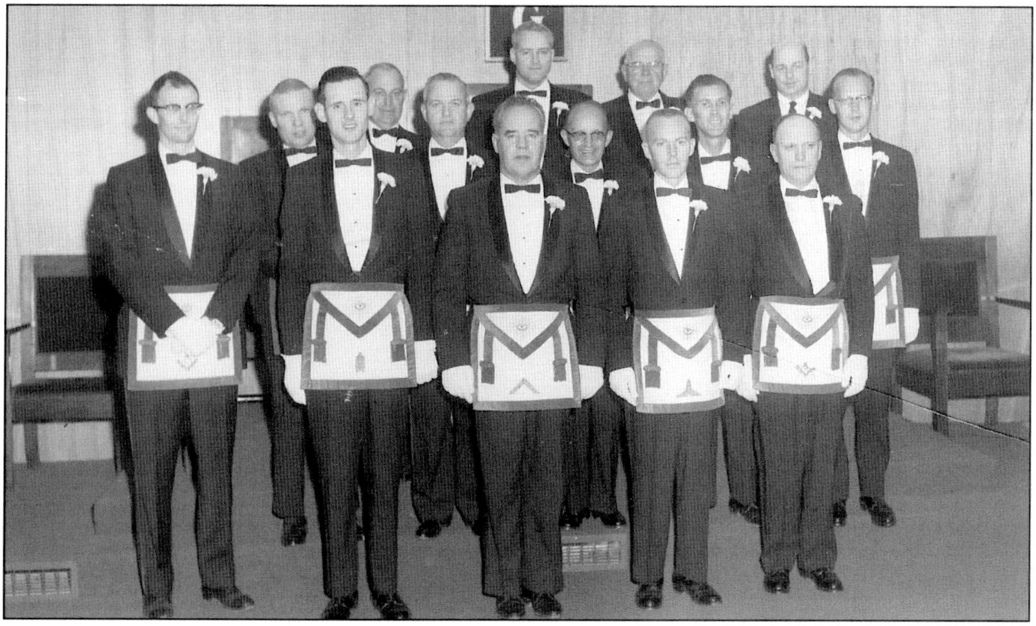

The Masonic Fraternity is founded on the principles first practiced by craftsmen in the Middle Ages. Modern Masonry dates from 1699, and promotes the brotherhood of man and the practices of charity to all people regardless of race, color, or creed. Mt. Zion Lodge was started in Hardwick in 1800 and moved to Barre in 1855. Seen here, from left to right, are as follows: (front row) M. Baker, H. Dennis, S. Ericson, G. Mennard, and R. Valley; (back row) J. Taugher, H. Clark, C. Clark, W. Flister, W. Schindler, M. Smith, R. Handy, A. Macintosh, and E. Miller.

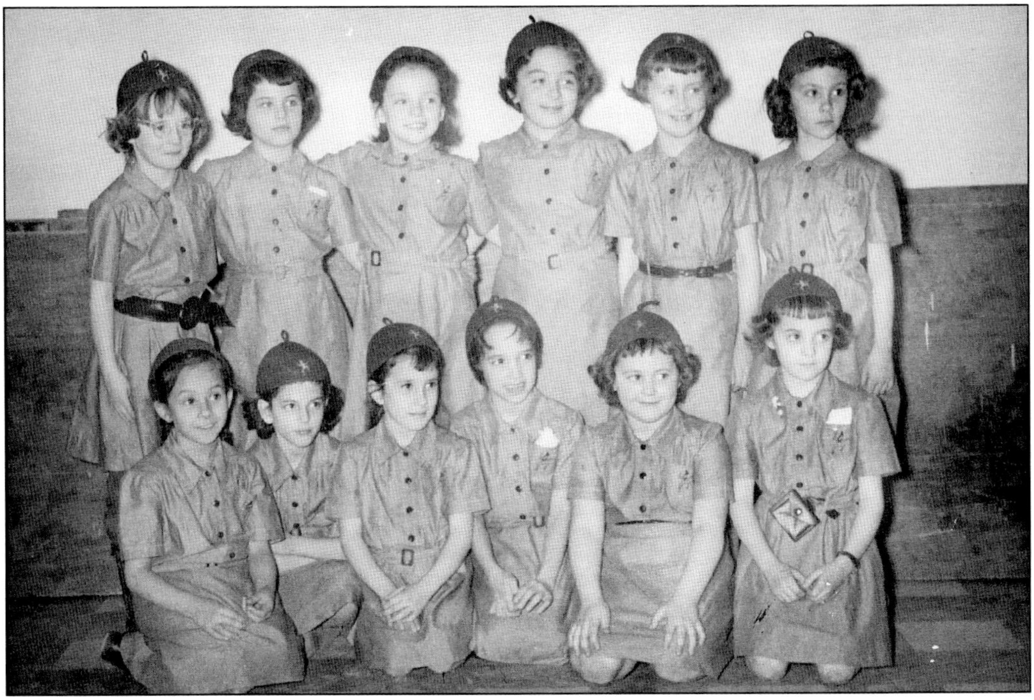

These smiling little Brownies may hold the key to the Legion Auxiliary's "Here Is Your Life" show on March 24, 1960, at the Ruggles Lane School in its sixth annual presentation.

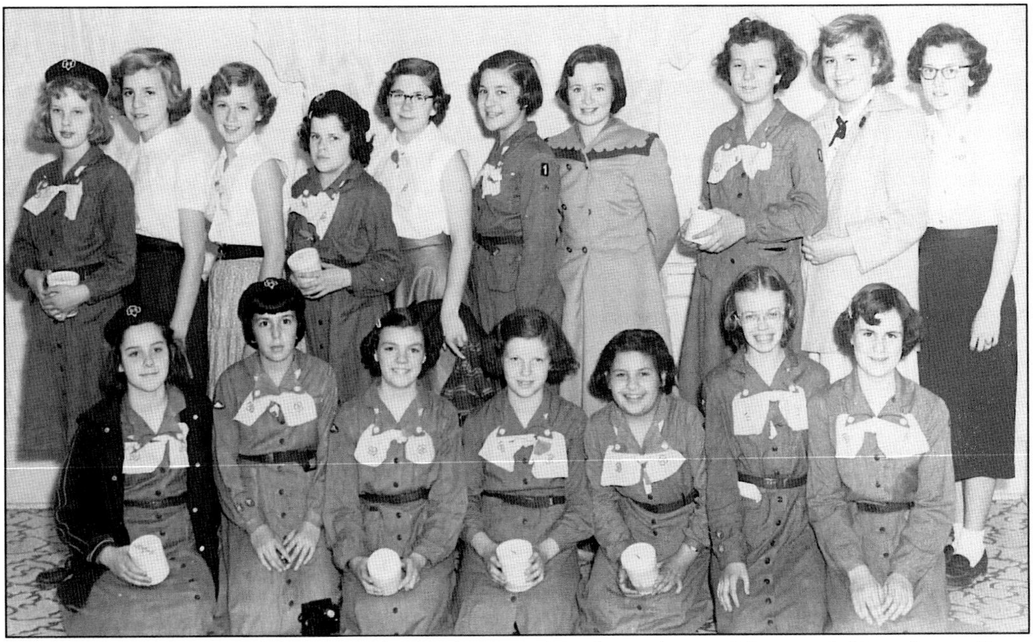

The Girl Scouts joined forces with the Legion Auxiliary for its Memorial Day drive. Seen here, from left to right, are as follows: (front row) Sonia Baker, Julie Mansueti, Nancy Bacon, Patsy Larabee, Ann Pitisci, Judy Baker, and Margaret Murphy; (back row) Betty Vaidulas, Joan Newcomb, Carol Ingle, Karen Langelier, Sue Gariepy, Virginia Varnot, Rebecca Bentley, Jean Loughman, Carol Newcomb, and Karen Swenberg.

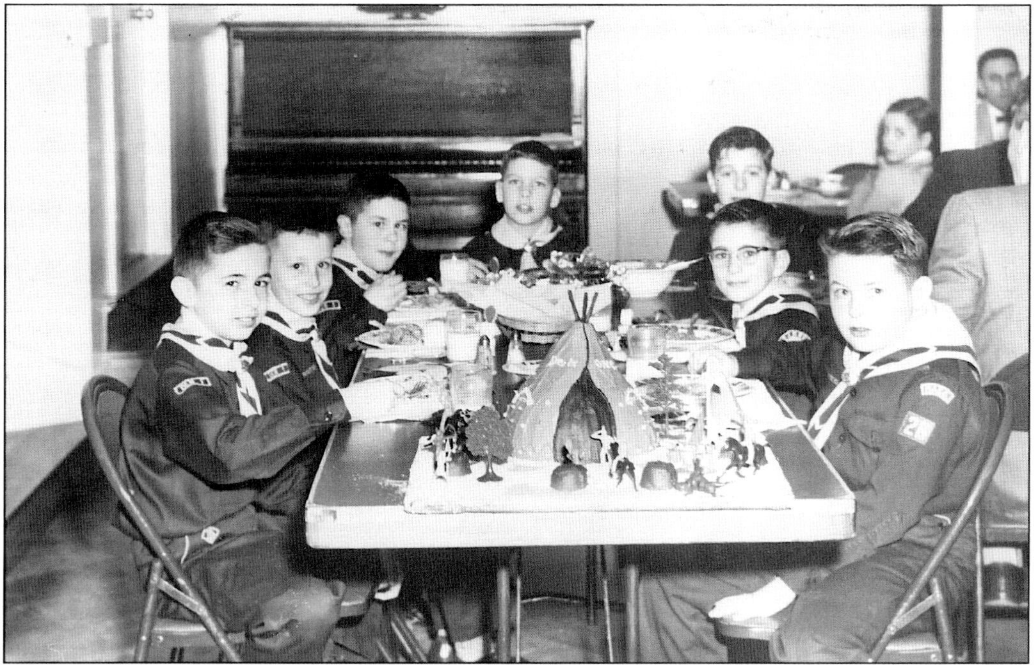

This 1959 Cub Scouts annual Blue and Gold Banquet was under the supervision of Margaret Bentley, the den mother of the group. The Barre Pack No. 26 has eight dens. The Cub Scouts work for their badges and participate in fund-raisers, food drives, overnight camping, and caroling in December. Shown here, from left to right, are Steven Bentley, John Flint, John Rogowski, David Spinney, Curtis Allen, Danny Trifilo, and Billy Neylon.

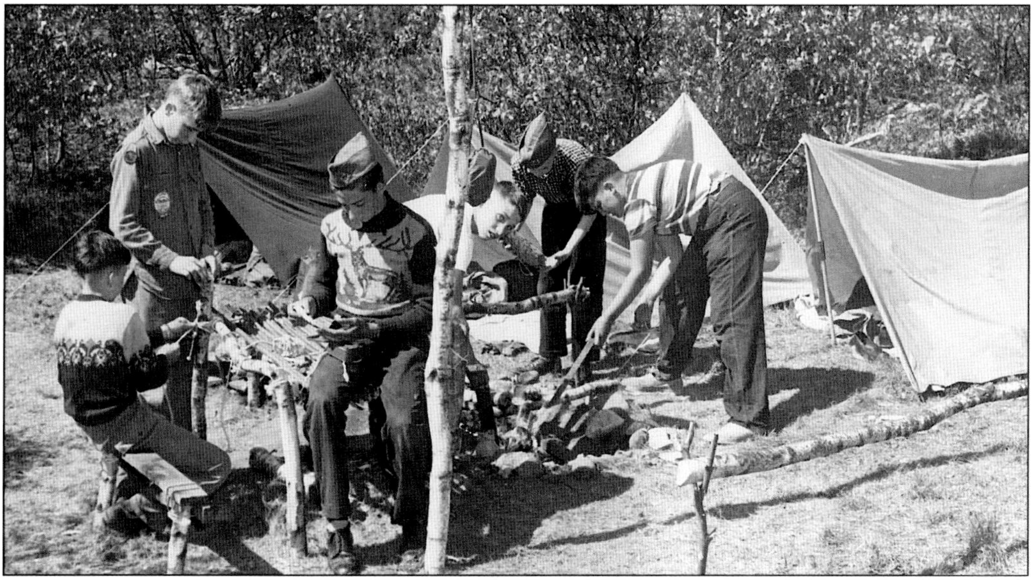

The Boy Scouts were first formed in Barre in 1913, at Christ Episcopal Church. Scouting has been an integral part of our community, helping with civic projects and, more recently, clearing around the grave site of Quork Walker, emancipated slave of the 1700s. Shown here, from left to right, are Michael Hudson, David McQueston, Roger Varnot, Robert Dunbar, Peter Flynn, and Robert Clough.

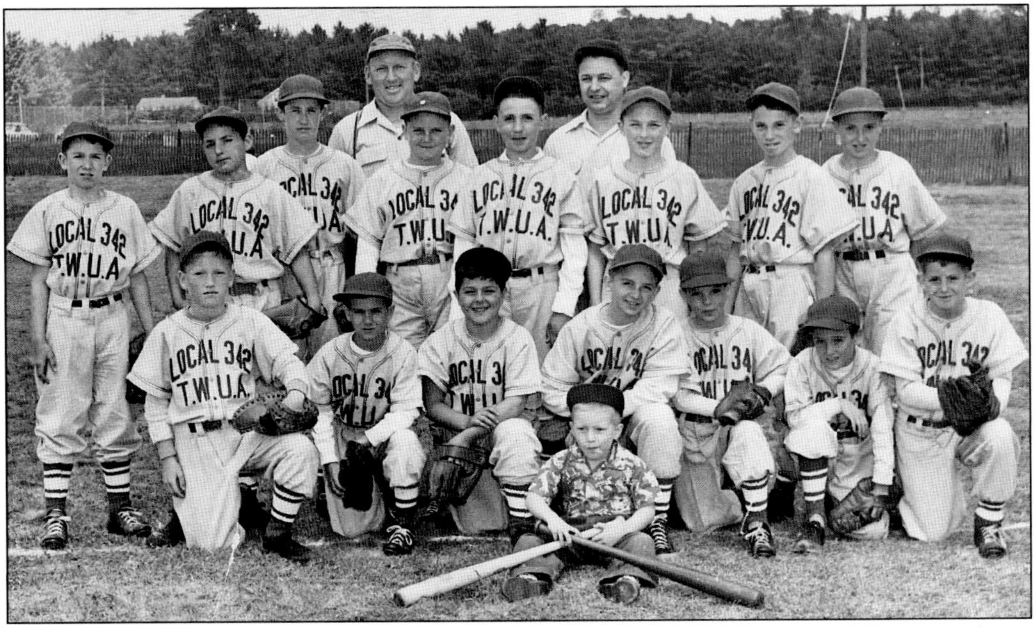

Walter Talancy started the Little League in Barre in 1953. Little League members seen here, from left to right, are as follows: (front row) Doug Phillips, George Marshall, Peter Inzerillo, Walter Talancy, Richard Crowley, Greg Mirabile, and John Mason; (middle row) Frank Mertzic, Eddie White, Dave Paquin, Paul Mann, John Panzic, Harry Corbett, Bob Dunbar, and Donald Raffier; (back row) Doug Phillips and Frank Varnot.

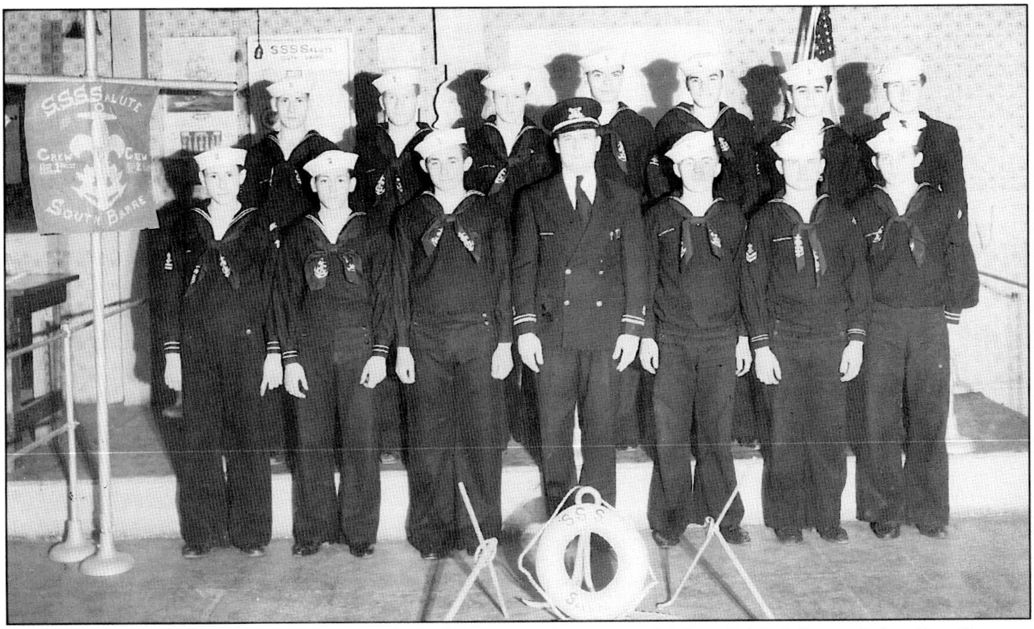

The South Barre Sea Scouts was for boys between the ages of 15 and 18. Most of the Sea Scouts in this 1935 photograph had previously been Boy Scouts. Seen above, from left to right, are as follows: (front row) Salvatore Puliafico, Michael Cadella, Armand Cornacchia, Walter Hosley (skipper), Elwin Hodges, Fred Thorng, and Leslie Albrecht; (back row) Anthony Matulaitis, Albert Clark, Herbert Hudson, Leo Crowley, Oswald Marconi, Peter Gareau, and Ed Crevier.

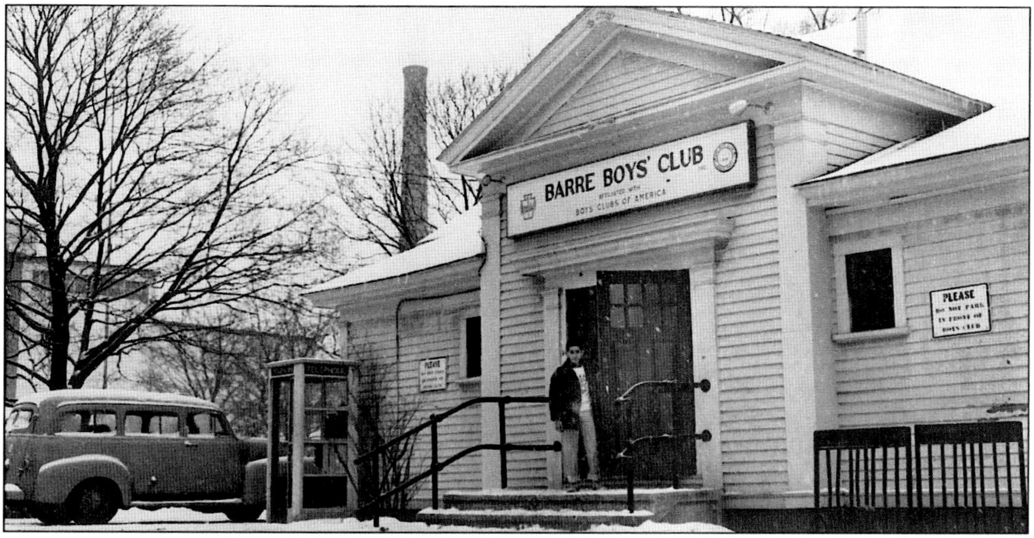

The Barre Wool Combing Co. Ltd. provided this building, the former Florence Hall in South Barre, for the Barre Boys Club, which opened its doors in 1960.

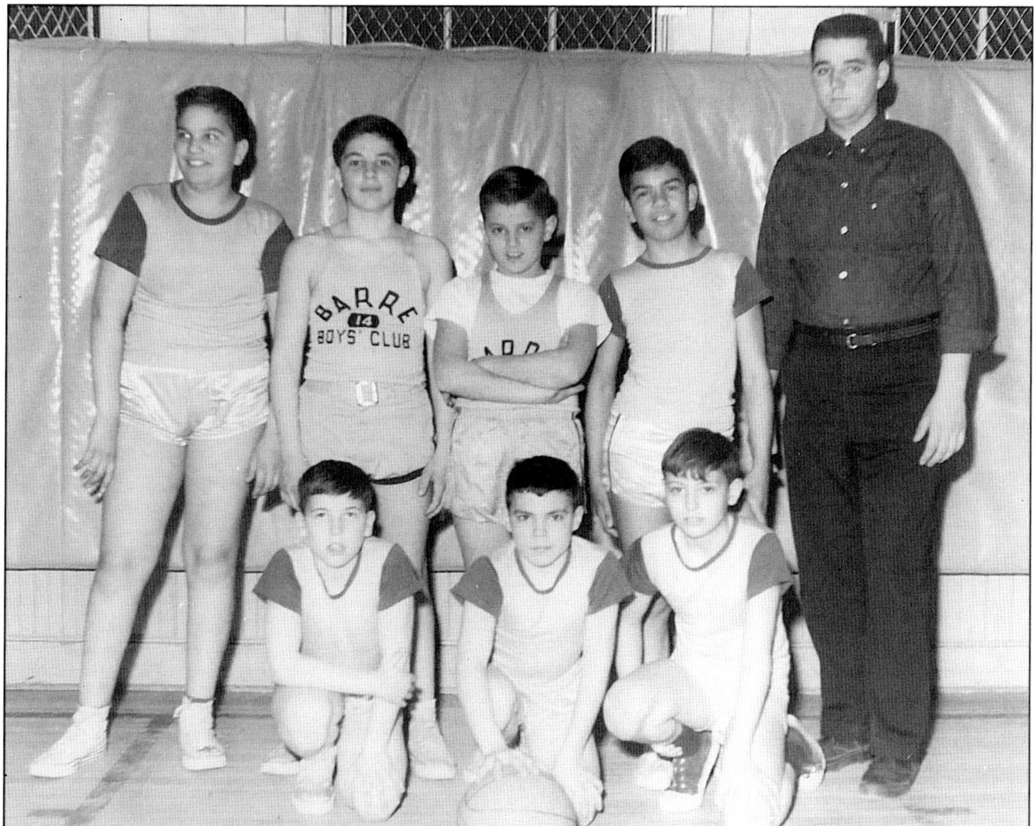

The Barre Boys Club members seen here, from left to right, are as follows: (front row) Anthony Shimanski, Peter Fargnoli, and Tommy Jordan; (back row) John Coppolino, John Benedict, Paul Staiti, unidentified, and Fran Gromelski.

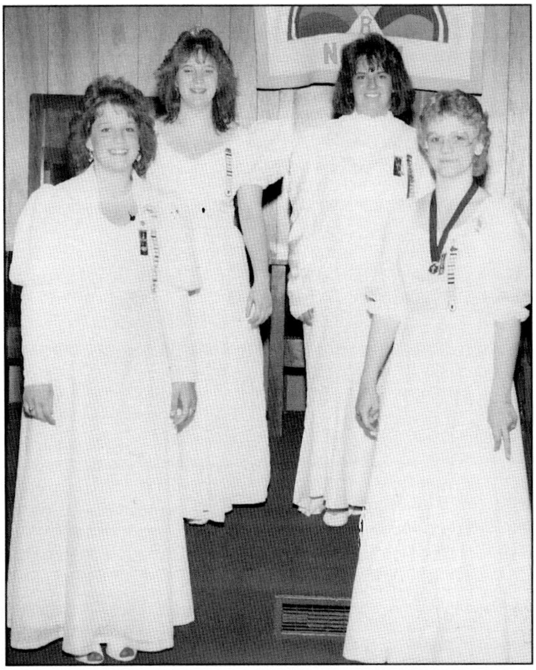

Barre Assembly No. 114, International Order of the Rainbow for Girls, was instituted in 1964. The Barre Assembly is sponsored by the Cradle Rock Chapter No. 125, Order of the Eastern Star (OES). There are Rainbow assemblies in every state as well as many foreign countries. Seen here, from left to right, are Christine Erickson, Julie Mennard, Pamela Barkman, and Shelley Modzeleski.

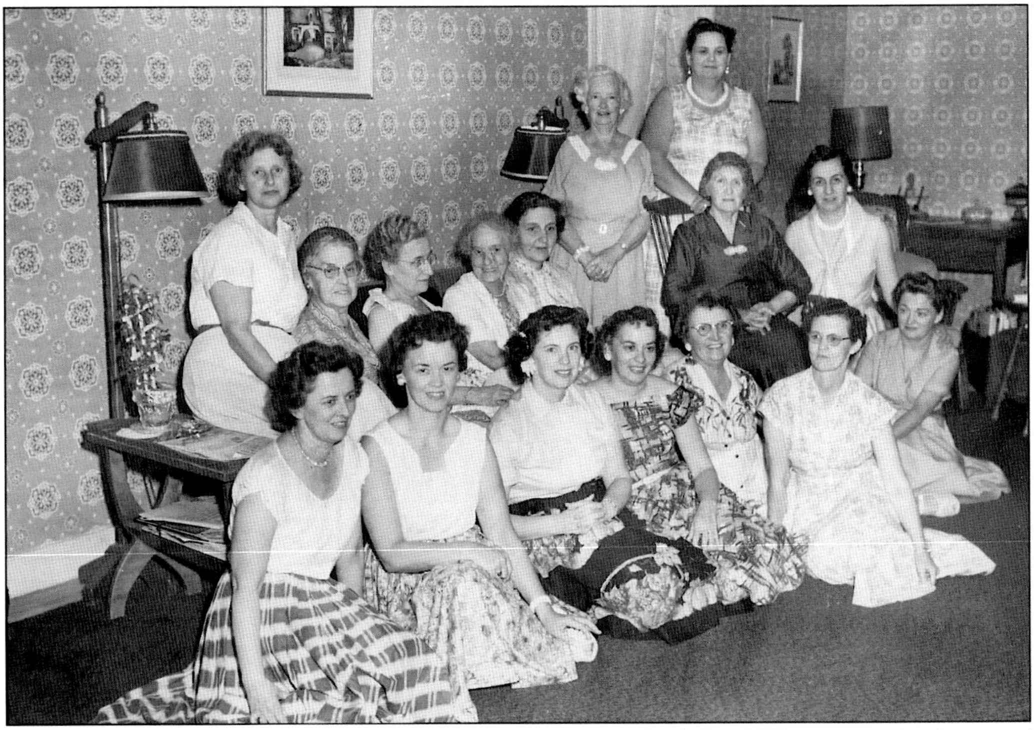

These past matrons of the Cradle Rock Chapter No. 125 of the OES pose at the home of Ruth Clark in 1958. They are, from left to right, as follows: (front row) Ruth Clark, Jule Flister, Diana Rogers, Ethel Smith, Emma Blake, Marion Damon, and Bessie Difley; (back row) Esther Freeman, Gertrude Damon, Mae Case, Cora Upham, Natita Loughman, Della Hillman, Ruth Waite, Mame Babcock, and Margaret Bentley.

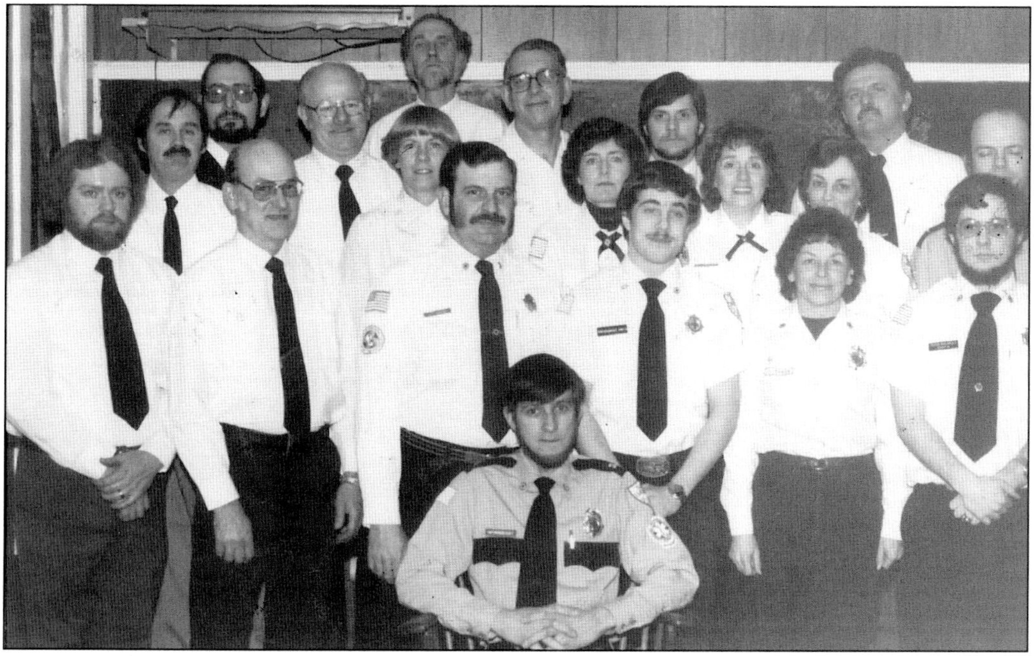

The Barre Emergency and Rescue Squad was founded in 1971 as an all-volunteer group to provide the town with better ambulance service and qualified attendants having medical knowledge. Seen in this 1982 photograph are as follows: (seated) Captain Ray Howard; (front row) Mark Larson, Fran Castonguay, Jim Higgins, Tim Guilbault, Sue Fullam, and Peter Guilbault; (back row) Rick Paula, Don Benson, Abe Harrington, Al Clark, Fran White, Bill McWilliams, Ken Clarkson, Judy Benson, Audrey Stevens, Sandy Fritcher, Sally Harrington, and Charlie Fullam.

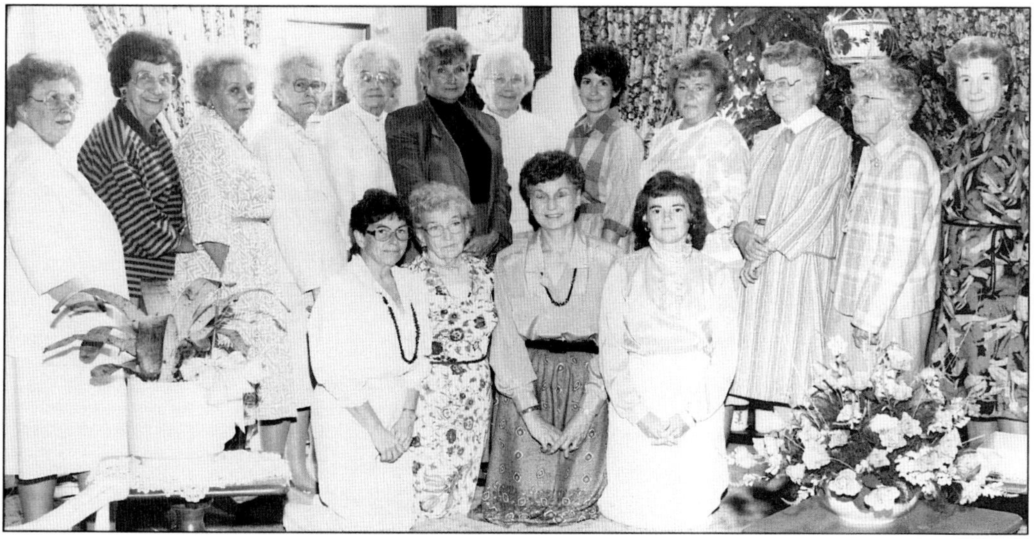

The Friday Club, shown here in 1987, is one of Barre's oldest clubs, founded in 1907. It is dedicated to cultural pursuits. It sponsors the annual spelling bee for grammar school students and buys books for the schools and town library. Over the years the club has sponsored many musicals, dances, lectures on health, given parties for children, held Gentlemen's Nights, helped needy families, and assisted children from foreign countries.

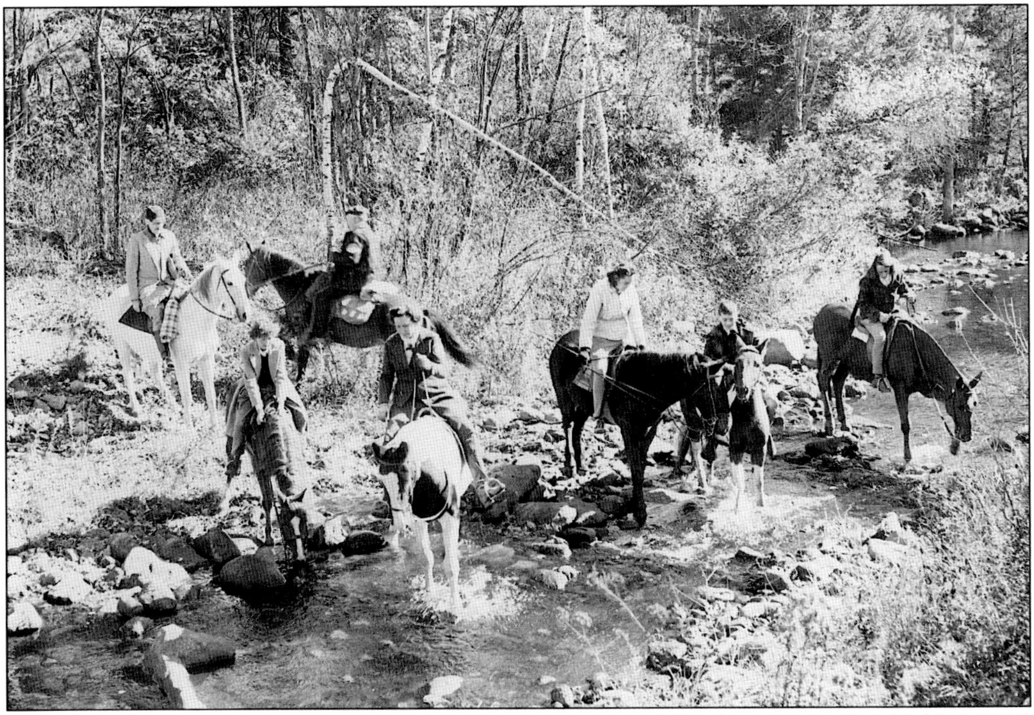

This is the Barre Riding and Driving Club off Route 62, *c.* 1942. The active group holds regular meetings, raises money for scholarships, conducts trail rides, and has sponsored 35-mile annual competitive events. Seen here, from left to right, are Herbert Rice, Irene Finan, Ed Glidden, Bertyne Rice Smith, Helen W. Connington, ? Glidden, and Betty Clark.

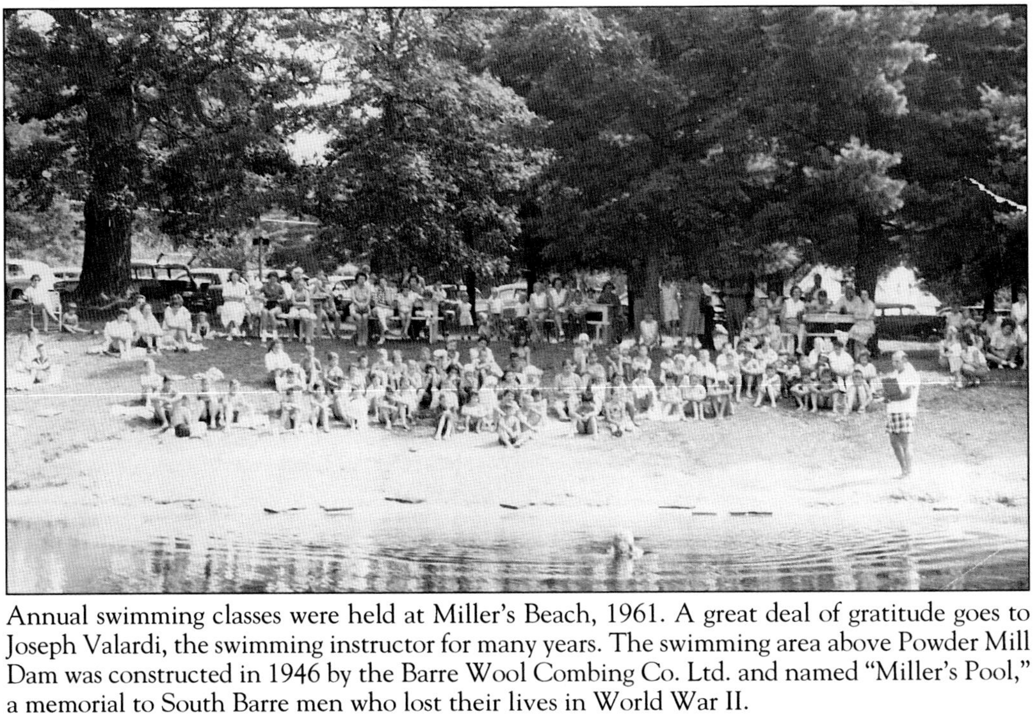

Annual swimming classes were held at Miller's Beach, 1961. A great deal of gratitude goes to Joseph Valardi, the swimming instructor for many years. The swimming area above Powder Mill Dam was constructed in 1946 by the Barre Wool Combing Co. Ltd. and named "Miller's Pool," a memorial to South Barre men who lost their lives in World War II.

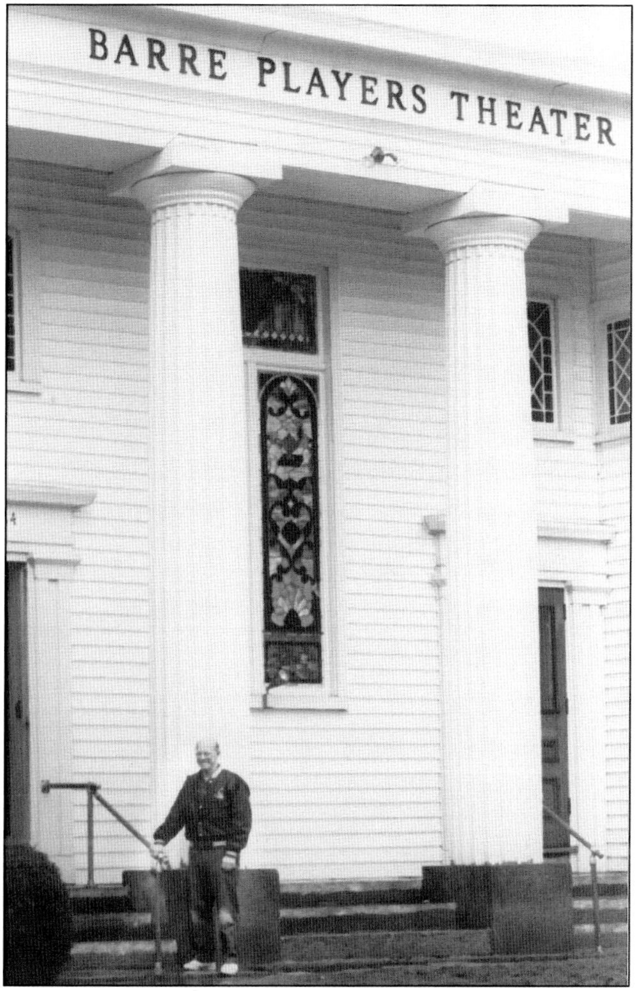

The event that set the stage for the formation of Barre Players was the 1921 presentation of *A Midsummer Night's Dream*. About 1,000 people were present at this performance staged by local talent at the old iron bandstand on the North Common. The play was under the direction of George Vivian (Victoria Hopkins' grandfather), a summer resident of Barre who was one of New York's leading producers. Nearly 30 residents of the town were actors in the play. Tradition has it that most of the town participated in the production as extras.

After Mr. Vivian left this area to form his own theater company in Washington, D.C., interest in local theater declined for a while. Barre Players became a functioning group again in 1957, when another man of the theater came to town, the Reverend Dr. Robert S. Illingworth, minister of the Congregational Church. One of his earliest innovations was breathing life into Barre Players and providing space for it in Fellowship Hall of the church. By 1960, Barre Players membership had grown so large and varied they became a community organization.

In 1992, the club incorporated to become Barre Players Inc. The following year, they purchased the Golden Age Meeting House, becoming one of only a few theater groups to own their building. The primary purpose of Barre Players remains the same as always, to provide quality productions. Since 1957, more than 125 plays, reviews, and musicals have been offered. Past president of Barre Players Tim Waite is shown here.

In 1998, after the deaths of Victoria (Vicki) and Russell Hopkins, the lobby of the theater was named in their memory for their many years of devoted service.

ACKNOWLEDGMENTS

With great appreciation acknowledgement is given to the authors of the chapters and for the opportunity to reproduce photographs borrowed from some collections: the *Barre Gazette*, the Barre Historical Society, Eleanor Caranci, Gabrielle Carroll, Albert Clark, Marilyn Collins, Roland Ethier, Walter Flister, Burt Frost, Rebecca Hamel, Howard Hastings, Jinx Hastings, R. Wes. Hopkins, Mary Kelley, Victoria King, Bill Neylon, the No. 4 Schoolhouse Inc., Lester Paquin, C. Ronald Potter, Rita Robinson, James Sullivan, Dolly Thorng, Matthew Trifilo, Olive Tuttle, Barbara Warren, Ed Yaglou, and George Yonker.